A SHORT WALK IN THE HINDU KUSH

By the same author:

THE LAST GRAIN RACE
SOMETHING WHOLESALE
LOVE AND WAR IN THE APPENINES
SLOWLY DOWN THE GANGES

and with Diana Petry
THE WONDERS OF BRITAIN
THE WONDERS OF IRELAND

ERIC NEWBY

A Short Walk in the Hindu Kush

HODDER AND STOUGHTON
London Sydney Auckland Toronto

Copyright © 1958 by Eric Newby. First printed 1958. This edition 1972. ISBN
o 340 16589 8. Reproduced from the original setting by arrangement with Secker
& Warburg Ltd. All rights reserved. No part of this publication may be reproduced
or transmitted in any form or by any means, electronic or mechanical, including
photocopy, recording, or any information storage and retrieval system, without permission in writing from the publisher. Printed in Great Britain for Hodder and
Stoughton Limited, St. Paul's House, Warwick Lane, London EC4P 4AH by
Richard Clay (The Chaucer Press) Limited, Bungay, Suffolk.

*This book is dedicated to Hugh
Carless of Her Majesty's Foreign
Service, without whose determination, it must be obvious to anyone
who reads it, this journey could
never have been made.*

'Il faudrait une expédition bien organisée
et pourvue de moyens matériels puissants
pour tenter l'étude de cette region de
haute montagne dont les rares cols sont
à plus de 5000 mètres d'altitude.'

L'Hindou Kouch et le Kaboulistan.
RAYMOND FURON

PREFACE
by
EVELYN WAUGH

M R. ERIC NEWBY must not be confused with the other
English writer of the same surname. I began reading A
SHORT WALK IN THE HINDU KUSH in the belief that it was the
work of his namesake, whom I have long relished. I found something equally delightful but quite different.

Mr. Eric Newby, I have since learned, is the author of an
exciting sea-log, THE LAST GRAIN RACE, an account of how at
the age of eighteen he signed on as an apprentice of the Finnish
barque *Moshulu*, lived in the fo'c'sle as the only Englishman,
worked the ship, rounded both capes under sail in all the vicissitudes
of the historic and now extinct passage from Australia to the
United Kingdom of the grain-carrying windjammers. His
career in the army was heroic and romantic. The bravado and
endurance which had briefly made him a sailor were turned to
the King's service, and were rewarded with the Military Cross
and a wife. After the war he went into the most improbable
of trades, *haute couture*. It would strain the imagination to picture
this stalwart young adventurer selling women's clothes. We are
relieved of the difficulty by his own deliciously funny description,
which immediately captivates the reader of the opening chapters
of A SHORT WALK. One can only use the absurdly trite phrase
"the call of the wild" to describe the peculiar impetus which
carried Mr. Newby from Mayfair to the wild mountains
of Afghanistan. He was no sailor when he embarked in the
Moshulu; he was no mountaineer when he decided to climb the
Hindu Kush. A few days scrambling on the rocks in Wales,
enchantingly chronicled here, were his sole preparation. It was
not mountaineering that attracted him; the Alps abound in
opportunities for every exertion of that kind. It was the longing,
romantic, reasonless, which lies deep in the hearts of most
Englishmen, to shun the celebrated spectacles of the tourist and
without any concern with science or politics or commerce, simply
to set their feet where few civilised feet have trod.

An American critic who read the manuscript of this book condemned it as "too English". It *is* intensely English, despite the fact that most of its action takes place in wildly foreign places and that it is written in an idiomatic, uncalculated manner the very antithesis of "Mandarin" stylishness. It rejoices the heart of fellow Englishmen, and should at least illuminate those who have any curiosity about the odd character of our Kingdom. It exemplifies the essential traditional (some, not I, will say deplorable) amateurism of the English. For more than two hundred years now Englishmen have been wandering about the world for their amusement, suspect everywhere as government agents, to the great embarrassment of our officials. The Scotch endured great hardships in the cause of commerce; the French in the cause of either power or evangelism. The English only have half (and wholly) killed themselves in order to get away from England. Mr. Newby is the latest, but, I pray, not the last, of a whimsical tradition. And in his writing he has all the marks of his not entirely absurd antecedents. The understatement, the self-ridicule, the delight in the foreignness of foreigners, the complete denial of any attempt to enlist the sympathies of his readers in the hardships he has capriciously invited; finally in his formal self-effacement in the presence of the specialist (with the essential reserve of unexpressed self-respect) which concludes, almost too abruptly, this beguiling narrative—in all these qualities Mr. Newby has delighted the heart of a man whose travelling days are done and who sees, all too often, his countrymen represented abroad by other, new and (dammit) lower types.

Dear reader, if you have any softness left for the idiosyncrasies of our rough island race, fall to and enjoy this characteristic artifact.

EVELYN WAUGH

CONTENTS

LIST OF ILLUSTRATIONS

Badar Khan loading his horse at the col on the Arayu
Frontispiece

ACKNOWLEDGEMENTS

MY thanks are due to the Afghan Government for their
kindness and co-operation in allowing me to travel in
Nuristan, and to *Vogue* for permission to reproduce *Meeting an
Explorer* which first appeared in it and which is now incorporated
in Chapter 20.

The map to illustrate the journey is based on the maps of the
Survey of India and a traverse made by Wilfred Thesiger, D.S.O.,
in 1956.

CHAPTER ONE

Life of a Salesman

WITH all the lights on and the door shut to protect us from the hellish draught that blew up the backstairs, the fitting-room was like an oven with mirrors. There were four of us jammed in it: Hyde-Clarke, the designer; Milly, a very contemporary model girl with none of the normal protuberances; the sour-looking fitter in whose workroom the dress was being made; and Newby.

Things were not going well. It was the week before the showing of the 1956 Spring Collection, a time when the *vendeuses* crouched behind their little cream and gold desks, doodling furiously, and the Directors swooped through the vast empty showrooms switching off lights in a frenzy of economy, plunging whole wings into darkness. It was a time of endless fittings, the girls in the workrooms working late. The corset-makers, embroiderers, furriers, milliners, tailors, skirt-makers and matchers all involved in disasters and overcoming them—but by now slightly insane.

This particular dress was a disaster that no one was going to overcome. Its real name, the one on the progress board on the wall of the fitting-room, pinned up with a little flag and a cutting of the material, was *Royal Yacht*, but by general consent we all called it *Grand Guignol*.

I held a docket on which all the components used in its construction were written down as they were called up from the stockroom. The list already covered an entire sheet. It was not only a hideous dress; it was soaking up money like a sponge.

"How very odd. According to the docket *Grand Guignol's* got nine zips in it. Surely there must be some mistake."

Hyde-Clarke was squatting on his haunches ramming pins into *Grand Guignol* like a riveter.

"This dress is DOOMED. I know it's doomed. BOTHER, I've swallowed a pin! Pins, quickly, pins."

The fitter, a thin woman like a wardress at the Old Bailey and with the same look of indifference to human suffering, extended a bony wrist with a velvet pincushion strapped to it like a watch. He took three and jabbed them malevolently into the material; Milly swore fearfully.

"Mind where you're putting those . . . pins. What d'you think I am—a bloody yoga?"

"You MUST stand still, dear; undulation will get you nowhere," Hyde-Clarke said.

He stood up breathing heavily and lit a cigarette. There was a long silence broken only by the fitter who was grinding her teeth.

"What do you think of it now, Mr. Newby?" he said. "It's *you* who have to sell it."

"Much worse, Mr. Hyde-Clarke." (We took a certain ironic pleasure in calling one another Mister.) "Like one of those flagpoles they put up in the Mall when the Queen comes home."

"I don't agree: I think she looks like a Druid in it; one of those terrible runny-nosed old men dressed in sheets at an *Eisteddfod*. How much has it cost up to now?"

I told him.

"Breathe OUT, dear. Perhaps you'll look better without any air. I must say there's nothing more gruesome than white jersey when it goes wrong." 'Dear' breathed out and the dress fell down to her ankles. She folded her arms across her shoulders and gazed despairingly at the ceiling so that the whites of her eyes showed.

"There's no need to behave like a SLUT," said Hyde-Clarke. He was already putting on his covert coat. "We'll try again at two. I am going to luncheon." He turned to me. "Are you coming?" he said.

We went to 'luncheon'. In speech Hyde-Clarke was a stickler in the use of certain Edwardianisms, so that beer and sandwiches in a pub became 'luncheon' and a journey in his dilapidated sports car 'travel by motor'.

Today was a sandwich day.   As we battled our way up Mount Street through a blizzard, I screeched in his ear that I was abandoning the fashion industry.

"I saw the directors this morning."

"Oh, what did they say?"

"That they were keeping me on for the time being but that they make no promises for the future."

"What did you say?"

"That I had just had a book accepted for publication and that I am staying on for the time being but I make no promises for the future."

"It isn't true, is it?   I can hardly visualise you *writing* anything."

"That's what the publishers said, originally.   Now I want to go on an expedition."

"Aren't you rather old?"

"I'm just as old here as on an expedition.   You can't imagine anything more rigorous than this, can you?   In another couple of years I'll be dyeing my hair."

"In another couple of years you won't have any to dye," said Hyde-Clarke.

On the way back from 'luncheon', while Hyde-Clarke bought some Scotch ribs in a fashionable butcher's shop, I went into the Post Office in Mount Street and sent a cable to Hugh Carless, a friend of mine at the British Embassy, Rio de Janeiro.

CAN YOU TRAVEL NURISTAN JUNE?

It had taken me ten years to discover what everyone connected with it had been telling me all along, that the Fashion Industry was not for me.

CHAPTER TWO

Death of a Salesman

THE rehearsal was set for four o'clock on Tuesday. At eleven o'clock on Tuesday morning I was called to the telephone. It was the London agent of one of the great New York stores.

"Miss Candlemass is coming to see your Collection this afternoon."

"We're only having the rehearsal this afternoon. The opening's tomorrow."

"Miss Candlemass has a very tight schedule." (I wanted to say I was sorry and hoped that it would be better soon.) "She's on her way home from Paris. She's open to buy."

"We'll be very happy if she comes to the rehearsal. It's at four o'clock."

"She's only free at one-thirty. Make it one-thirty and you'll have to be READY. She doesn't like to be kept waiting."

He went on to say that Miss Candlemass was only interested in tweed suits and that the material had to be of a precise weight and proof against the corruptions of moth and rust and every other natural and unnatural ailment.

I told the Managing Director. He pretended to be unimpressed. I told the Head of the Boutique, who was not unnaturally furious. We told the workrooms that they had two and a half hours less to make the final adjustments in the suits and one of the skirt-makers had hysterics and had to lie down on the couch reserved for those suffering from female disorders; we told the model girls that they would have to lunch in the canteen, all four had lunch dates; the Commissionaire was warned to man the *porte cochère*; the counting-house was ordered to stand by from one o'clock onwards to be ready to answer any difficult questions about shipping and customs. I set off in a taxi on a circular tour of London cloth merchants to obtain swatches of the sort of material required by Miss Candlemass. Then I came back and re-costed the collection.

By one-thirty the atmosphere was electric. The Commissionaire was in position; the Head of the Boutique was ready to receive Miss Candlemass; the model girls were poised on the threshold of the changing-room with the first suits strapped on, like racehorses under starter's orders. I had just finished heavily annotating three programmes in dollars. The only person not present was Hyde-Clarke.

"I do not propose to change the habits of a lifetime to suit the convenience of a citizen of the United States," he remarked, and departed to luncheon. He proved to be the only one of us who had correctly appreciated the situation.

At half-past three Miss Candlemass arrived. It was quite obvious, without her saying so, which she did incessantly during her brief stay on the premises, that she had been lunching at Claridges.

The party consisted of the Shoe Buyer from the same store, readily identifiable because he was wearing a pair of brown crocodile shoes; the Agent, normally a man of briskness and decision, now reduced to a state of gibbering sycophancy by the proximity of Miss Candlemass; and Miss Candlemass herself. All three were a uniform, bright shade of puce. I must say in my lunchless state I envied them. The Head of the Boutique, a Scotswoman of character, refused to admit their existence, for which I admired her deeply, so that it was left for me to escort them to their seats.

Miss Candlemass was about nine feet high and hidden behind smoked glasses in mauve frames studded with semi-precious metal. She was like a lath, with very long legs, just too thin to be healthy, but she was very hygienic, smelled good and had fabulous shoes and stockings. With her dark glasses, the general effect was that of being engaged in watching an eclipse of the earth from the moon.

She didn't get as far as the showroom. As she clicked across the hall, she was attracted by the scent counter. She swooped on the largest bottle of scent we put out, a Rajah size flagon as big as a port decanter, and began to croon over it.

"Why don't you take it, Minnie?" said the man in the crocodile shoes, to whom I had already taken a violent dislike.

"Well, I rather think I will. I just adore these people's perfume." She opened an enormous black gladstone bag and dropped it in.

They sat down and the model girls came streaming in wearing our beautiful new suits. I handed Miss Candlemass the annotated programme and a nicely arranged pattern card with the fruits of my morning's labours neatly arranged on it.

Miss Candlemass wasn't paying any attention. She was well away describing the Duke of Norfolk who had been lunching at the next table, in minute, ecstatic detail, for the benefit of the agent who, by reason of his status, had been given a seat with his back to the engine.

"What do you think of them, Miss Candlemass?" Sixteen suits had passed in front of her.

"A very lovely family; and so old."

"Yes, but the suits?"

"Suits. I don't want any suits, do I? I'm filled up with suits. I want to see some dresses."

"But, surely, Miss Felsheim buys the dresses?"

"Yes, Lulu buys the dresses, but I just adore to see dresses. You know all that lovely perfume makes me feel in the mood for dresses."

We showed the dresses. Finally *Grand Guignol* hove into sight. Great changes had taken place but it still looked ghastly. Miss Candlemass loved it and swore to tell Miss Felsheim about it. As Milly wore round for the long beat to the changing-room, she passed me two envelopes. One contained the perfectly enormous bill for the scent, beaten out in a white heat of rage by the ladies in the counting-house. The other contained a cable. I read it.

It came from the British Embassy, Rio de Janeiro, and was addressed to 'Eric Rubey, Shammersmith' (I lived in Hammersmith), which would account for the slight delay. How it had arrived at all was a mystery. It bore three words.

OF COURSE, HUGH.

The showroom, already large, suddenly expanded. I understood what Sassoon meant when he wrote, 'Everyone suddenly burst out singing.'

Miss Candlemass was saying, "I'm afraid you haven't got it, Mr. Newby."

"Splendid, splendid."

"We did much better with Raymond Beale; he really studies the American Market."

"Mr. Beale has since gone bankrupt. Hi-de-ho."

As they were leaving I handed the bill for the scent to the agent.

"I think Miss Candlemass is expecting that as a *pourboire*."

"So do I, very strict firm this, tum-te-tum, very businesslike."

"I don't think she's going to like this, Mr. Newby. It may make things more difficult."

"She can put it down to the shoe department, tra-la-la."

"I'd better give you a cheque if you insist. You're very cheerful for someone who hasn't had an order. Are you always like this?"

"No, hardly ever. I've just had some really good news."

He wrote a cheque. When they had gone I gave it to Madame Fifi, the aged *vendeuse* who ran the scent department.

"Good boy," she croaked, patting my cheek. "That was a dummy bottle—full of coloured wattair."*

Hugh Carless, who had replied so opportunely to my cable, entered the Foreign Service in 1950. The son of a retired Indian Civil Servant, himself a man of unusual intellectual attainments, he is, like so many Englishmen, in love with Asia. For a time he was posted to the School of Oriental Studies, from which he emerged with a good knowledge of Persian; then to the Foreign Office, from which he frequently disappeared on visits to industrial plants; once he went down a coalmine. It was even suggested that he should visit a couture house and he approached me with this project, which did seem to have a certain educative value. It at least accorded far more with my pre-conceived

* Fortunately this was merely a *plaisanterie*.

ideas of the Higher Diplomacy, which derived from an intensive study of the works of. E. Phillips Oppenheim, than the visits to atomic piles and computer factories that the spirit of the age demanded.

His Persian being both fluent and academic, he was lucky to be posted to our Embassy at Kabul where he could actually make use of his talents.

From time to time he wrote me long letters, which came to me by way of the District Postmaster, Peshawar, which I read with envy in the bedrooms of the provincial hotels I stayed in when I 'travelled'. They were not the sort of letters that third secretaries in the Foreign Service usually write, full of details of the compound, the current indiscretions, the cocktail parties and the people passing through. Instead, they spoke of long, arduous, and to me fascinating, journeys to the interior, under-taken with horses and mysterious beings called Tajik drivers.

It was early in 1952 that he first mentioned Nuristan.

'An Austrian forestry expert, a Herr von Dückelmann has recently dined with me,' he wrote. 'He has been three or four times in Nuristan. Food there is very scarce, he says, and although he himself is a lean, hardy man he lost twelve pounds in weight during a ten day trip to the interior.'

Later in 1952 he wrote again.

'I have just returned from an expedition to the borders of Nuristan, *The Country of Light*. This is the place for you. It lies in the extreme N.E. of Afghanistan, bordering on Chitral and enclosed by the main range of the Hindu-Kush mountains. Until 1895 it was called Kafiristan, *The Country of the Unbelievers*. We didn't get in but we didn't expect to, the passes are all over 15,000 feet and we didn't have permission. So far as I can discover no Englishman has been there since Robertson in 1891. The last Europeans to visit it—von Dückelmann apart—were a German expedition in 1935, and it's possible that no one has visited the north-west corner at all. I went with Bob Dreesen of the American Embassy.'

I had heard of Dreesen. He was one of the American party

which escaped from the Chinese Communist advance into
Turkestan in 1950, evacuating the Consulate from Urumchi by
lorry to Kashgar and then crossing the Karakoram Range into
India with horses.   Hugh went on to speak of a large mountain,
nearly 20,000 feet high, that they had attempted to climb and of
one of his men being hit on the head by a great stone.   At that
time it had all seemed infinitely remote, and subsequently Hugh
had been transferred to Rio de Janeiro; but the seed had been
planted.

Hugh's telegram was followed by a great spate of letters which
began to flow into London from Rio.   They were all at least
four pages long, neatly typed in single spacing—sometimes two
would arrive in one day.   They showed that he was in a far
more advanced state of mental readiness for the journey than I
was.   It was as if, by some process of mental telepathy, he had
been able to anticipate the whole thing.

'Time', he wrote, 'is likely to prove a tricky factor for
me.   I have been posted at Tehran.   I hope to leave here on
May 12th and fly home via the United States where I must
spend five days in New York with a friend' (the sex of the
friend was unspecified but he subsequently married her).   'I
could meet you in Stamboul on June 20th.   We can be in
Kabul on July 1st.   I have heard from my Ambassador in
Tehran who hopes I will be there by August.   He will probably allow late August.'

In answer to my unspoken question about how I was to be in
Stamboul on June 20th, he continued.

'I have ordered a vehicle for delivery at Brighton' (why
Brighton, I wondered) 'on May 25th.   It will be a station
wagon with sleeping accommodation for two and will have a
wireless set and two extra wheels.'   It was typical of Hugh
that he could invest a car radio with all the attributes of a
transmitting set without actually saying so.   'You will have
to leave England on June 1st whether you drive to Stamboul
or ship from Genoa or Trieste.'

This was heady stuff but then, quite suddenly, the tone of
the letters changed.

'I don't think we should make known our ambition to go
to Nuristan. Rather I suggest we ask permission to go on a
Climbing Expedition. There are three very good and un-
climbed peaks of about 20,000 feet, all on the marches of
Nuristan. One of them, Mir Samir (19,880) I attempted with
Bob Dreesen in 1952 (*vide* my letter of 20.9.52). We climbed
up to some glaciers and reached a point 3,000 feet below the
final pyramid. A minor mishap forced us to return.'

He was already deeply involved in the clichés of mountaineering jargon. I re-read his 1952 letter and found that the 'minor
mishap' was an amendment. At the time he had written, 'one
of the party was hit on the head by a boulder': he didn't say
who. He continued remorselessly:

'This will leave us free to approach the War Office for
equipment' (I had rashly mentioned a Territorial Regiment
with which I was associated) 'and the Everest Foundation for
a grant. It will be honest, honourable, and attainable, and
if only partially so leaves us free to return to that part NEXT
YEAR.'

I was filled with profound misgiving. In cold print 20,000
feet does not seem very much. Every year more and more
expeditions climb peaks of 25,000 feet, and over. In the Himalayas a mountain of this size is regarded as an absolute pimple,
unworthy of serious consideration. But I had never climbed
anything. It was true that I had done some hill walking and a
certain amount of scrambling in the Dolomites with my wife,
but nowhere had we failed to encounter ladies twice our age
armed with umbrellas. I had never been anywhere that a rope
had been remotely necessary.

It was useless to dissemble any longer. I wrote a letter protest-
ing in the strongest possible terms and received by return a list
of equipment that I was to purchase. Many of the objects I
had never even heard of—two Horeschowsky ice axes; three
dozen Simond rock and ice pitons; six oval karabiners (2,000 lb.
minimum breaking strain); five 100 ft. nylon ropes; six abseil
slings; Everest goggles; Grivel, ten point crampons; a high
altitude tent; an altimeter; Yukon pack frames—the list was

an endless one. 'You will also need boots. I should see about
these right away. They may need to be made.'

I told Wanda, my wife.

"I think he's insane," she said, "just dotty. What will
happen if you say no?"

"I already have but he doesn't take any notice. You see
what he says here, if we don't go as mountaineers we shan't
get permission."

"Have you told the Directors you're leaving?"

"Yes."

"You *are* in a spot. We're all in a spot. Well, if you're
going I'm coming too. I want to see this mountain."

I wrote to Hugh. Like an echo in a quarry his reply came
back, voicing my own thoughts.

'I don't think either of you quite realize what this country is
like. The Nuristanis have only recently been converted to Islam;
women are less than the dust. *There are no facilities for female
tourists.* I refer you to *The Imperial Gazetteer of India*, volume
on Afghanistan, page 70, line 37 *et seq.* This is somewhat out
of date but the situation must be substantially the same today.'

I found the book in a creepy transept of the London Library.

"What does it say?" asked Wanda. "Read it."

"'There are several villages in Kafiristan which are places of
refuge, where slayers of their fellow tribesmen reside perma-
nently!'"

"It says 'fellow tribesmen' and I thought you were going to
Nuristan. This says Kafiristan."

"Don't quibble. It was called Kafiristan until 1895. It
goes on; listen to this: 'Kafir women are practically slaves,
being to all intents and purposes bought and sold as household
commodities.'"

"I'm practically a slave, married to you."

"'The young women are mostly immoral. There is little
or no ceremony about a Kafir marriage. If a man becomes
enamoured of a girl, he sends a friend to her father to ask her
price. If a price is agreed upon the man immediately proceeds
to the girl's house, where a goat is sacrificed and then they are

considered to be married.   The dead are disposed of in a peculiar manner.' "

"Apart from the goat, it sounds like a London season.   Besides he admits it's all out of date.   I'm coming as far as I jolly well can."

"What about the children?"

"The children can stay with my mother in Trieste."

I was heavily involved on all fronts: with mountaineering outfitters, who oddly enough never fathomed the depths of my ignorance; possibly because they couldn't conceive of anyone acquiring such a collection of equipment without knowing how to use it: with the Consuls of six countries, and with a Bulgarian with whom I formed an indissoluble entente in a pub off Queen's Gate.   He was a real prototype Bulgarian with a big moustache and lots of black hair.

"Have a pint of Worthington, Mr. Kolarov."

"I SHALL like it."   He threw his head back and it was gone.

"You like it?"

"Not strong enough.   I shall have a cognac, then I shall have a Worthington, then perhaps another cognac, then perhaps I shall be more gay."

More soberly with the Foreign Office, who had to obtain permission from the Ambassador at Kabul for Hugh to visit Afghanistan.   I was interviewed by a representative of the Asian Desk in the sombre room full of hair sofas and broken umbrellas reserved for persons like myself, intruders from the outside world without credentials.   We faced each other across a large mahogany table.   Like all such encounters it was not a success.

"We have sent the Ambassador a long cable."

"But that was a month ago."

"It is not as simple as you think."   Without undue subtlety he managed to convey that I never thought at all.   "You can hardly blame *us* if you leave a request of this kind until the last moment, besides, there is nothing to stop you going to Afghanistan, the cable only refers to Carless."

"Grr."

With the Autumn Collection.   It was now the second week in May.   I was leaving in a fortnight.   To add to my troubles

I now received a letter from Hugh. It was extremely alarming. I read it to Hyde-Clarke.

"'These three climbs will certainly be a good second-class mountaineering achievement. But we shall almost certainly need with us an experienced climber.'"

"I thought you said he was an experienced climber."

"So I did. Do listen!

"'What about Adam Arnold Brown who is now in India as a head of a public school at Begumpet?'" Here Hyde-Clarke chuckled. "'He was head of the Outward Bound Mountaineering School in Eskdale, and has done a good deal of Alpine climbing. He and I were at Trinity Hall together. I have sent him a cable asking him to join us in Kabul by air for a five-week assault on three 20,000 feet peaks but he may be on leave. His address in London is *V/C (WRATH) W.C.1.*'"

"Very appropriate, but what a terrifying cable to receive."

"That's only the beginning. Listen to this.

"'It is just possible that he may not be able to come. In which case we must try elsewhere. In my opinion the companion we need should not only have climbing ability and leadership but round out our party's versatility by bringing different qualities, adding them to ours.'"

"It sounds like the formula for some deadly gas."

"Will you listen! This isn't funny to me.

"'Perhaps he would be a Welsh miner, or a biologist, or a young Scots doctor. Someone from quite another background, bringing another point of view . . .'"

"For the first time," said Hyde-Clarke, "I'm beginning to be just a little bit jealous. I'd just love to listen to you all lying on top of one another in one of those inadequate little tents, seeing one another's points of view."

"Why don't you come too? I don't see why Hugh should be the only one to invite his friends.

"'All proper expeditions seem to have a faithful administrative officer, who toils through the night to get everyone and everything off from London on time and then is forgotten.'"

"I like the part about being forgotten."

"'I know how busy you must be but couldn't you find one?'"

"With a ginger moustache and a foul pipe . . ."

"Captain Foulenough?"

"Why don't you write to Beachcomber?"

We pursued this fantasy happily for some time.

"'Have you approached the Everest Foundation? They are there to assist small parties such as ours.'"

"Not quite like yours, I should have thought," said Hyde-Clarke. "I should try the Oxford Group. Ring up Brown's Hotel."

I received only one more letter before Hugh left Rio.

'If you want to take a Folboat you could make the passage down the Kabul River from Jalalabad, through the frontier gorge in Mahsud Territory, just north of the Khyber, past Peshawar and Nowshera to Attock where the waters of the Kabul and Indus rivers flow together through a magnificent defile. There on the cliffs Jelal ud Din, the young ruler of Bokhara and Samarqand, made a last stand against the Mongol hordes and, having lost the day, galloped his horse over the cliffs, which as far as I can remember are 150 feet high, swam the river, went to Delhi and carved out another kingdom.'

CHAPTER THREE

Birth of a Mountain Climber

WHEN Hugh arrived from New York ten days later I went to meet him at London Airport. Sitting in those sheds on the north side which still, twelve years after the war, give the incoming traveller the feeling that he is entering a beleaguered fortress, I wondered what surprises he had in store for me.

His first words after we had greeted one another were to ask if there was any news from Arnold Brown.

"Not a thing."

"That's bad," he said.

"It's not so disastrous. After all, you have done some climbing. I'll soon pick it up. We'll just have to be careful."

He looked pale. I put it down to the journey. Then he said: "You know I've never done any *real* climbing."

It took me some time to assimilate this.

"But all that stuff about the mountain. You and Dreesen . . ."

"Well, that was more or less a reconnaissance."

"But all this gear. How did you know what to order?"

"I've been doing a lot of reading."

"But you said you had porters."

"Not porters—drivers. It's not like the Himalayas. There aren't any 'tigers' in Afghanistan. No one knows anything about mountaineering."

There was a long silence as we drove down the Great West Road.

"Perhaps we should postpone it for a year," he said.

"Ha-ha. I've just given up my job!"

Hugh stuck out his jaw. Normally a determined-looking man, the effect was almost overwhelming.

"There's nothing for it," he said. "We must have some lessons."

Wanda and I were leaving England for Istanbul on June 1st. Hugh and I had just four days to learn about climbing.

The following night after some brisk telephoning we left for Wales to learn about climbing, in the brand new station wagon Hugh had ordered by post from South America. He had gone to Brighton to fetch it. Painted in light tropical colours it had proved to be rather conspicuous in Hammersmith. Soon it had been covered with swarms of little boys and girls whose mothers stood with folded arms silently regarding it.

We had removed all the furniture from the drawing-room to make room for the equipment and stores. Our three-piece suite was standing in the garden under a tarpaulin. The drawing-room looked like the quartermaster's store of some clandestine force. It was obvious that Hugh was deeply impressed.

"How long have you been living like this?"

"Ever since we can remember. It's not all here yet. There's still the food."

"What food?" He looked quite alarmed.

"Six cases of Army ration, compo. in fibre boxes. It's arriving tomorrow."

"We can always leave it in England. I don't know about you but food doesn't interest me. We can always live off the country.'

I remembered von Dückelmann, that hardy Austrian forester without an ounce of spare flesh on him, who had lost twelve pounds in a fortnight in Nuristan.

"Whatever else we leave behind it won't be the food."

"Well, I suppose we can always give it away." He sounded almost shocked, as if for the first time he had detected in me a grave moral defect. It was an historic moment.

With unconcealed joy my wife watched us load some of the mountaineering equipment into the machine.

"We'd better not take all of it," Hugh said. "They might

wonder why we've got so much stuff if we don't know how to use it."

Over the last weeks the same thought had occurred to me constantly.

"What about the tent?"

The tent had arrived that morning. It had been described to me by the makers as being suitable for what they called 'the final assault'. With its sewn-in ground-sheet, special flaps so that it could be weighed down with boulders, it convinced me, more than any other single item of equipment, that we were going, as the books have it, 'high'. It had been specially constructed for the curious climatic conditions we were likely to encounter in the Hindu Kush.

"I shouldn't take *that*, if I were you," said my wife with sinister emphasis. "The children tried to put it up in the garden after lunch. Whoever made it forgot to make holes for the poles."

"Are you sure?"

"Quite sure. You know it's got those poles shaped like a V, that you slip into a sort of pocket in the material. Well, they haven't made any pockets, so you can't put it up."

"It's lucky you found out. We should have looked pretty silly on Mir Samir."

"You're going to look pretty silly at any rate. I shouldn't be surprised if they've done the same thing to your sleeping-bags."

"Have you telephoned the makers?"

"That's no use. If you send it back to them, you'll never see it again. I've sent for the little woman who makes my dresses. She's coming tomorrow morning."

We continued to discuss what we should take to Wales.

"I should take your Folboat," said Hugh. "There's bound to be a lake near the inn. It will be a good chance of testing it BEFORE YOU PASS THROUGH THE GORGES. The current is tremendously swift."

I had never had any intention of being either drowned or ritually mutilated in Mahsud Territory. I told him that I hadn't got a Folboat.

"I was almost certain I wrote to you about getting a Folboat. It's a pity. There's not much time now."

"No," I said, "there isn't."

It was nearly midnight when we left London. Our destination was an inn situated in the wilds of Caernarvonshire. Hugh had telephoned the proprietor and explained to him the peculiar state of ignorance in which we found ourselves. It was useless to dissemble: Hugh had told him everything. He was not only an experienced mountaineer, but was also the head of the mountain rescue service. It is to his eternal credit that he agreed to help us rather than tell us, as a more conventional man might have done, that his rooms were all booked.

We arrived at six o'clock the following morning, having driven all night, but already a spiral of smoke was issuing from a chimney at the back of the premises.

The first thing that confronted us when we entered the hotel was a door on the left. On it was written EVEREST ROOM. Inside it was a facsimile of an Alpine hut, done out in pine wood, with massive benches round the walls. On every side was evidence of the presence of the great ones of the mountain world. Their belongings in the shape of ropes, rucksacks, favourite jackets and boots were everywhere, ready for the off. It was not a museum. It was more like the Royal Enclosure. Sir John and Sir Edmund might appear at any moment. They were probably on the premises.

"Whatever else we do I don't think we shall spend much time in the *Everest Room*," said Hugh, as we reverently closed the door. "For the first time I'm beginning to feel that we really do know damn all."

"EXACTLY."

At this moment we were confronted by a remarkably healthy-looking girl.

"Most people have had breakfast but it's still going on," she said.

The only other occupant of the breakfast room was a compact man of about forty-five, who was eating his way through the sort of breakfast I hadn't been able to stomach for ten years. He was wearing a magnificent sweater that was the product of peasant industry. He was obviously a climber. With an hysterical attempt at humour, like soldiers before an attack, we tried to turn him into a figure of fun, speaking in whispers. This proved difficult, as he wasn't at all comic, just plainly competent.

"He looks desperately healthy." (His face was the colour of old furniture.)

"Everyone looks healthy here, except us."

"I don't think it's real tan."

"Perhaps he's making a film about mountain rescue."

"How very appropriate."

"Perhaps he'll let us stand-in, as corpses."

After breakfast the proprietor introduced us to the mystery man. We immediately felt ashamed of ourselves.

"This is Dr. Richardson," he said. "He's very kindly agreed to take you out and teach you the rudiments of climbing."

"Have you ever done any?" asked the Doctor.

It seemed no time to bring up my scrambles in the Dolomites, nor even Hugh's adventures at the base of Mir Samir.

"No," I said firmly, "neither of us knows the first thing about it."

We had arrived at seven; by nine o'clock we were back in the station wagon, this time bound for the north face of the mountain called Tryfan.

"Stop here," said the Doctor. Hugh parked the car by a milestone that read 'Bangor X Miles'. Rearing up above the road was a formidable-looking chunk of rock, the *Milestone Buttress*.

"That's what you're going to climb," said the Doctor. "It's got practically everything you need at this stage."

It seemed impossible. In a daze we followed him over a rough wall and into the bracken. A flock of mountain sheep watched us go, making noises that sounded suspiciously like laughter.

Finally we reached the foot of it. Close-to it didn't seem so formidable. The whole face was scarred by the nailed boots of countless climbers.

"This thing is like a by-pass," said the Doctor. "Later in

the season you'd have to queue up to climb it.   We're lucky to
have it to ourselves."

"If there's one thing we don't need it's an audience."

"First of all you've got to learn about the rope.   Without
a rope climbing is suicide.   It's the only thing that justifies it.
Chris told me what you're planning to do.   If anything happens
on that mountain, it may not get into the papers, and at least no
one else will have to risk their necks to get you off if anything
goes wrong.   If I thought that you were the sort of people who
would take risks, I wouldn't have come with you today."

He showed us how to rope ourselves together, using the proper
knots; the bowline for the leader and the end man; the butter-
fly noose, a beautifully symmetrical knot, for the middleman;
how to hold it and how to coil it so that it would pay out without
snarling up, and how to belay.

"You never move without a proper belay.   I start to climb
and I go on until I reach a knob of rock on to which I can belay.
I take a *karabiner*" (he produced one of the D-shaped steel rings
with a spring-loaded clip) "and attach a sling to the loop of
rope round my waist.   Then all I have to do is to put the sling
over the knob of rock, and pass the rope under one shoulder
and over the other.   If possible, you brace your feet against a
solid block.   Like that you can take the really big strain if the
next man comes off."

"When the second man reaches the leader, the leader unclips
the *karabiner* with the sling on it, and the second man attaches
it to *his* waist.   He's now belayed.   The second man gives his
own sling to the leader who goes on to the next pitch.   Like
this."

"What I don't see," I whispered to Hugh, "is what happens
if the leader falls on the first pitch.   According to this he's
done for."

"The leader just mustn't fall off."

"Remind me to let you be leader."

The Doctor now showed what I thought was a misplaced
trust in us.   He sent us to the top of a little cliff, not more than
twenty feet high, with a battered-looking holly tree growing on
it.   "I want you to pretend that you're the leader," he said to

Hugh. "I want you to belay yourself with a sling and a *karabiner* to the holly tree. On the way up I am going to fall off backwards and I shan't tell you when I'm going to do it. You've got to hold me." He began to climb.

He reached the top and was just about to step over the edge when, without warning, he launched himself backwards into space. And then the promised miracle happened, for the rope was taut and Hugh was holding him, not by the belay but simply with the rope passed under one shoulder and over the other. There was no strain on the sling round Hugh's waist at all, his body was like a spring. I was very impressed—for the first time I began to understand the trust that climbers must be able to have in one another.

"Now it's your turn," said the Doctor.

It was like a memorable day in 1939 when I fell backwards off the fore upper topsail yard of a four-masted barque, only this time I expected Hugh to save me. And he did. Elated we practised this new game for some time until the Doctor looked at his watch. It was 11.30.

"We'd better get on to the rock. We wouldn't normally but there's so little time and you seem to be catching on to the roping part. Let's go. We'll take the *Ordinary Route*. You may think it isn't much but don't just go bald-headed at it. I'm going to lead. It's about two hundred feet altogether. We start in this chimney." He indicated an inadequate-looking cleft in the rock face.

It seemed too small to contain a human being at all but the Doctor vanished into it easily enough. Like me, he was wearing nailed boots, not the new-fangled ones with rubber vibram soles. I could hear them screeching on the rock as he scrabbled for a foothold. There was a lot of grunting and groaning then he vanished from sight.

Hugh went next. It was easier for him as he was very slim.

Then it was my turn. Like a boa-constrictor swallowing a live chicken, I wriggled up it, with hideous wear and tear to my knees, until I emerged on a boulder slope.

"Now we begin," said the Doctor.

"What was that, if it wasn't the beginning?"

"The start. This is the beginning."

"How very confusing."

The worst part was what he called 'Over the garden wall', which entailed swinging round a projection, hanging over a void and then traversing along a ledge into a cave.

"I wish he'd wear rubbers," I said to Hugh, as the Doctor vanished over the wall with a terrible screeching of tricounis. "It's not the climbing I object to, it's the noise."

·There was still a twenty-foot chimney with a tree in it up which we fought our way and, at last, we lay on the top panting and admiring the view which was breathtaking. I was very impressed and proud. It wasn't much but I had done my first climb.

"What do you call this?" Hugh said, warily. "Easy, difficult or something in between?"

"Moderate."

"How do they go? I've forgotten."

"Easy, moderate, difficult, very difficult, severe, very severe, exceptionally severe, and excessively severe."

"Oh."

While we were eating our sandwiches the Doctor began to describe what he called 'The Free Rappel'. More than a year has passed since, for the first and last time, I practised this excruciatingly painful method of descending the face of a mountain. Even now I am unable to remember it without a shudder. Like the use of the bayonet, it was something to be learned and, if possible, forgotten for ever.

"You first," said the Doctor. In dealing with him we suffered the disadvantage that he wasn't retained at some handsome fee to teach us all this. He was in fact ruining his holiday, in order to give us a slightly more than even chance of surviving.

"Put a sling round the tree and run the double rope through it; now pass it round your right thigh, between your legs; now up the back and sling it over your left shoulder so that it falls down in front. That's right. Now walk backwards to the edge, keep the rope taut. Now keep your legs horizontal and walk down."

I walked down. It would have been perfect if only the face

of the cliff had been smooth; unfortunately it was slightly concave, which made it difficult to keep my legs at right angles to the face. I failed to do so, slipped and went swinging backwards and forwards across the face like a pendulum, with the rope biting into my groin.

"Well, you've learned one lesson," Hugh said cheerfully, when I reached the bottom after disengaging myself from the rope and swarming down in a more conventional manner.

"If it's a question of doing that again or being castrated by Mahsuds, I'll take the Mahsuds. My groin won't stand up to much more of this."

"You must be very sensitive," Hugh said. "Lots of girls do it."

"I'm not a girl. There must be some other way. It's impossible in thin trousers."

After a large, old-fashioned tea at the inn with crumpets and boiled eggs, we were taken off to the *Eckenstein Boulder*. Oscar Eckenstein was a renowned climber at the end of the nineteenth century, whose principal claim to fame was that he had been the first man in this or any other country to study the technique of holds and balance on rock. He had spent his formative years crawling over the boulder that now bore his name. Although it was quite small, about the size of a delivery van, his boulder was said to apparently embody all the fundamental problems that are such a joy to mountaineers and were proving such a nightmare to us.

For this treat we were allowed to wear gym shoes.

Full of boiled egg and crumpet, we clung upside down to the boulder like bluebottles, while the Doctor shouted encouragement to us from a safe distance. Occasionally one of us would fall off and land with a painful thump on the back of his head.

"YOU MUST NOT FALL OFF. Imagine that there is a thousand-foot drop under you."

"I am imagining it but I still can't stay on."

Back at the inn we had hot baths, several pints of beer, an enormous dinner and immediately sank into a coma. For more than forty hours we had had hardly any sleep. "Good training," was Hugh's last muffled comment.

By this time the waitresses at the inn had become interested in this artificial forcing process. All three of them were experienced climbers who had taken the job in the first place in order to be able to combine business with pleasure. Now they continued our climbing education.

They worked in shifts, morning and afternoon, so that we were climbing all the time. We had never encountered anything quite like them before. At breakfast on the last day, Judith, a splendid girl with auburn hair whose father had been on Everest in 1933, told us what she had in mind. "Pamela and I are free this afternoon; we're going to do the *Spiral Stairs* on Dinas Cromlech. It's an interesting climb."

As soon as we could get through our breakfast we looked it up in the Climbing Guide to the Snowdon District, Part 6.

'Dinas Cromlech,' said the book, 'is perhaps the most impressive cliff on the north side of the Llanberis Pass, its massive rhyolite pillars giving it the appearance of some grim castle . . . all routes have surprising steepness . . . on the whole the rock is sound, although *on first acquaintance it may not appear to be so.*'

Spiral Stairs was described as 'Very difficult' and as having 'an impressive first pitch with good exposure'. At the back was a nasty picture of the Cromlech with the routes marked on it. Besides *Spiral Stairs* there was *Cenotaph Corner*, *Ivy Sepulchre* and the *Sexton's Route*. It sounded a jolly spot.

"I wish we were doing *Castle Gully*. It says here, 'a pleasant vegetable route'."

"They might have decided on *Ivy Sepulchre*," said Hugh. "Just listen to this. 'Two hundred feet. Exceptionally severe. A very serious and difficult climb . . . loose rock overhangs . . . progress is made by a bridging type of lay-back movement, an occasional hold of a doubtful nature appearing *now* and *then*.' He doesn't say what you do when it doesn't."

"What's a lay-back?"

"You were doing a lay-back when you fell off the Eckenstein Boulder."

"This is only the beginning, it gets worse. 'At this point the angle relents . . .' "

"Relents is good," I said.

" '. . . to a small niche below the conspicuous overhang; no belay. Start the overhang by bridging. The climbing at this point is exceptionally severe, strenuous and in a very exposed position.' It goes on and on! 'A short groove leads to the foot of an old rickety holly tree and after a struggle with this and the crack behind it, a good hold can be reached on the left wall.' "

"I wonder why everything seems to end with a rickety old holly tree."

We decided to have a quiet morning. Just then the other two girls appeared loaded with gear.

"Hurry up," they said, "we've got to be back by half-past twelve. We're going to take you up *The Gauge*. You made a nonsense of it, the Doctor said. And you've both got to lead."

That afternoon, as Judith led the way up the scree from the road towards the base of Dinas Cromlech, we felt that if anything the guide book, in spite of its sombre warnings, had not prepared us for the reality. It was as if a giant had been smoothing off the sides of a heap of cement with a trowel and had then lost patience and left it half finished. Its most impressive feature was a vast, right-angled wall, shiny with water and apparently smooth.

"*Cenotaph Corner*," said Judith, "Hundred and twenty feet. When you can do that you really will be climbers."

It seemed impossible.

"Joe Brown led it in 1952, with Belshaw. Joe's a plumber in Manchester. He spends every moment he can here. You remember how awful it was last winter when everyone's pipes were bursting? In the middle of it he left a note on the door of his house: 'Gone climbing. Joe Brown.' People nearly went mad."

"Where is he now?"

"In the Himalayas."

We looked at what he had climbed with awe.

There were already three people on *Spiral Stairs*. I could see what the book meant by 'good exposure'. At that moment one of them was edging his way round the vertical left-hand edge of *Cenotaph Corner*.

"That's the part that always gives me a thrill," said Pamela, the other girl. "Pity. Let's not wait, let's do *Ivy Sepulchre* instead."

"Oh, Pamela, do you think we ought to? It may be too much for them."

She made us sound like a couple of invalids out on the pier for an airing. Nevertheless, this was no time for stubborn pride. I asked Hugh if that was the climb we had been reading about at breakfast. He said it was.

"I think Judith's right," I said. "It may be too much for us."

As we waited in the cold shadow under the lee of the *Cenotaph*, Judith explained what we were going to do.

"The beginning's rather nasty because of that puddle. It makes your feet slippery just when they need to be dry. We'll climb in two parties. Pamela will lead Hugh, I'll lead you. The first part's seventy feet; round the edge of the *Cenotaph* it's very exposed and you'll feel the wind. Don't come on until I shout and you feel pressure on the rope. I'll be belayed then. Even if you come off you won't fall far."

"What happens if someone does come off? You can't just leave them hanging."

"Send for the fire brigade," said Judith.

Both girls were shuffling their boots on the rock like feather-weight boxers.

Then Pamela was gone, soon to be followed by Hugh.

After what seemed an eternity it was Judith's turn. I had her belayed but at this stage it wasn't much use: I remembered the Doctor's warning, 'The leader must not fall off.' Then she vanished. I continued to pay out the rope. There was a long interval and I heard her shout very distantly to come on and the rope tautened.

It was impossible to get on to the rock without getting at least one foot wet.

Very slowly I worked my way out to the corner of the *Sepulchre*. As I edged round it into what seemed to be empty space I came on to the part with good exposure, the part that always gave Pamela a thrill. Below me was a huge drop to the rocks and as I came round the wind blew my hair into my eyes.

Two more pitches and we were on the top. I felt a tremendous exaltation. Sitting there on a boulder was a man in a bowler hat and white collar smoking a pipe.

"Early closing in Caernarvon," Judith said.

"He looks like an undertaker to me."

"We shall have to hurry, it's Pamela's day to serve tea." We went down a wide gully, then raced down the scree to the car. The others were waiting for us. The girls were pleased, so were we. Only the man with the bowler hat weighed on my mind. I asked Hugh if he had seen him.

"Which man? We didn't see a man."

"Now you're making me feel like one of those school-teachers at Versailles."

"We saw the other party, but we didn't see a man in a bowler hat."

As we were leaving for London, Judith gave me a little pamphlet costing sixpence. It showed, with the aid of pictures, the right and wrong ways of climbing a mountain.

"We haven't been able to teach you anything about snow and ice," she said, "but this shows you how to do it. If you find anything on the journey out with snow on it, I should climb it if you get the chance."

"I wish we were coming with you," she added, "to keep you out of trouble."

"So do we," we said, and we really meant it. Everyone turned out to say goodbye. It was very heart-warming.

"You know that elderly gentleman who lent you a pair of climbing boots," Hugh said, as we drove through the evening sunshine towards Capel Curig.

"You mean Mr. Bartrum?"

"Did you know he's a past President of the Alpine Club? He's written a letter about us to the Everest Foundation. He showed it to me."

I asked him what it said.

"He wrote, 'I have formed a high opinion of the character and determination of Carless and Newby and suggest that they should be given a grant towards the cost of their expedition to the Hindu Kush.' "

CHAPTER FOUR

Pera Palace

ELEVEN days later I arrived with Wanda in Istanbul. As we drove along the last long stretch of road, lurching into the pot-holes, the Sea of Marmara appeared before us, green and windswept, deserted except for a solitary caique beating up towards the Bosphorus under a big press of sail. Our spirits rose at the thought of seeing Istanbul when the sun was setting, but when we reached the outskirts it was already quite dark. We had planned to enter the city by the Golden Gate on the seaward side, for it sounded romantic and appropriate and we had been stoking ourselves all the way across Europe with the thought of it, not knowing that for several hundred years the gate had been sealed up. Instead we found ourselves on an interminable bypass lined with luminous advertisements for banks and razor blades. Of the wall constructed by Theodosius there was no sign. It was a fitting end to an uncomfortable journey.

We left the car in the courtyard of the old Embassy and changed our money with one of the gatekeepers. We asked him where we should stay.

"Star *Oteli*, clean *Oteli*, cheap *Oteli*, good *Oteli*, *Oteli* of my brodder."

"Is it far?"

"Not so far; take taxi, always taxi. Bad place, at night bad menses and girlses."

"Order a taxi."

He uttered some strange cries. As if by magic a taxi appeared. It was driven by a huge brute with a shaven head; sitting next to him was another smaller man. They were a sinister pair.

"What's the other one for?"

"He is not for anything. He is brodder."

"They don't look like brothers."

"He is brodder by other woman."

With a roar the taxi shot forward. After fifty yards it stopped and the brother opened the door.

"Star *Oteli*."

With sinking hearts we followed him up a nearly vertical flight of stairs to the reception desk. I prayed that the hotel would be full but it wasn't. We set off down a long brilliantly lit passage, the brother of the gatekeeper leading and the brother of the taxi man bringing up the rear to cut off our retreat. The doors on either side were open, and we could see into the rooms. The occupants all seemed to be men who were lying on their beds fully clothed, gazing at the ceiling. Everywhere, like a miasma, was the unforgettable grave-smell of Oriental plumbing.

"Room with bed for two," said the proprietor, flinging open a door at the extreme end. He contrived to invest it with an air of extreme indelicacy, which in no way prepared us for the reality.

It was a nightmare room, the room of a drug fiend or an epileptic or perhaps both. It was illuminated by a forty-watt bulb and looked out on a black wall with something slimy growing on it. The bed was a fearful thing, almost perfectly concave. Underneath it was a pair of old cloth-topped boots. The sheets were almost clean but on them there was the unmistakable impress of a human form and they were still warm. In the corner there was a washbasin with one long red hair in it and a tap which leaked. Somewhere nearby a fun-fair was testing its loud-hailing apparatus, warming up for a night of revelry. The smell of the room was the same as the corridor outside with some indefinable additions.

After the discomforts of the road it was too much. In deep gloom we got back into the taxi. The driver was grinning.

"Pera Palace!"

As we plunged down the hill through the cavern-like streets, skidding on the tramlines, the brothers screwed their heads round and carried on a tiresome conversation with their backs to the engine.

"Pera very good."

Never had a city affected me with such an overpowering sense of melancholy.

"No."

"Very good Istanbul."

"Very good taxi." We were heading straight for a tram that was groaning its way up the hill but passed it safely on the wrong side of the road.

I asked if anyone was ever killed. "Many, many, every day."

"How many?"

"Two million."

At the Pera Palace we took a large room. Originally it must have had a splendid view of the Golden Horn, now there was a large building in the way. We sent our clothes to the laundry and went to bed.

There had been no news of Hugh at the Embassy, but before sinking into a coma of fatigue, we both uttered a prayer that he would be delayed.

Early on the following morning he was battering on our door. He had just arrived by air and was aggressively fit and clean. Between his teeth was a Dunhill pipe in which some luxurious mixture was burning; under his arm was a clip board full of maps and lists. His clothes had just the right mixture of the elegant and the dashing. He was the epitome of a young explorer. We knew what he would say. It was an expression that we were to hear with ever-increasing revulsion in the weeks to come.

"We must leave at once."

"We can't, the wagon's got to be serviced."

"I've already arranged that. It'll be ready at noon."

Like survivors of an artillery bombardment we were still shaking from the spine-shattering road we had taken through Bulgaria. What the pre-war guide had described as 'another route':

"It's been rather a long drive." We enumerated the hardships we had undergone, how we had been stripped by customs officials on the Jugoslav frontier, the hailstones as big as pigeons' eggs in the Balkans, the floods, landslips, mosquitoes, all the tedious mishaps of our journey; but lying in our splendid bed we were not objects for obvious sympathy.

"I shall drive. You two can rest."

"You don't seem to realise," I said, "there's no rest in that machine, there's so much stuff in it. After a bit we were fighting one another to drive. Besides, damn it, we want to see Istanbul."

"You can always see Istanbul some other time. It's been here for two thousand years."

"You mean *you* can always see it another time."

He looked at his watch reluctantly.

"How long do you want?"

Only Wanda had the courage to answer. "Three days," she said.

We grew fond of the Pera Palace; the beds had big brass knobs on and were really comfortable. Our room seemed the setting for some ludicrous comedy that was just about to begin. Probably it had already been played many times. It was easy to imagine some bearded minister of Abdul Hamid pursuing a fat girl in black stockings and garters round it and hurting himself on the sharp bits of furniture. In the bathroom the bath had the unusual facility of filling itself by way of the waste pipe without recourse to the taps. We watched this process enthralled.

"I think it's when the current's running strongly in the Bosphorus."

"It can't be that. It's warm."

"Why don't you taste it?"

"I can't remember whether the Bosphorus is salt or not. Besides it's a very curious colour sometimes."

It was Wanda who discovered the truth. I found her with her ear jammed hard against the wall of the bathroom.

"It's the man next door. He's just had a bath. Now he's pulled out the plug. Here it comes."

For the second time that day the bath began to fill silently.

By contrast the staff were mostly very old and very sad and, apart from our friend in the next bathroom, we never saw anyone. There was a restaurant where we ate interminable meals in an atmosphere of really dead silence. It was the hotel of our dreams.

Three days later we left Istanbul. The night porter at the Pera Palace had been told to call us at a quarter to four; knowing that he wouldn't, I willed myself to wake at half-past three. I did so but immediately fell into a profound slumber until Hugh arrived an hour later from his modern *Oteli* up the hill, having bathed, shaved, breakfasted and collected the vehicle. It was not an auspicious beginning to our venture. He told us so.

There was a long wait for the ferry to take us to Scutari and when it did finally arrive embarkation proceeded slowly. Consumed by an urgent necessity, I asked the ferry master who bowed me into his own splendidly appointed quarters, where I fell into a delightful trance, emerging after what seemed only a moment to see the ferry boat disappearing towards the Asian shore with the motor-car and my ticket. At the barrier there was a great press of people and one of three fine-looking porters stole my wallet. It was the ferry master himself who escorted me on to the next boat, '*pour tirer d'embarras notre client distingué*' as he ironically put it. For the second time in my life I left Europe penniless.

CHAPTER FIVE

The Dying Nomad

ON the road from Istanbul we were detained by a series of misadventures in Armenia. At Horasan, a small one-street town on the Aras river, instead of turning right for Agri and the Persian frontier, Hugh roared straight on. There was a long climb, followed by a descent on hairpin bends into a canyon of red, silver and green cliffs, with a castle perched on the top, down to a village where the air was cool under the trees and women were treading something underfoot in a river, and a level stretch under an overhanging cliff where gangs working on a narrow gauge railway were bringing down avalanches of stones. On the right was the same fast running river.

We were tired and indescribably dirty. In the last of the sunlight we crossed a green meadow and bathed in a deep pool. It was very cold.

"What river do you think this is?" Bathed and shaved we sat in the meadow putting on clean socks. Behind a rock, further downstream Wanda was washing her hair.

"It's the Aras."

"But the Aras flows west to east; this one's going in the opposite direction."

"How very peculiar. What do you make of it?"

"It can't be the Aras."

With night coming down we drove on beside the railway, over a wooden bridge that thundered and shuddered under our weight, through a half-ruined village built of great stone blocks where two men were battering one another to death and the women, black-skirted and wearing white head-scarves, minded their own business, up and up through a ravine with the railway

always on our left, into pine forests where the light was blue and
autumnal—partisan, Hemingway country, brooding and silent—
past a sealed-up looking house, with Hugh's dreadful radio blaring
all the time louder and louder until suddenly we realised that
what we were listening to was Russian, crystal clear and getting
stronger every minute.

Hugh stopped the car and switched on the light and we huddled
over the map, which Wanda had been studying with a torch.

"Do you know where we are?" He looked very serious.

"About sixty kilometres from Kars," she said.

"But we're on the wrong road. That's on the Russian
Frontier."

"Not quite on it. The frontier's here"—she pointed to the
map—"on the river, a long way from the town."

"How long have you known this?" I had never seen him so
worried.

"Since we had that swim: the current was going the wrong
way. I thought you realised it."

At first I thought he was going to hit her. Finally, he said
in a strangled sort of voice, "We must go back immediately."

"Whatever for? Look, there's a road along the Turkish side
of the river, south to Argadsh, just north of Ararat. It's a
wonderful chance. If we're stopped all we've got to say is that
we took the wrong road."

"It's all very well for you. Do you realise *my* position?
I'm a member of the Foreign Service but I haven't got a diplomatic visa for Turkey. We have permission to cross Anatolia
by the shortest possible route. In this vehicle we've got several
cameras, one with a long-focus lens, a telescope, prismatic com-
passes, an aneroid and several large-scale maps."

"The maps are all of Afghanistan."

"Do you think they'll know the difference at a road block?
We've even got half a dozen daggers."

"They weren't *my* idea. I always said daggers were crazy."

"That's not the point. You saw what the Turks were like
in Erzerum. We shall all be arrested. We may even get shot.
It's got all the makings of an incident. And you're not even
British."

"By marriage," said Wanda, "but I think you're making it sound much worse than it really is."

We argued with him in the growing darkness, even made fun of him, but it was no use, he was beyond the reach of humour. On his face was a look that I had never seen. He spoke with an air of absolute certainty, like a man under the influence of drugs. Like the Mole in *The Wind in the Willows* picking up the scent of his old home, Hugh was in direct contact with the Foreign Office, S.W.1, and the scent was breast-high.

It took me some moments to remember where I had encountered this almost mad certainty before, then it came to me—at the memorable interview with the man from the Asian Desk.

We were ninety kilometres from Horasan. Finally he agreed to continue to the next town, Sarikamis, and return the following day.

But the next day had brought disaster and tragedy. Towards evening we had arrived at Bayazid. 'Fortress town on the Persian Frontier; close to Ararat on the great caravan road from Tabriz to Erzerum with the Serail of Ezak Pasha on a rock.' The ancient guide to Turkey had made it sound romantic, but the splendours of the caravan road had departed and several earthquakes and countless massacres had made of Bayazid a sad, shanty town without a skyline, full of soldiers clumping down the single street in great boots, and debased-looking civilians in tattered western suits and cloth caps.

Determined to sleep in Persia we set off at breakneck speed towards the east. Night was coming on. The road was deserted; it ran through an arid plain; to the right were low mountains with, close under them, the black tents of the nomad people. All day, in the upland country about Ararat, we had seen bands of them on the march, driving their bullocks loaded with tent poles and big tribal cooking pots; vicious-looking donkeys with pack saddles, flocks of goats and sheep; the men and women on foot, the women in full red skirts with a sort of black surcoat and black balaclavas, the younger ones in pill-box hats and plaits, the boys wearing lambskin caps, the smallest children sitting, on white cushions, astride lean little horses; all moving westward along the line of the telegraph poles, each family enveloped in its own cloud of dust.

Less than a mile from the Customs House on the Turkish side, travelling in the last of the light, something dark loomed up on the road in front. Wanda shouted but Hugh was already braking hard. There was going to be an accident and it was going to take a long time to happen. I wondered whether he would swerve off the road and whether we should turn over when he did. He shouted to us to hold on, the wheels locked and we went into a long tearing skid, with the horn blaring and all our luggage falling on us, pressing us forward on to the windscreen, everything happening at once as we waited for the smash but instead coming to a standstill only a few feet from whatever it was in the road.

There was a moment of silence broken only by awful groans. We were fearful of what we should see but the reality was worse than anything we imagined. Lying in the road, face downwards, a shapeless black bundle covered with dust, was one of the nomads. He was an old man of about seventy, blackened by the sun, with a cropped grizzled head. Something had run him down from behind and his injuries were terrible; his nose was almost completely torn off and swelling up through a tear in the back of his shirt was a great liquid bulge; but he was still conscious and breathing like a steam engine.

We wrapped him in a blanket, put a big shell dressing on the maw where his nose had been, stopped the bleeding from the back of his head and wondered what to do next. We dared not move him off the road because we had no idea what internal injuries he had, nor could we give him morphia because it seemed certain that his brain must have been injured.

Now the men of the tribe came running, attracted by the lights. They were followed by the children and then by the women. With the women came the man's wife, a windswept black-haired creature of about thirty, who flung herself down in the dust with a jangling of gold ornaments and set up a great wailing. The rest stood in a half-circle in the light of the head-lamps and looked at us silently.

At the same moment a jeep arrived, full of soldiers. One of them was a doctor who spoke English. It seemed a miracle.

He lifted the shell dressing and winced. Then he saw the great blue swelling, now growing bigger.

"You must take him to the camp." (There was a military camp five miles back on the road.)

"But if he's moved he may die."

"He is going to die. You see that"—he pointed at the bulge—"haemorrhage. He may live till morning. He is strong old man but there is nothing to do."

"You will come with us?"

"I am going to ——" (He named a place none of us had ever heard of.) "It is you must take him."

We told him that we were going to Persia. Still we did not realise our predicament.

Then it came, like a bombshell.

"YOU CANNOT KILL MAN AND GO AWAY. THERE WILL BE INQUIRY."

"BUT WE DIDN'T. WE FOUND HIM. LOOK HERE." We showed him the tyre marks. They ended about seven feet from the body.

"To do such damage you must travel fast." He pointed to the crushed offside wing, legacy of Hugh's encounter with a London taxi. "But do not worry, *he* is only nomad. I am sorry for *you*."

His men helped us place the wounded man in the back seat. When he had gone we realised that we didn't know his name.

At the camp, a few huts under the mountains, there was no doctor. Nor could anyone speak Persian, French or German—only Turkish.

"Bayazid, Bayazid," was all they could say, waving us on. With the groans of the old man in our ears and the heartrending cries of his wife from the back seat where she supported him, we drove the fifteen miles to the town.

All night we sat under the electric light in the corridor of the military hospital, smoking cigarettes, dozing, going into the room where he was, to listen to his breathing as it became louder and louder. He died horribly, early the next morning on a canvas stretcher just as it was growing light, surrounded by judges and prosecutors and interpreters screaming at him, trying to find out what had run him down, the members of his family elbowed out by official observers.

As soon as the man was dead, the nightmare of the day began. In a convoy of vehicles we returned to the scene of the accident. In ours was a Judge, who seemed hostile; a young Pubhc Prosecutor, who didn't; a tall Colonel with a broken nose, hard as nails like a Liverpool policeman; a Captain, who was indifferent, neither unamiable nor amiable—nothing; an interpreter, who looked as though he had been routed out of a house of ill-fame, who spoke extraordinarily bad Levantine French of a purely declamatory kind; a number of really smelly policemen and two or three soldiers. Apart from the Interpreter, the Prosecutor spoke a few words of French but tried hard with them; the Captain not more than a dozen words of English but he was useless. All the rest spoke nothing but their native tongue. By a paradox it was the Prosecutor who seemed to offer the greatest hope. Worst of all was the interpreter, who seemed intent on destroying us.

"*Vous êtes Carless?*" he enquired sardonically as I was getting into the car to drive to the place of the accident. With all the more important officials in our car, which had been emptied of luggage in order to transport them, it seemed better that Hugh shouldn't drive.

"*Non, M'sieur.*"

"*Il faut que M. Carless conduit l'automobile.*"

"*Pourquoi?*"

"*M. Le Juge l'a dit.*"

All the way to the scene of the accident they watched Hugh like a hawk. It looked very bad for him. There on the gravel road was the long swerving mark of the skid ending practically where the body had been. The space between was already ploughed up by countless footmarks, but if we had hit the old man, the force of the blow would have thrown his body almost precisely into the position in which we found it.

The interrogation went on right through the baking noonday heat until evening. Half a dozen times we were made to re-enact the accident; the road was measured; the nomad children were made to collect stones to mark the key points; drawings were made; statements were taken. All we could say was that we had found him and that there had been no other witnesses— the nearest nomads had been nearly a mile from the road. It was not our fault, we said, you must believe us. But then there were the men of the tribe committing perjury, describing the accident, offering flowers to the Judge; while the Interpreter, sensing the dislike that we were trying so hard to conceal, redoubled his own efforts to destroy us by garbling everything we said. Worst of all they told us that ours was the only vehicle travelling towards the Customs House from the Turkish side on the evening of the accident.

Hugh was in a spot. The only hope seemed to be the Prosecutor, who had ordered the beating of several members of the tribe. "They are lying," he said, as he watched the policeman thumping them in the incandescent heat. "I am only interested in the *truth*. And I shall discover it." He was a remarkable man. But when we were alone we begged Hugh to send a cable to Ankara. He was absolutely immovable.

"I'm going to see it through myself," he said. "If it comes to a trial there's going to be the most shocking scandal at any rate. Whether they find me guilty or innocent, somebody. will always bring it up. The only thing is to convince them that I didn't do it at this stage before they charge me. Besides, what will my Ambassador think if I arrive in Persia under a cloud."

Exhausted we returned to the town. On the way one of the jeeps full of policemen broke down. The Judge ordered us to abandon them. No one was sorry, they were a brutal lot. We left them honking despairingly in the darkness; the soldiers were delighted.

But there were inexhaustible supplies of policemen; at the station in Bayazid half a dozen more poured out of the building, surrounding us.

"My God, they're going to lock me up for the night." All day Hugh had behaved with the most admirable calmness. Now for the first time he showed signs of strain.

"*Malheureusement*," said the Interpreter, turning to Wanda and myself and showing a set of broken yellow teeth, "*M. Carless doit rester ici mais VOUS, VOUS êtes libre.*"

"I don't need a policeman," Hugh said. I had never seen him so angry. "You have my word. I shan't run away."

"You are not arrested yet. It is to protect you from incidents. Perhaps people will be angry."

With a policeman outside the inn shooing away the passers-by, the three of us ate rice and kebab and some very odd vegetables and drank a whole bottle of raki. We were famished, having eaten nothing since the previous night.

At the next table was a medical officer in battledress. He was an Armenian and had the facility with languages of his race. "My name is Niki," he said. After dinner we sat with him on the roof under a rusty-looking moon. "This is a town of no-women," he said, pointing at the soldiery milling in the street below. "Look, there are thousands of them. They are all becoming mad because there is nothing here for them—or for me," he added more practically.

"This is your country?"

"This was my country. There is no Armenia any more. All those shops"—pointing at the shop fronts now shuttered and barred—"Armenian—dead, dead, all dead. Tomorrow they will decide whether you will be tried or not," he went on to Hugh. "If you need me I will come. I think it is better that you should not be tried. I have heard that there is a German from Tehran here, a lorry driver who has cut off a child's foot with his lorry. He has been three months awaiting a trial. They keep him without trousers so that he shall not escape."

Next morning all three of us took pains with our appearance. The internal arrangements at the inn were so loathsome that I shared a kerosene tin of water with Hugh and shaved on the roof, the cynosure of the entire population who were out in force. Wanda, debarred from public appearance, was condemned to the inside. As a final touch our shoes were cleaned by a boot-black who refused to charge. I was impressed but not Hugh.

"I don't suppose they charge anything at the Old Bailey." Nothing could shake his invincible gloom.

At nine o'clock, sweltering in our best clothes, we presented ourselves at the Courthouse and joined a queue of malefactors.

After a short wait we were called. The room was simple, whitewashed, with half a dozen chairs and a desk for the Prosecutor. On it was a telephone at which we looked lovingly. Behind the Prosecutor lurked his evil genius, the Interpreter.

The Prosecutor began to speak. It was obvious that one way or the other he had made his mind up. He was, he said, interested only in Justice and Justice would be done. It was unfortunate for M. Carless that he did not possess a Diplomatic Visa for Turkey otherwise it would be difficult to detain him. We now knew that Hugh was doomed. But, he went on, as his visa only applied to Iran, he proposed to ask for proceedings to be stayed for a week while he consulted the authorities in Ankara.

"*Malheureusement, c'est pas possible pour M. Carless,*" said the Interpreter winding up with relish, "*mais vous êtes libre d'aller en Iran.*"

For two hours we argued; when Hugh flagged I intervened; then Wanda took up the struggle; arguments shot backwards and forwards across the room like tennis balls: about diplomatic immunity, children languishing in Europe without their mother, ships and planes missed, expeditions ruined, the absence of witnesses.

"Several beatings were given yesterday for the discouragement of false witnesses and their evidence is inadmissible," said the Prosecutor, but he was remote, immovable.

"*Malheureusement vous devez rester ici sept jours pour qu'arrive une réponse à notre telegramme,*" said the Interpreter in his repulsive French.

"*Monsieur le Procureur a envoyé une telegramme?*"

"*Pas encore,*" replied the Interpreter, leering triumphantly. I had never seen him look happier.

We implored Hugh to send a telegram to Ankara. He was adamant but he did agree to send for Niki, the Armenian doctor. It was not easy to find an un-named Armenian M.O. in a garrison town but he arrived in an hour, by jeep, round and fat but to us a knight in armour. The Interpreter was banished and Niki began translating sentence by sentence, English to Turkish,

Turkish to English.   Hugh spoke of N.A.T.O. and there was a
flicker of interest, of how the two countries had fought together
on the same side in Korea, of the great qualities of the Turkish
Nation, of the political capital that the Russians would make when
the news became known, that such a situation would not happen
in England.   Finally, Hugh said he wanted to send a telegram.
We knew what agony this decision cost him.

"It is extremely difficult.   There is no direct communication.
We shall first have to send to Erzerum."

"Then send it to Erzerum."

"It will take three days.   You still wish?"

"Yes, I wish."

Hugh wrote the telegram.   It looked terrible on paper.   I
began to understand why he had been so reluctant to send it.

'Detained Bayazid en route Tehran awaiting formulation
of charge killing civilian stop Diplomatic visa applicable
Iran only.'

Niki translated it into Turkish; holding the message, the
Prosecutor left the room.   After a few minutes he returned with
a heavily moustached clerk in shirt-sleeves.   For more than ten
minutes he dictated with great fluency.   It was a long document.
When it was finished Niki read it aloud.   It gave an account of
the entire affair and expressed Hugh's complete innocence.

The last stamp was affixed; the Prosecutor clapped his hands,
coffee was brought in.

It all happened so quickly that it was difficult to believe that
it was all over.

"But what made him change his mind?"   It was an incredible
volte-face.

"The Public Prosecutor asks me to say," said Niki, "that it
is because M. Carless was gentlemanly in this thing, because you
were all gentlemanly," bowing to Wanda, "that he has decided
not to proceed with it."

CHAPTER SIX

Airing in a Closed Carriage

IN Tehran Wanda left us to return to Europe.

On the 30th June, eleven days from Istanbul, Hugh and I reached Meshed, the capital of the province of Khurasan, in north-east Persia, and drove through streets just dark to the British Consulate-General, abandoned since Mussadiq's coup and the breaking off of diplomatic relations in 1953.

After a long wait at the garden gate we were admitted by an old, grey-bearded sepoy of the Hazarah Pioneers. He had a Mongolian face and was dressed in clean khaki drill with buttons polished. Here we were entertained kindly by the Hindu caretaker.

The place was a dream world behind high walls, like a property in the Deep South of the United States. Everywhere lush vegetation reached out long green arms to destroy what half a century of care had built up. The great bungalows with walls feet thick were collapsing room by room, the wire gauze fly nettings over the windows were torn and the five-year-old bath water stagnant in the bathrooms. In the living rooms were great Russian stoves, standing ceiling high, black and banded like cannon set in the walls, warming two rooms at once, needing whole forests of wood to keep them going.

The Consulate building itself was lost and forgotten; arcades of Corinthian columns supported an upper balcony, itself collapsing. The house was shaded by great trees, planted perhaps a century ago, now at their most magnificent. Behind barred windows were the big green safes with combination locks in the confidential registry. I asked Hugh how they got them there.

"In the days of the *Raj* you could do anything."

"But they must weigh tons. There's no railway."

"If Curzon had anything to do with it, they were probably dragged overland from India."

On the wall in one of the offices we found a map of Central Asia. It was heavily marked in coloured pencil. One such annotation well inside Russian territory, beyond a straggling river, on some sand dunes in the Kara-Kum desert read, 'Captain X, July, '84' and was followed by a cryptic question mark.

"The Great Game," said Hugh. It was a sad moment for him, born nearly a century too late to participate in the struggle that had taken place between the two great powers in the no-man's-land between the frontiers of Asiatic Russia and British India.

Apart from Hugh and myself, everyone inside the Consulate firmly believed that the British would return. In the morning when we met the old man from Khurasan who had been in the Guides Cavalry, the younger one who had been in a regiment of Punjabis and the old, old man who was the caretaker's cook, I felt sad under their interrogation about my health and regiment. To them it was as though the Indian Army as they had known it still existed.

"*Apka misaj kaisa hai, Sahib?*"

"*Bilkul tik hai.*"

"*Apka paltan kya hai?*"

I had acquired Urdu rapidly sixteen years before. It had vanished as quickly as it came. Soon I dried up completely and was left mouthing affirmatives. "*Han, han.*"

"For God's sake don't keep on saying, '*Han, han*'. They'll think you're crazy."

"I've said everything I can remember. What do you want me to say. That we're not coming back, ever?"*

With all the various delights of Meshed to sample it was late when we set off. Driving in clouds of dust and darkness beyond the outer suburbs the self-starter began to smoke. Grovelling under the vehicle among the ants and young scorpions, fearful

* The latest news (1957) is that the British Government has allotted a sum of money for the repair of the Consulate-General.

of losing our feet when the great American lorries roared past, we attained the feeling of comradeship that only comes in moments of adversity.

The starter motor was held in place by two inaccessible screws that must have been tightened by a giant. It was a masterpiece of British engineering. With the ants marching and counter-marching over me, I held a guttering candle while Hugh groped with the tinny spanner that was part of the manufacturers' 'tool kit'.

"What does the book say?"

It was difficult to read it with my nose jammed into the earth.

"The starter is pre-packed with grease and requires no main-tenance during the life of the vehicle."

"That's the part about lubrication but how do you GET IT OFF?"

It was like trying to read a first folio in a crowded train. I knocked over the candle and for a time we were in complete darkness.

"It says: 'Loosen the retaining screws and slide it.'"

"There must be a place in hell for the man who wrote that."

"Perhaps you have to take the engine out first."

Late at night we returned unsuccessful to the city and in the *Shāri Tehran*, the Warren Street of Meshed, devoted to the motor business, hammered on the wooden doors of what until recently had been a caravanserai, until the night watchman came with stave and lantern and admitted us.

In the great court, surrounded by broken-down droshkies and the skeletons of German motor-buses, we spread our sleeping bags on the oily ground beside our vehicle. For the first time since leaving Istanbul we had achieved Hugh's ambition to sleep 'under the stars'.

Early the next morning the work was put in hand at a work-shop which backed on to the courtyard. It was the sort of place where engines are dismembered and never put together again. The walls of the shop were covered with the trophies of failure, which, together with the vast, inanimate skeletons outside, gave me the same curious feelings of fascination and horror that I still experience in that part of the Natural History Museum devoted to prehistoric monsters.

The proprietor Abdul, a broken-toothed demon of a man, conceived a violent passion for Hugh. We sat with him drinking coffee inside one of the skeletons while his assistant, a midget ten-year-old, set to work on the starter with a spanner as big as himself, shaming us by the ease with which he removed it.

"Arrrh, CAHARLESS, Soul of your father. You have ill-used your motor-car." He hit Hugh a violent blow of affection in the small of the back, just as he was drinking his coffee.

"Urggh!"

"What do you say, O CAHARLESS?"

Hugh was mopping thick black coffee from his last pair of clean trousers.

"I say nothing."

"What shall I say?"

"How should I know."

"You are angry with me. Let us go to my workshop and I shall make you happy."

He led us into the shop. There he left us. In a few minutes he returned with a small blind boy, good-looking but with an air of corruption. Abdul threw down his spanner with a clang and began to fondle him.

"CAHARLESS!" he roared, beckoning Hugh.

"NO!"

Presently Abdul pressed the boy into a cupboard and shut the door. There followed a succession of nasty stifled noises that drove us out of the shop.

Later, when we returned, Hugh was given a tremendous welcome.

"CAHARLESS, I thought you were departed for ever. You have come back!"

"You still have my motor-car."

To me he was less demonstrative but also less polite, snatching my pipe from my mouth and clenching it between his awful broken teeth in parody of an Englishman.

"CAHARLESS, when you take me to *Englestan* I shall smoke the pipe."

All through the hot afternoon he worked like a demon with his midget assistant, every few minutes beseeching Hugh to take him to England. After two hours the repairs were finished. Now he wanted to show us how he had driven to Tehran in fourteen hours, a journey that had taken us two days and most of one night.

In breathless heat he whirled us through the streets, tyres screeching at the corners. We were anxious to pay the bill and be off. Never had we met anyone more horrible than Abdul, more energetic and more likely to succeed.

"How much?"

"CAHARLESS, my heart, CAHARLESS, my soul, you will transport me to *Englestan*?"

"Yes, of course."

"We shall drive together?"

What a pair they would make on the Kingston By-Pass.

"Yes, of course, Bastard" (in English). "How much?"

The machine almost knocked down a heavily swathed old lady descending from a droshky and screamed to a halt outside a café filled with evil-looking men, all of whom seemed to be smitten with double smallpox.

"CAHARLESS, I am your slave. I will drive you to Tehran."

"Praise be to God for your kindness (and I hope you drop dead). THE BILL."

"CAHARLESS, soul of your father, I shall bring you water. Ho, there, Mohammed Gholi. Oh, bring water for CAHARLESS, my soul, my love. He is thirsty."

He screamed at the robbers in the shop, who came stumbling out with a great *chatti* which they slopped over Carless.

"Thank you, that is sufficient."

"CAHARLESS, I love you as my son."

"This bill is enormous."

It was enormous but probably correct.

A little beyond Meshed we stopped at a police post in a miserable hamlet to ask the way to the Afghan Frontier and Herat. I was already afflicted with the gastric disorders that were to hang like a cloud over our venture, a pale ghost of the man who had climbed the *Spiral Stairs* on Dinas Cromlech less than a month before. Hugh seemed impervious to bacilli and, as I sat in the vehicle waiting for him to emerge from the police station, I munched sulphaguanadine tablets gloomily and thought of the infected ice-cream he had insisted on buying Kazvin on the road from Tabriz to Tehran.

"We must accustom our stomachs to this sort of thing," he had said and had shared it with Wanda, who had no need to accustom herself to anything as she was returning to Italy.

The germs had been so virulent that she had been struck down almost at once; only after three days in bed at the Embassy with a high temperature had she been able to totter to the plane on the unwilling arm of a Queen's Messenger. I had rejected the ice-cream. Hugh had eaten it and survived. It was unjust; I hated him; now I wondered whether my wife was dead, and who would look after my children.

I had succumbed much later. In the fertile plain between Neishapur and Meshed we had stopped at a *qanat* for water. The *qanat*, a subterranean canal, was in a grove of trees and this was the place where it finally came to the surface after its journey underground. It was a magical spot, cool and green in the middle of sunburnt fields. There was a mound grown with grass like a tumulus with a mill room hollowed out of it and a leat into which the water gushed from a brick conduit, the *qanat* itself flowing under the mill. In several different spouts the water issued from the far side of the mound. It was as complex as a telephone exchange.

"Bound to be good," Hugh said, confronted by the crystal jets. "*Qanat* water. Comes from the hills."

It was delicious. After we had drunk a couple of pints each we discovered that the water didn't come from the *qanat* but from the conduit which came overland from a dirty-looking village less than a mile away.

"I can't understand why you're so fussy," he said, "it doesn't affect me."

Now, as I sat outside the police station brooding over these misfortunes, there was a sudden outburst of screams and moans from the other side of the road, becoming more and more insistent and finally mounting to such a crescendo that I went to investigate.

Gathered round a well or shaft full of the most loathsome
sewage was a crowd of gendarmes in their ugly sky-blue uniforms and several women in a state of happy hysteria, one screaming more loudly than the rest.

"What is it?"

"Bābā," said one of the policemen, pointing to the seething
mess at our feet and measuring the length of quite a small baby.
He began to keen; presumably he was the father. I waited a
little, no one did anything.

This was the moment I had managed to avoid all my life; the
rescue of the comrade under fire, the death-leaper from Hammersmith Bridge saved by Newby, the tussle with the lunatic with
the cut-throat razor.

Feeling absurd and sick with anticipation I plunged head first
into the muck. It was only four feet deep and quite warm but
unbelievable, a real eastern sewer. The first time I got hold of
something cold and clammy that was part of an American
packing case. The second time I found nothing and came up
spluttering and sick to find the mother beating a serene little
boy of five who had watched the whole performance from the
house next door into which he had strayed. The crowd was
already dispersing; the policeman gave me tea and let me change
in the station house but the taste and the smell remained.

Five miles beyond the police post the road forked left for the
Afghan frontier. It crossed a dry river bed with banks of gravel
and went up past a large fortified building set on a low hill.
After my pointless immersion I had become cold and my teeth
were chattering. It seemed a good enough reason to stop the
vehicle and have a look. Only some excuse such as this could
halt our mad career, for whoever was driving seemed possessed
of a demon who made it impossible ever to stop. Locked in
the cab we were prisoners. We could see the country we
passed through but not feel it and the only smells, unless we
put our heads out of the window (a hazardous business if we
both did it at the same time), were the fumes of the exhaust and
our foul pipes; vistas we would gladly have lingered over had

we been alone were gone in an instant and for ever. If there is any way of seeing less of a country than from a motor-car I have yet to experience it.

The building was a caravanserai, ruined and deserted, built of thin flat bricks. The walls were more than twenty feet high, decorated on the side where the gate was with blind, pointed arches. Each corner was defended by a smooth round tower with a crumbling lip.

Standing alone in a wilderness of scrub, it was an eerie place. The wind was strong and under the high gateway, flanked by embrasures, it whistled in the machicolations. Inside it was a warren of dark, echoing tunnels and galleries round a central court, open to the sky, with the same pointed arches as on the outer wall but here leading into small cells for the accommodation of more important travellers. In time of need this was a place that might shelter a thousand men and their animals.

The roof was grown thick with grass and wild peas, masking open chimney holes as dangerous as oubliettes. The view from the ramparts was desolate.

The air was full of dust and, as the sun set, everything was bathed in a blinding saffron light. There was not a house or a village anywhere, only a whitewashed tomb set on a hill and far up the river bed, picking their way across the grey shingle, a file of men and donkeys. Here for me, rightly or wrongly, was the beginning of Central Asia.

We drove on and on and all the time I felt worse. Finally we reached a town called Fariman. A whole gale of wind was blowing, tearing up the surface of the main street. Except for two policemen holding hands and a dog whose hind legs were paralysed it was deserted. Through waves of nausea I saw that Hugh had stopped outside some sort of café.

"I think we'd better eat here." To my diseased imagination he seemed full of bounce.

"I don't think I can manage any more."

"You are a funny fellow: always talking about food, now you don't want any."

"You forget I've already eaten."

He disappeared for a moment, then I saw him in the doorway semaphoring at me. With my last remaining strength I tottered into the building. It was a long room, brilliantly lit, empty except for the proprietor. He was bald, but for a grubby-looking frizz of grey curls, and dressed in a long, prophetic sort of garment. Hanging like a miasma over him and everything else in the building was a terrible smell of grease.

"*Ovis aries*, fat-tailed sheep, they store it up in their tails for the winter."

"I've never smelt a sheep like this, dead or alive."

"It's excellent for cooking," Hugh said. Nevertheless, he ordered boiled eggs.

I had '*mast*'. Normally an innocuous dish of curdled milk fit for the most squeamish stomach, it arrived stiff as old putty, the same colour and pungent.

While I was being noisily ill in the street, a solitary man came to gaze. "*Shekam dard*," I said, pointing to my stomach, thinking to enlist his sympathy, and returned to the work in hand. When next I looked at him he had taken off his trousers and was mouthing at me. With my new display of interest, he started to strip himself completely until a relative led him away struggling.

That night we huddled in our sleeping-bags at the bottom of a dried-out watercourse. It seemed to offer some protection from the wind, which howled about us, but in the morning we woke to find ourselves buried under twin mounds of sand like dead prospectors. But for the time being I was cured: sixteen sulphaguanadine tablets in sixteen hours had done it.

Full of sand we drove to the frontier town, Taiabad. It was only eight o'clock but the main street was already an oven. The military commander, a charming colonel, offered us sherbert in his office. It was delicious and tasted of honey. Hugh discussed the scandals of the opium smuggling with him. "It is a disgraceful habit," the Colonel said. "Here, of course, it is most rigorously repressed but it is difficult to control the traffic at more remote places." (In the Customs House the clerks were

1. Hugh and pilgrim photographer at Meshed.

2. The bridge at Gulbahar.

3. Hugh and Badar Khan in the wood at Kaujan.

4. Shepherd in the Panjshir Valley on the way to Kabul with a flock of fat-tailed sheep.

5. Abdul Rahim with the snow cock.

6. The Carless–Newby expedition approaches the mountain.

7. Mir Samir from the west.

8. The way to east glacier from the Chamar Valley. Summit in the background.

9. Abdul Ghiyas on the rock wall.

10. Mir Samir from the Chamar Pass.

11. Looking down on the east glacier from the ridge.

12. The way to the east ridge.

13. Hugh on the east ridge.

14. "On the face of this abominable castle our capacity for humour finally deserted us."

already at this hour enveloped in clouds of smoke.) "You are going to Kabul. Which route are you proposing to take?"

We asked him which he thought the best.

"The northern is very long; the centre, through the Hazara country, is very difficult; the way by Kandahar is very hot. We are still awaiting the young American, Winant. He set off to come here by the northern route in May."

"But today's the second of July."

"There was a Swedish nurse with him. Also he was very religious. It was a great mistake—a dangerous combination. Now we shall never see them again. In some respects it is a disagreeable country. Unless you are bound to go there, I counsel you to remain in Iran. I shall be delighted to put you up here for as long as you wish. It is very lonely for me here."

We told him our plans.

"You are not armed? You are quite right. It is inadvisable; so many travellers are, especially Europeans. It only excites the cupidity of the inhabitants. I should go by Kandahar. Your visas are for Kandahar and that is the only route they will permit anyway. That is if anyone at the customs post can read," he added mischievously.

Reluctantly we took leave of this agreeable man and set off down the road through a flat wilderness, until we came to a road block formed by a solitary tree-trunk. In the midst of this nothingness, pitched some distance from the road, was a sad little tent shuddering in the wind. After we had sounded the horn for some minutes a sergeant appeared and with infinite slowness drew back the tree-trunk to let us pass and without speaking returned to the flapping tent. Whatever indiscretion the Colonel may have been guilty of to land himself in such a place as Taiabad paled into utter insignificance when one considered the nameless crimes that this sergeant must have been expiating in his solitary tent.

After eight miles in a no-man's-land of ruined mud forts and nothing else we came to a collection of buildings so deserted-looking that we thought they must be some advanced post evacuated for lack of amenity. This time the tree-trunk was whitewashed. As Hugh got down to remove it, angry cries came from the largest and most dilapidated building and a file of soldiers in hairy uniforms that seemed to have been made from old blankets poured out of it and hemmed us in. As we marched across the open space towards the building, the wind was hot like an electric hair dryer and strong enough to lean on.

Inside the customs house in a dim corridor several Pathans squatted together sharing a leaky hubble-bubble. They had semitic, feminine faces but were an uncouth lot, full of swagger, dressed in saffron shirts and *chaplis* with rubber soles made from the treads of American motor tyres. In charge of them was a superior official dressed in a round hat and blue striped pyjamas whom they completely ignored. It was he who stamped our passports without formality.

The customs house was rocking in the wind which roared about it so loud that conversation was difficult.

"Is it always like this?" I screamed in Hugh's ear.

"It's the *Bād-i-Sad-o-Bist*, 'the Wind of Hundred and Twenty Days'."

"Yes," said one of the Pathans, "for a hundred and twenty days it blows. It started ten days ago. It comes from the north-west, but God only knows where it goes to."

After the half-light of the building, the light in the courtyard was blinding, incandescent; the dust in it thick and old and bitter-tasting, as if it had been swirling there for ever.

We were in Afghanistan.

Now the country was wilder still, the road more twisting, with a range of desolate mountains to the west dimly seen in the flying sand of the *Bād-i-Sad-o-Bist*. The only people we met were occasional roadmenders, dessicated heroes in rags, imploring us for water. To the left was the Hari-Rud, a great river burrowing through the sand, and we pointed to it as we swept past, smothering them in dust, but they put out their tongues and waved their empty water skins and cried, *"namak, namak"* until we knew that the river was salt and we were shamed into stopping. It was a place of mirage. At times the river was so insubstantial that it tapered into nothingness, sometimes it became a lake, shivering like a jelly between earth and sky.

At Tirpul the road crosses the river by a battered handsome bridge, six arches wide, built of brick. We swam in a deep pool under an arch on the right bank that was full of branches as sharp as bayonets, brought down by the floods. Nevertheless, it was a romantic spot. The air was full of dust and the wind roared about the bridge, whipping the water into waves topped with yellow froth that falling became rainbows. Upstream a herd of bullocks were swimming the river, thirty of them, with the herdsmen astride the leaders and flankers, urging them on. Beyond the river was Tirpul itself, a small hamlet with strange wind machines revolving on mud towers, with an encampment of black nomad tents on the outskirts and a great square caravanserai deserted on a nearby hill.

Out of the water, we dried out instantly and were covered with a layer of glistening salt. Hugh was a wild sight crouching on the bank in Pathan trousers, *shalvār*, far removed from the Foreign Office figure conjured up by the man at the Asian Desk. Here Hugh was in his element, on the shores of the Hari-Rud, midway between its source in the Kōh-i-Bāba mountains and the sands of the Kara-Kum, its unhealthy terminus in Russian Turkestan which holds the secret and perhaps the bones of the enigmatic Captain X whose name endures on the map in the Consulate at Meshed.

Sixty miles farther on we arrived at Herat. On the outskirts of the city, raised by Alexander and sieged and sacked by almost everyone of any consequence in Central Asia, the great towers erected in the fifteenth century by Gauhar Shah Begum, the remarkable wife of the son of Timur Leng,* King Shah Rukh, soar into the sky. Only a few of the ceramic tiles the colour of lapis-lazuli, that once covered these structures from top to bottom, still remain in position.

In the city itself the police stood on platforms of timber thick enough to withstand the impact of a bus or a runaway elephant, directing a thin trickle of automobiles with whistles and ill-tempered gestures, like referees.

In the eastern suburbs, where the long pine avenues leading to

* Tamerlane.

the *Parq Otel* were as calm and deadly as those round Bourne-
mouth, the system became completely ludicrous. At every inter-
section a policeman in sola topi drooped in a coma of boredom
until, galvanised into activity by our approach, he sternly blew'
his whistle and held up the non-existent traffic to let us pass.

The *Parq Otel* was terribly sad. In the spacious modernistic
entrance hall, built in the thirties and designed to house a worldly,
chattering throng, there was no one. Against the walls sofas
of chromium tubing, upholstered in sultry red uncut moquette,
alternated with rigid-looking chairs, enough for an influx of
guests, who after thirty years had still not arrived. On the
untenanted reception desk a telephone that never rang stood next
to a letter rack with no letters in it. A large glass showcase
contained half a dozen sticky little pools that had once been
sweets, some dead flies and a coat hanger.

Besides ourselves the only other occupants of the Parq were
two Russian engineers. We met them dragging themselves
along the corridors from distant bathrooms in down-at-heel
carpet slippers. They had gone to pieces. Who could blame
them?

While Hugh washed in one of the fly-blown bathrooms, I
went to photograph the great towers. Maddened by gaping
crowds, fearful of committing sacrilege, I drove the vehicle off
the road on to what I took to be a rubbish dump. It turned out
to be a Moslem cemetery from which there was an excellent view
but the camera refused to wind the film and, as I struggled with it,
the sun went down. From all sides the faithful, outraged by
my awful behaviour, began to close in. Gloomily I got back
into the car and drove away.

By the time we left Herat it was dark. All night we drove
over shattering roads, taking turns at the wheel, pursued by a
fearful tail wind that swirled the dust ahead of us like a London
fog. If it had been possible we should have lost the way, but
there was only one road.

Until midnight we had driven in spells of an hour; now we
changed every 30 minutes. It was difficult to average twenty
miles in an hour and trying to do so we broke two shock
absorbers. It was also difficult to talk with our mouths full of

dust but we mumbled at one another in desultory fashion to keep awake.

"The aneroid shows seven thousand."

"I don't care how high we are, I'm still being bitten."

"It's something we picked up at that tea place."

"Perhaps if we go high enough they'll die."

"If they're as lively as this at this altitude, they're probably fitted with oxygen apparatus."

Finally even these ramblings ceased and we were left each with the thoughts of disaster and bankruptcy that attend travellers in the hour before the dawn.

The sun rose at five and the wind dropped. We were in a wide plain and before us was a big river, the Farah-Rud. As the owner of a tea-house had prophesied, the bridge was down. It was a massive affair but two arches had entirely vanished. It was difficult to imagine the cataclysm that had destroyed it.

We crossed the river with the engine wrapped in oilskin, the fan belt removed, and with a piece of rubber hose on the exhaust pipe, to lift it clear of the water, led by a wild man wearing a turban and little else, one of a crew of three stationed on the opposite bank. In the middle the water rose over the floorboards and gurgled in our shoes.

It was a beautiful morning; the sky, the sand and the river were all one colour, the colour of pearls. Over everything hung a vast silence, shattered when the ruffians on the other side started up a tractor.

Because we were tired, having driven all night, we had forgotten to discuss terms for this pilotage. Now, safe on the other bank, too late we began to haggle.

"This is a monstrous charge for wading a river." It was necessary to scream to make oneself heard above the sound of the tractor.

"It is fortunate that we did not make use of the tractor," said the man in the ragged turban. "It is rare for a motor to cross by its own power. With the tractor you would have had greater cause for lamentation."

"That being so by now you must be men of wealth."

Back came the unanswerable answer.

"But if we were not poor, *Āghā*, why should we be sitting on the shores of the Farah-Rud waiting for travellers such as you?"

The walls of the hotel at Farah were whitewashed and already at six o'clock dazzling in the sun. Breakfast was set in the garden: it was a silly idea of our own; runny eggs and flies and dust and hot sun all mixed inextricably together in an inedible mass.

We passed the day lying on *charpoys* in a darkened room: Hugh was out completely, like a submarine charging its batteries, naked but for his Pathan trousers. Except for a brief interval for lunch, mildly curried chicken and good bread, he slept ten hours.

I could not sleep. I tried to read but it was too hot. Outside beyond the shutters the world was dead, sterilised by sun. At a little distance, shimmering in the heat, were the turreted walls of old Farah. I longed to visit it but the prospect of crossing the sizzling intervening no-man's land alone was too much. This was the city that Genghis Khan had captured and vainly attempted to knock down in the thirteenth century, that was re-occupied in the eighteenth and finally abandoned voluntarily in the nineteenth, so miserable had life within its walls become.

The sun expired in a haze of dust and the long, terrible day was over. In the early evening we set off. To the left were the jagged peaks of the Siah Band range; there were no trees and no sign of water, but by the roadside wild melons were growing, and we halted to try them but they were without taste. As we grew sticky eating bought melons from Farah, using the bonnet of the vehicle as a table, two nomad men passed with a camel, followed at a distance of a quarter of a mile by a youngish woman who lurched along in an extremity of fatigue. Neither of the men paid the slightest attention to her but they saluted us cheerfully as they went past.

It seemed impossible for the road to get worse, but it did: vast pot-holes large enough to contain nests of machine-gunners; places where it was washed away as far as the centre, leaving a six-foot drop to ground level; things Hugh called 'Irish Bridges', where a torrent had swept right through the road leaving a steep natural step at the bottom; all provided a succession of spine-shattering jolts. Whereas the previous night we had only met two lorries in the hours of darkness, there were now many monster American vehicles loaded with merchandise to the height of a two-storeyed house, each with its complement of piratical-looking men hanging on the scramble nettings, who jumped off to wedge the wheels on the steep gradients, while the passengers huddled together, making the crossing on foot groaning with apprehension.

Sticky with melon we arrived at a town called Girishk on the Helmand river. There, under a mulberry tree, squatted the proprietor of a *chaie khana*, a long-headed, grey-bearded Pathan, chanting a dirge on the passing of a newly-founded civilisation, no new thing in this part of the world.

"There is no light in the bazaar. The Americans brought light when they came to build the great dam" (the Helmand River Barrage) "but when they left they took the machine with them and now there is no more light."

"There is no more light and I am alone in the desert" (this was an exaggeration—Girishk has eight thousand inhabitants) "with nothing but these tins and a tea pot. Once I worked in a German woollen mill but now I am poor; we are all poor."

This was not the first time we had listened to these sad night intimacies of the tea-house. Nevertheless the old man's lament was strangely impressive. Perhaps because of the time—the unearthly hour before the dawn; because of the outlandish noises—the cries of shepherds calling to one another in the open country beyond the town and the barking of their dogs, like them, bolstering their courage in the darkness; but most of all because of the place itself—the tea-house that was nothing but a rug under a tree with a fire of yellow scrub to warm it, round which lay sleeping figures wrapped like sarcophagi, with their feet pointing towards the flames. All these, together with the heaps of empty tins that were the proprietor's inheritance and the giant fleas that invested us immediately we sat down, are not easily forgotten.

We asked him about the dam, that vast scheme of which so much vague ill had been spoken all along the way.

"It is all salt," he moaned, "the land below the American Dam. They did not trouble to find out and now the people will eat *namak* (salt) for ever and ever."

The oil lanterns that were tied to the mulberry trees and which illuminated the street began to flicker and go out one by one.

We rose to leave.

"You will be in Kandahar in two hours," he went on. "The Americans built the road; they have not taken that away."

It was as he said. The road was like a billiard table. The following morning we arrived at Kabul and drove down the great ceremonial avenues, newly asphalted, past Russian steam-rollers still ironing out the final bumps, to the principal hotel. We were five days late. It was Friday, July 5th. In a month we had driven nearly 5,000 miles. Our journey was about to begin.

CHAPTER SEVEN

A Little Bit of Protocol

IT was good to be separated from our motor-car, for which we had conceived a loathing normally reserved for the living, but no sooner were our feet planted on solid earth than difficulties of a ludicrous but nonetheless irksome kind began to pile up around us. The two most memorable were the affair of the Afghan bicyclist and the problem of Hugh's old cook.

Rather incautiously, but with the best of intentions, Hugh had suggested in one of his letters from South America that we should take with us one of the local inhabitants in order to impart what he called 'an Afghan flavour' to our climb, his idea being that it would, if nothing else, convince the authorities of our good intentions. But then he appeared to have forgotten about it—and so had I. Unfortunately he had incorporated his suggestion in the letter he wrote to the Foreign Office when he applied for permission to be allowed to make the journey, but without specifying any particular sort of companion.

On the afternoon of our arrival, suitably clothed, washed and shaved, we presented ourselves at the Afghan Foreign Ministry. There, in the Protocol Department, we met the young hopes of the Afghan Foreign Service, elegant, intelligent young men who treated us with a courtesy, consideration and lack of curiosity superior to that shown by our own side when we had proposed our expedition. The difficulties that had appeared insuperable in London seemed to diminish when dealing with these splendid fellows. Hugh was so overcome with enthusiasm that he, unwisely I thought, raised the subject of an Afghan climber.

"We should, of course, be delighted if someone nominated by you would like to accompany us."

"My dear chap," said Abdul Ali, "if you take my advice you will forget about it. You are only likely to land yourself with some fellow who will bore you stupid in a couple of days. Besides, no one here knows the first thing about climbing."

"I only mention it because I wrote officially."

"I should think no more about it if I were you."

"What about coming yourself?" He seemed an excellent companion. We really meant it.

"Unfortunately, we are extremely busy with the arrangements for the visit of the Pakistan Minister, otherwise I should be delighted."

He invited us to a splendid tea. Afghanistan is a man's country, so that it was our host who hovered behind a battery of silver teapots, hot water, cream and milk jugs, handing out dainty sandwiches. Afterwards he spoke of his hunting experiences in some detail, and I fell into a coma from which I emerged refreshed and confident. But the next day brought bad omens.

As a result of our long drive we were extremely unfit. Our three days in Wales had worked wonders with us, like one of those courses in physical culture on which you make a muscle-bound colossus of yourself in next to no time simply by pressing one hand hard against the other. But our fitness, like my knowledge of Urdu during the war, had been acquired swiftly in exceptional circumstances; now, equally rapidly, it had melted away.

"We must do some climbing," said Hugh, as we reeled off to bed that evening after returning from a gramophone recital at one of the Embassies. "Ropework, that's what we need. Mir Samir's a terrific mountain."

I was as apprehensive as he was about our appalling condition. It may have been something to do with the altitude but we were finding it almost impossible to keep awake. At the recital, like the rest of the audience, we had both slept solidly through the entire performance. I had woken up with my head nestling on the bosom of a jolly female Turk to find her husband glowering at me; there are other dangers in Afghanistan besides tribal warfare.

Then I remembered Hugh's last letter from South America. "Acclimatisation should be no great problem," he had written. "The Turcoman's Throne (15,447) just above Kabul can be climbed in a day and we should probably spend a couple of days up there before setting out in earnest." But now that the need for acclimatisation had become acute, Hugh changed his mind.

"We'll climb Legation Hill," he said. "I'll set the alarm for five. We'd better wear our windproof suits." And fell asleep.

The British Embassy lies beyond the town. Built at the express order of Lord Curzon to be the finest Embassy in Asia, it is strategically situated so far from the bazaars that none but the most heavily subsidised mob would dream of attacking it. Above the compound there is a small hill, perhaps a thousand feet high, up which young secretaries pelt in gym shoes after a heavy night. This is Legation Hill. In the early morning we set out to scale it, laden with heavy boots and all the impedimenta of our assumed trade.

As we marched out of the front gate of the Embassy, roped together and in our windproof suits, the guards saluted.

"They remember me," said Hugh, returning it with satisfaction. "Wonderfully faithful fellows, these Pakistanis."

"If you made a practice of this sort of thing while you were here, they'd have to be absolutely ga-ga not to."

As we tottered up the winding track, dripping with perspiration, tripping over the rope, our ice-axes clinking mockingly on the unfriendly soil, I was filled with gloomy forebodings. My legs felt like putty. I had a splitting headache and my tongue was covered with a thick unwholesome rime. It took us twenty-five minutes to reach the top.

"Archie used to do it in ten," said Hugh, as panting and feeling sick, we sprawled on the summit, pretending to admire the extensive view of the suburbs of Kabul spread out below us.

"He must be a superman."

"Not at all. He had to leave the Foreign Service because he drank too much."

In low spirits we descended for breakfast.

"We're certainly going to need those days on the Turcoman's Throne."

"I'm afraid there's not going to be time. We shall have to limber up on the glaciers of Mir Samir. There's plenty of scope there."

Back at the Protocol Department Abdul Ali looked serious. "Your permissions have come through."

"That's wonderful. It's very quick."

"I'm glad that you're pleased. But there's something else. A man has been chosen to accompany you."

"But you said you thought we would be better advised to go alone."

"I know. It's most curious. It's nothing to do with us here. None of us know anything about it. It came from some-one outside our Department, and on the highest level. Until yesterday it was in the hands of the Ministry for Defence."

"Ah," said Hugh, with a return of satisfaction. "It must be the Nuristani I hoped for from the Army. I did mention him in my letter to the Ambassador. Just the man we want."

"He isn't a Nuristani," said Abdul Ali. "I only wish for your sake he was. The thing's out of the hands of the Defence Ministry. They've passed it to the Olympic Committee. This man's just come back from riding round the world on a bicycle. He's never been on a mountain in his life."

Quite soon, summoned by telephone, the candidate appeared. He was a large, muscular man with a lot of black hair laced with brilliantine, like something out of a Tarzan film. His appear-ance belied his character, which was retiring. It was true about riding round the world on a bicycle. He had performed this feat on a massive roadster of the sort issued to policemen, carrying with him 150 lb. of baggage. It was difficult to imagine him on the Simplon Pass but he had undoubtedly been there. Against my will I found myself conducting a sort of viva voce examination of this formidable being.

"Have you had any previous climbing experience?"

"None at all," he said and my heart warmed to him. "But I did run in the ten thousand metres in the Asian Games," he added modestly.

"I see."

Like all similar interviews this one was not a success, owing to the complete lack of qualifications of the interviewer.

"How did you come to apply for this? It's going to be very arduous." I glared horribly, trying to discourage him.

"I didn't apply. The Olympic Committee only told me that I was going this morning."

"I see."

"Don't keep on saying that," Hugh hissed in my ear. "You make it sound like the B.B.C."

"Are you keen to come on this trip?"

"If you wish me to come I shall come."

Hugh was just about to say yes when I kicked him violently under the table.

"Everything is a little complicated at the moment. We'll let you know in the morning."

"Of course, we shall have to take him," said Hugh as soon as he had gone.

"But why? He doesn't want to go. You heard what he said, he's been ordered to. It's going to be bad enough with two of us knowing nothing; with one more it'll be suicide."

"You don't seem to realise that because the Government has selected him, we *must* take him. If we don't they'll be very offended."

"But even the Protocol think we'd be better alone. You heard what Abdul Ali said."

"That was before he knew about this man. You don't understand these people at all. A thing like this might have a very bad effect on Anglo-Afghan relations."

I looked at Hugh closely when he said this but he was quite serious. Here it was again breaking the surface, that massive but elusive entity, the Foreign Office Mind, like an iceberg with most of its bulk hidden below the surface but equally menacing.

Hugh had no more wish to take the cyclist than the cyclist had to come with us, but he was not able to see that the machinery that had produced him could be put in reverse. For two hours I argued with him. It was in vain.

"Sometimes I don't think you have any sense of moral responsibility at all," he said after a particularly heated exchange. "This man has virtually been given to us by Protocol."

"Well, if he was given to us by Protocol, give him back by Protocol. Perhaps he hasn't got any boots."

"That's an idea," said Hugh, unexpectedly. "He couldn't come if he didn't have any boots."

Although it was late he went to telephone. Soon he was back. "He hasn't got any boots."

"Then he can't come."

"But I telephoned Abdul Ali and he's promised to do his best to get some. He'll let us know in the morning. He's going to try the Army. I said we'd try the Embassy."

"You are an ass."

"It's all right, he's got very small feet. There's no one with feet like that in the whole compound."

"How do you know?"

"If you'd lived in the compound for a couple of years you get to know the size of everything."

The next morning Abdul Ali telephoned.

"I'm afraid there is not a pair of boots to fit our friend in the whole of Kabul."

"Could you lend him a pair yourself? He's about your size."

I could have strangled Hugh at this moment.

"Unfortunately I only have two pairs and I shall be using them myself on a hunting trip quite soon."

"I am extremely sorry that he won't be able to come. Please convey our regrets to him and my thanks to the Olympic Committee."

"For a man who has only been in the Foreign Service since the war I must say you've made remarkable progress," I said as Hugh replaced the receiver. "You're almost inhuman."

He considered this for a moment before replying.

"Yes, I think on the whole the training is excellent," he said with a smile.

Even more far-reaching in its effects on the welfare of our expedition was the business of Ghulam Naabi, Hugh's old cook, who had accompanied him on his previous ventures into the interior and had been present at the abortive attempt to scale the mountain.

All the way from Istanbul, a lean period of abstinence from food, *chez Carless*, I had been upheld in spirit, if nothing else, by a continual flow of reminiscence about Ghulam Naabi; his prodigious appetite that would at least, I thought, ensure the regular supply of victuals that had up to now been denied me; his resourcefulness that enabled him in a rather oblique way to overcome the everyday disasters of the road; the ludicrous misadventures that befell him and which would probably provide us with an inexhaustible supply of anecdote. All gave promise of a sympathetic, fallible character who would lend a certain humanity to the rather austere project on which we were embarking, and be a far more rewarding companion than the young biologist with whom I had been threatened at one stage of our planning but to whom, mercifully, no further reference had been made.

Even Dreesen, the companion of Hugh's earlier journey whom I had from the outset regarded as a semi-mythical character but who had eventually materialised in the guise of United States Consul at Tabriz in north-western Persia, had spoken well of him, as we sat on the Consular terrace in the gloaming, drinking *Perrier Jouet*, and recovering from the horrors of our passage through Anatolia.

"If Hugh takes Ghulam Naabi you'll have some chance of survival," he said when Hugh was out of earshot. "If not, God help you."

I asked him why. These were the early days before Hugh had endeavoured to destroy us with infected food.

"The man's a fiend. He never eats. I got so hungry on that mountain I thought I'd die. He doesn't seem to realise you can't go charging about at seventeen thousand feet on an empty stomach."

My heart warmed to Dreesen, but he continued:

"That's one of the reasons we're having champagne this evening. I'm celebrating too; because I'm not going."

He had been joking but nevertheless I had felt a certain chill of apprehension. If this lean, husky individual who had crossed the Karakorams on foot, had felt the strain what was it going to be like for me, relatively enfeebled by years in the dress business?

One of Hugh's first acts on arriving in Kabul was to summon Ghulam Naabi.

"He's working for an Australian," he explained. "But I think he should come on the preliminary reconnaissance before we set off. Besides, he'll be very useful when we choose our Tajik drivers."

"But this man he's working for. What's he going to say if you take his cook away from him?"

"It's only for a month," Hugh said, as if this was some extenuation for robbing a man of his cook. "Besides he's an Australian."

"What's that got to do with it? It doesn't seem to make it any more legitimate to me."

"I mean, being an Australian he's pretty certain to be an easy-going sort of fellow."

I thought of some of the Australians I had met and how little I should have liked to deprive them of anything without asking first.

When Ghulam Naabi finally appeared, he seemed a perfect choice. He was round and brown and fat and jolly and resembled a Christmas pudding. His eyes were like shiny currants and he was even done up in something that was like a white pudding cloth but was really an old white mess jacket. He wore a Karakul cap and on his feet were *chaplis* from Peshawar with soles three inches thick, constructed from the treads of American motor tyres. He was delighted at the prospect of an·outing; about the greater scheme he said nothing.

In the afternoon Hugh suggested that I accompany Ghulam Naabi to the bazaar to buy provisions for the journey.

"We've really got plenty for ourselves," he said in the particularly off-hand voice he always employed when speaking of food (I thought of the four boxes of army rations that so far constituted our only guard against death by starvation and my blood ran cold). "It's really for the drivers; they expect it, it's the custom."

"I've made a list," he went on, handing me a minute slip of paper. "I think you should go too, to see that he doesn't overdo it. Besides it will be a good opportunity for you to *chaffer* for bargains."

The list was very short:

> 3 seers of flour
> 8 pau of sugar
> 12 pau of salt
> 6 doz. safety matches
> 2 hurricane lanterns.

There was no doubt that, whatever sufferings we were about to undergo, Hugh intended that the drivers should participate equally.

"Aren't we going to take any rice? I always thought it was a staple food in this part of the world."

"Too heavy. We must think of the horses; probably we'll only have three."

I was reluctant to ask him to explain the weights and measures. He was already irritated that I had not made any appreciable advances in my knowledge of Persian and I wanted to reserve my interrogations for the journey. It seemed simple enough but, in order not to be entirely at the mercy of the stall holders, I looked up the weights and measures in an official handbook, where they were set out with devilish ingenuity.

"At Kabul," said the book, "16 *khurds* = 1 *charak*; 4 *charaks* = 1 *seer*." This seemed straightforward enough. I turned the page expecting to find what the *seer* equalled and learned that it equalled 7 *seers* 13½ *chittaks* British Indian Weight.

"But at Kandahar," it went on triumphantly, "20 *miskals* = 1 *seer*, which is 8⅝ *tolas* British while at Mazar-i-Sharif, 1 *Mazar seer* = 1¾ *Kabuli seers*—that is 14 British *Seers*." There was no mention at all of the *pau* of which I was supposed to buy 8 of sugar and 12 of salt.

It was obvious that with the limited time at my disposal I was not destined to learn much about the weights and measures of the country, so for the time being I abandoned the attempt and let Ghulam Naabi do the haggling. I only intervened once, when he was about to buy the hurricane lanterns.

"Ask the man if he's got any other lanterns. *Better* lanterns." The ones we were being offered had 'Bulldog Lantern' marked on them and, less prominently, 'Made in Japan'. It seemed an appropriate occasion to buy British, or at least Empire.

"They are very good lanterns. You do not like them? Here everyone uses them."

"Haven't they got any others? Not Japanese."

The owner of the shop vanished into the dark recesses. After a long interval he re-appeared with two more lanterns. They appeared to have been in stock for some considerable time. When he had blown the dust from them, I saw that they were precisely the same as the Japanese lanterns, except that this time the name was 'Lifeguard' embossed with a picture of a trooper of the Household Cavalry, and the label 'Made in Germany' was more prominent.

The shopkeeper named a price two and a half times the Japanese. I gave up the struggle to support the Empire.

"It is always better to buy Japanese," remarked Ghulam Naabi, when some twenty minutes later he had effected a fifty per cent reduction in the price of the Japanese lanterns. "Much cheaper. Everything Japanese comes by railway, through Russia."

We made one last stop to buy six dozen boxes of Russian safety matches, which effectively undercut in price even the Japanese matches, and our shopping was at an end.

I asked Ghulam Naabi whether we should have enough food. He must have understood where my anxiety lay, for he winked and said, "Sahib, all will be well. Do not be worried. Am I not a fat man?"

Readers who are not interested in the history and geography of Nuristan should leave off here and start again at Chapter 8.

The country which was our final goal is still, in the second half of the twentieth century, one of the least known in the world. As late as 1910 Colonel Sir Thomas Holdich, in his book, *The Gates of India*, could write of Nuristan:

'Who will unravel the secrets of this inhabited outland, which appears at present to be more impracticable to the explorer than either of the poles?'

Nearly fifty years have passed since the Chief Survey Officer of the Indian Section made this challenging statement but, even allowing for a certain exaggeration, there is no doubt that the means of getting into it have not become any easier; neither the aeroplane nor the motor car has made the slightest difference. To get there you still have to walk.

But it is not only the absence of roads that makes Nuristan difficult. The Afghan Government has displayed understandable reluctance in allowing travellers to enter it; partly because the inhabitants are unpredictable in their reception of foreigners and partly because potential visitors are suspected of being agents who would stir up trouble.

Nuristan, 'The Country of Light', is a mountainous territory in the north-east of Afghanistan, lying between latitudes 34 and 36 north and longitudes 70 and 71-50 east, although some authorities consider that its southern limits extend a few more minutes southwards.

It is walled in on every side by the most formidable mountains. To the north by the main Hindu Kush range, which is the watershed between the Oxus and the deserts of Central Asia and the Indus and the rivers that flow into the Indian Ocean; to the north-east by the Bashgul range, eastwards of the river of that name; to the east and south-east its boundary is the Kunar river to its junction with the Kabul river; and to the south and south west the mountains which rise on the left bank of the Kabul river.

To the west, the side from which we were approaching it, the boundary is a spur of the Hindu Kush on the east bank of the Panjshir, whose crowning points are Mir Samir and another unnamed mountain to the north-east. The whole of this area including the parts in Chitral has been estimated to cover an area of 5,000 square miles and has been known since early times as Kafiristan, 'The Country of the Unbelievers'; the larger part, that inside Afghanistan, having been called Nuristan since 1895.

Nuristan is drained by three main rivers. They all have their origins on its northern frontier and they all flow towards the Kabul river, from the great ox-bow bend that the Hindu Kush makes south-west of its junction with the Pamirs and the Karakoram range. The one farthest east is the Bashgul river; in the centre is the Pech and on the west, next to the Panjshir, is the Alingar whose upper waters are called the Ramgul; the Bashgul and the Pech discharging into the Kunar, the Alingar into the Kabul river above Jalalabad. Eventually all are united where the Kunar joins the Kabul and they continue together to the Indus and the Indian Ocean.

These three valleys, all of which have innumerable subsidiary streams pouring into them, are linked indirectly by passes between 12,000 and 16,000 feet high, only negotiable on foot and closed by deep snow between October and March. Many of the valleys are heavily wooded and so deep that in autumn and winter they are said to remain in perpetual shadow.

Each valley is inhabited by different tribes and each speaks its own language. All these languages belong to the group known as Dardic, which is said to be an offshoot from the original Aryan spoken by the inhabitants of the Khiva oasis in Trans-Caspia. But there coherence ends.

It was at one time assumed that, because there were two main tribal divisions within the country, the *Siah-Posh* or Black-Robed Kafirs and the *Safed-Posh* or White-Robed Kafirs, who took their names from the dress they adopted, so also there were only two languages. But it is now known that while the *Siah-Posh**
who inhabit the north and east all speak various dialects of Bashguli, the language spoken on the Bashgul river, all appear

---

* Of the *Siah-Posh* the most numerous are the Katirs; the Bashgul Katirs, the Kti or Kantiwar Katirs, the Kulam Katirs and the Ramgul Katirs living in the north-west.

to be able to understand one another. With the *Safed-Posh* the language problem is so wildly complicated that one's mind reels. Expressed in the simplest terms the situation seems to be as follows: the *Safed-Posh* occupy the centre and south-east and consist of three tribes, the Wai, the Presun or Parun and the Ashkun. The Wai live to the south-east of the Bashgul in the mountains above the Kunar river; the Presun on the upper part of the Pech river, and the Ashkun somewhere completely inaccessible in the mountains of the Alingar in the south-west. Of these the Wai and the Presun speak different languages that are mutually unintelligible and unintelligible to all the *Siah-Posh*, except for one small section of the Wai who speak a mixture of *Siah-Posh* Bashguli and Parun. To whom they are intelligible is not clear. The Ashkuns are reputed to speak a variant of the language of the Wai but, as no one has ever visited them who was qualified to express an opinion, their language and everything else about them remain a mystery.*

The origins of the Kafirs are uncertain. There is a popular legend that they are descended in the male line from stragglers from the army of Alexander the Great, who skirted Kafiristan on the road to India.

Having passed the winter of 327 B.C. with his army at Alexandreia ad Caucasum (near the present town of Charikar which lies at the junction of the Panjshir and Ghorband rivers at the foot of the Hindu Kush), Alexander despatched one of his generals, Hephæston, through the Khyber with the main body of the army to capture Taxila in the Upper Punjab. He himself set off with a lighter force along the north bank of the Kabul river and entered the Kunar Valley, where he defeated a blond, warlike people, the Aspasians, who may well have been indigenous Kafirs. It was in these operations against the Aspasians that Ptolemy, the son of Lagos, who later became King of Egypt, distinguished himself.

Somewhere east of the Kunar, possibly in the province of

* Anyone wishing to study this formidable, though fascinating, subject may refer to the *Linguistic Survey of India*, Vol. VIII, Part II, by Sir G. A. Grierson.

Swat, at a point that has been the despair of archaeologists in their efforts to determine it, he came to the city of Nysa.

Of Nysa, Arrian speaks as follows:

'The city was built by Dionysos or Bacchus when he conquered the Indians, but who this Bacchus was, or at what time or from whence he conquered the Indians, is hard to determine. Whether he was that Theban who from Thrace or he who from Tmolus a mountain of Lydia undertook that famous expedition into India . . . is uncertain.'

Beyond the city was a mountain called Meros where the ivy grew. Being reminded by the inhabitants of the reverence expected of him, Alexander made a sacrifice to Bacchus and his troops made garlands, calling on Dionysos. What a scene it must have been, like some painting of Poussin!*

To this day Nuristan is overgrown with ivy and vines and until lately the inhabitants were notable drinkers. As late as 1857 a missionary, the Reverend Ernest Trumpp, wrote that three Kafirs sent by Major Lumsden as recruits for the Corps of Guides demanded a *mashak* of wine a day, a leather water bag holding equal to six English gallons. Yet he also says that with this ration they were never drunk. Trumpp's Kafirs never spoke of Kafiristan, which they regarded as an insulting epithet: they called it Wamasthan.

Whether or not the Nysæans were pre-Alexandrian invaders from Greece, at the time Alexander crossed the Hindu Kush, the plains of Kabul and the passes over the Hindu Kush from Andarab were certainly held by Greeks, descendants of those transported to Asia by Darius Hystaspes after the fall of Miletus. Equally certainly Kafiristan and its inhabitants in those days covered a far wider area than is occupied by Nuristan today, taking in considerable parts of Badakshan, the Panjshir, Swat and Chitral. The admixture of Greek blood, which gives to many of the inhabitants of Nuristan today a startlingly South European look, had certainly begun long before the arrival of

* This interesting theory concerning the origin of the Kafirs is dealt with more fully in *Geographical Journal*, VII, London, 1896, 'The Origin of the Kafirs of the Hindu Kush', Col. T. H. Holdich.

the Macedonian army.   All that Alexander's stragglers did when
they encountered the Kafir women, who have the reputation of
being sluttish, accommodating and extremely handsome, was to
strengthen it.

Travellers in Kafiristan have always been few and far between.
From the sixth century onwards Chinese Buddhists make passing reference to Kafiristan on their way to the holy places of
India—travellers like Sung Yün who crossed the Pamirs to the
Oxus in A.D. 519 and entered India by way of Kafiristan to
avoid an even more dreadful crossing of the upper Indus by a
bridge constructed from a single iron chain.   But for the most
part, when entering Afghanistan, they seem to have passed on
either side of it.

Genghis Khan refers to the Kafirs in the thirteenth century;
Timur Leng fought them in the fourteenth without conspicuous
success, although he is reputed to have acquired a Kafir wife;
in the fifteenth the Emperor Babur drank their wines without
rapture.   In 1602 a Portuguese Jesuit, Benedict de Goès,
coadjutor to the Superior of the Order in the Mogul's Empire,
set off from Lahore for China (where he died), attaching himself
to a caravan of five hundred merchants, and passed through a
part of eastern Afghanistan which he calls 'Capherstam'.   He
says that the soil was fertile and yielded plenty of grapes; offered
a cup of wine he found it very good.   Thereafter, as far as I can
discover, no travellers through Kafiristan have left any record
for two hundred years, although there must have been others.

A most colourful traveller who was supposed to have visited
Kafiristan was Colonel Alexander Gardner.   He was a soldier
of fortune employed as commandant of a picked body of horse
by the nephew and deadly enemy of the reigning Amir, Dost
Muhammad Khan.   According to his own account he went
there twice.*

The first time was in 1826 when he had to flee for his life
through west Kafiristan on his way to Yarkand after the Amir
had slaughtered and mutilated his followers together with his
beautiful Afghan wife and small son by way of reprisal.   (Gardner had captured her from a caravan in which she had been

* *Colonel Alexander Gardner* by Major H. Pearse.   Edinburgh, 1898.

travelling as lady-in-waiting to a princess who was related to the Amir and had installed her in a *castello* in the Hindu Kush.)

The second occasion was in 1828 when he returned from Yarkand by way of northern Kafiristan and the Kunar Valley.

Subsequently Gardner entered the service of the great Sikh ruler Ranjit Singh.

A photograph of him survives, taken when he was seventy-nine. He is dressed from head to foot in a suit of tartan of the 79th Highlanders. Even his turban decorated with egret's plumes is of tartan. With his Sikh's beard and alert look he is himself rather like an eagle. He died in bed at Jammu at the age of ninety-two, a pensioner of the Sikhs. (*See note p.* 92.)

In the 1830's the almost equally remarkable American traveller Charles Masson made his extensive journeys in Afghanistan disguised in the local dress, living with the inhabitants in a way which would be difficult today. Although he did not penetrate far into Kafiristan, he followed the Alingar as far as its junction with the Alishang and then followed the Alishang itself, a journey no European was to accomplish again until 1935.

Less well known is the visit of a Christian missionary, Fazl Huq, in 1864. Fazl Huq was a Pathan, the son of a *Mullah*, who had been converted to Christianity at Peshawar. To avoid any imputation of changing faith to curry favour with missionaries, he joined the Corps of Guides as a sepoy, a regiment in which Christian other ranks were anathema to the Muslim rank and file and as much in danger of losing their lives as they were in civilian life.

Together, with an ex-*Mullah* named Narullah, who was also a Christian convert, he set off for Kafiristan in September 1864, at the invitation of a Kafir soldier of whom there were several in the Guides, taking with him medicine and presents from the Church Missionary Society. The treatment they received from their own people, fanatic Muslims, on the road through Swat was as disagreeable as anything they were to encounter in Kafiristan itself, but after overcoming the most formidable difficulties they finally reached the Kunar river, floated down it on a raft of inflated skins, and entered Jalalabad disguised as women.

Eventually they reached a place somewhere on the southern marches of Kafiristan where the Kafirs came to barter for salt. Here the two faithful bodyguards they had hired in Jalalabad left them and, having abandoned their disguise, they continued into the country alone.

At the village to which they had been invited by the sepoy they carried on their missionary work for twenty days and were well received, the Kafirs reserving the martyr's crown for Muslims.

Each day Huq kept a journal, using lime juice as an invisible ink.

Adultery was unknown, he wrote, only the unmarried ever being suspected of immorality which was extirpated with ferocity; married couples having a sort of laisser-passer in such matters. He also noticed that the Kafirs watched their relatives die in silence and that they put them in wooden boxes on the mountainside with the lids weighed down with heavy stones. Some of the houses he saw were five storeys high. During his stay he saw a variety of birds and beasts—crows, parrots, leopards, bears and wolves.

Huq and Narullah stayed in Kafiristan until the first snows fell, then returned by the way they had come. Reaching the Kabul river at Jalalabad they floated down it on a raft as far as Peshawar, which they reached after an absence of two months. It was a remarkable exploit.

It was not until the eighties, when the great game of espionage between Britain and Russia was being played flat out beyond the frontiers of India, that another serious attempt was made to enter Kafiristan. In 1883 W. W. Macnair, an enterprising officer of the Indian Survey, disobeying the strict orders of the Indian Government that no European should cross the frontier without permission, penetrated the eastern marches as far as the Bashgul Valley. Macnair wore the dress of a Muhammadan *Hakim* and stained himself with a disagreeable mixture of weak caustic soda and walnut juice. He was accompanied by a native 'known in *The Profession* as the Saiad' and two Kaka Khel Pathans, a tribe respected by the Afghans and to some extent by the Kafirs. With him he took an enormous book decorated with cabalistic signs which concealed within it a plane table for mapping and other surveying instruments. As *Hakim* he was much given to solitary meditation and generally chose high peaks for this purpose.

Macnair reported that the inhabitants were celebrated for their beauty and their European complexions; that they worshipped idols; drank wine from silver cups and vases; used chairs and tables, and spoke a language unknown to their neighbours; that brown eyes were more common than blue; that their complexions varied between pink and a bronze as dark as that of a Punjabi; that the infidelity of wives was punished by mild beating and that of men by a fine of cattle, and that one of their prayers ran:

> Ward off fever from us.
> Increase our stores.
> Kill the Mussulmans.
> After death admit us to Paradise.

Macnair estimated the population at 200,000.

On his return to India he was officially reprimanded by Lord Ripon, the Viceroy, and later congratulated in private.

Two years later in 1885 the Bashgul Valley was more fully explored by Colonel Woodthorpe of the Indian Survey when he visited it with Sir William Lockhart on a mission whose object was to examine the passes of the Hindu Kush. But it was not until Sir George Robertson, the British Political Agent in Gilgit, made his prolonged journeys in Kafiristan in 1890 and 1891, visiting the upper reaches of the Bashgul and penetrating farther westwards than any other explorer had so far succeeded in doing into the upper part of the Pech Valley, that any real knowledge was gained of the country and the people. His book *The Káfirs of the Hindu Kush* gives the only complete picture that has come down to us of the Kafirs living in their pristine state of paganism. And it was to be the final one. Already Robertson was encountering tribes who had been converted to Islam and his was the last opportunity that any European was to have before the old pagan religion of the country was obliterated.

In the twentieth century the names of the countless secret

agents of all nations who must have visited Nuristan have so far not been revealed. The first recorded visitors seem to have been two Russians, Vavilov and Bukinitsh, who spent four days in the Pech Valley in 1924.

It is the Germans who have held almost the entire monopoly of travel and exploration in Nuristan during the last thirty years. There is something about the place that appeals to the German character: the dark forests and gloomy valleys; the innate paganism of the *grosse blonde vollhaarige menschen* whose origins *nicht indo-arisches, sondern ein europaisch-arisches Restvolk der Indo-germanen sind*.

In 1925 two Germans tried to enter from the southwards without success; one a geologist, Dr. Herbordt, the other a Baron von Platen. Both reached the frontier north of Jalalabad but got no farther.

In 1928 Dr. Martin Voigt and Herr Seydack, a Prussian State Forester, both of whom were working for King Amanullah, went up the Kunar Valley and the Bashgul, reached the Hindu Kush divide and descended the Pech river to its confluence with the Kunar. They did not, however, visit the western part, the Alingar-Ramgul Valley which no European had so far seen.

In 1935 there came the Deutsche Hindu Kush Expedition. This, like everything else emanating from Germany in the middle thirties, was grandiloquent and slightly less thorough than it cracked itself up to be. It was certainly big. Its members travelled with forty mules specially imported for the job, fifteen mule drivers, three Afghan officers and sixteen soldiers. It worked methodically, establishing supply depots for itself en route. The objects of the expedition were rather ambiguous but its members seem to have spent most of their time, when they might have been looking for the Ashkuns, studying the comparative anatomy of the inhabitants. On their return to civilisation they embalmed their findings, the result of the thorough measuring to which they had subjected the inhabitants, in a large almost unreadable volume printed in excruciating gothic type.

After the last war there were the enterprising journeys of von Dückelmann, an Austrian who had spent the last war interned in India, and Hans Neubauer, a botanist in the employ of the Afghan Government.

In November 1951 a young American called Mackenzie spent fifteen days in Nuristan, reaching a point where there was a rock inscribed by Timur Leng.

There was the Danish Henning-Haslund expedition on which the leader Haslund unfortunately died, which visited East and Central Nuristan on several occasions between 1948 and 1954.

And in 1956 it seemed that there was to be the Carless-Newby expedition, consisting of a man from the dress trade and a career diplomat, who were setting off to visit the Ramgul Katirs in Nuristan for no other reason than to satisfy their curiosity.

According to *European Adventurers of Northern India, 1785–1849* by C. Grey and H. L. O. Garrett, Lahore, 1929, he was an Irish deserter from the British Service who never went to Kafiristan and was made a colonel because he was the only man in the Sikh Army who was willing to cut off the right thumb, nose and ears of a Brahmin who had struck an officer.

CHAPTER EIGHT

Panjshir Valley

"Panjhīr is another tuman; it lies close to Kafiristan, along the
Panjhīr road, and is the thoroughfare of Kafir highwaymen who
also, being so near, take tax of it. They have gone through it,
killing a mass of persons, and doing very evil deeds, since I came
this last time and conquered Hindustan."
(932 A.H.–1526 A.D.)   *Mem. Bābur*, p. 214

WE left Kabul on July 10th ("Probably for ever," we said,
jesting in the tedious fashion that explorers employ to
keep up their spirits). Our destination was the Panjshir Valley
and The Mountain.

The last hope of recruiting an expert mountaineer had now
expired. During our short stay in the capital we had been
extremely discreet about our capabilities, or rather the lack of
them, but still no one had come forward, except the cyclist, and
he could scarcely be regarded as anything but a liability. It is
true that we had met several people of different nationalities who
said that they were just about to set off for Nuristan; so often
did they say it that our project began to seem almost commonplace. However, we were reassured by an old inhabitant.

"I've lived here thirty years," he said, "and I can't remember
a time when someone from the town wasn't threatening to go to
Nuristan. But it's all talk—and then only when they're in
their cups," he added picturesquely. "You're not likely to find
it overcrowded."

With us in the vehicle were Ghulam Naabi and one of the
private servants from the Embassy, a fine-looking, bearded man
with loyal eyes. This is nearly always a bad sign in Asia where
fine-looking, bearded men with loyal eyes have a habit of leaving

you in the lurch at the most inconvenient moments—but this particular specimen really was faithful. He was to drive us to the Panjshir Valley and return to Kabul after dumping us there. It was a tight squeeze with all our equipment and the four of us sweated morosely.

The road climbed a pass where gangs of Hazaras, slit-eyed, round-headed Mongols in the uniform of the Afghan Labour Corps, were widening it, using Russian steamrollers with cruel-looking spiky projections on the rolling part. Immediately the lugubrious air that hangs over the visitor to Kabul in an almost visible cloud was dispelled, and we entered the Koh-i-Daman, rich upland country. Our spirits rose.

In spite of being hot it was a beautiful day and puffs of white cloud floated at regular intervals in a deep blue sky, as if discharged by a cannon. Mulberry trees, loaded with fruit, shaded the abominable surface of the road from the heat of the afternoon; vines grew in profusion and everywhere there was running water, dancing in the sunlight and gurgling in the irrigation ditches on whose banks minute, bare-bottomed nomad children from the encampments that were everywhere along the road risked death happily.

To the west the more distant prospect was magnificent. The high crest of the Paghman range formed an imposing backcloth with the Takht-i-Turkoman, on whose summit we should already have planted our ice-axes, rising impressively at its southern end. It was from this range of mountains that the richness of the land proceeded, the parallel rivers which flowed down from it forming a series of oases, rich with orchards, in the plain between the road and the mountains.

Of these oases, the oasis of Istalif is reputedly the most beautiful.

"Istalif produces pottery of a delightful blue colour," Hugh remarked, whetting my interest. "The name comes from *stafiloi*, the vine—from the time when the Koh-i-Daman was Greek-speaking."

"He who has not seen Istalif has nothing seen," said Ghulam Naabi. Nevertheless, true to our policy of stopping for nothing, we thundered past the road that leads to it.

Presently we reached Charikar (Alexandreia ad Caucasum)

where Alexander spent the winter of 327 B.C. with his army
before moving on to Nikaia (a city on the site of modern Kabul),
and the conquest of India. Now, ahead of us, the Hindu Kush
mountains rose spiky and barren-looking out of the plain.
Nesting under them was a small town built at the junction of
two rivers, both emerging from narrow defiles, the Shatul and
the Panjshir itself, which comes racing out of a great gorge and
spreads over banks of grey shingle on its way to join the Kabul
river and eventually the Indus and the sea. This was Gulbahār—
'The Rose of Spring'.

Not far from Gulbahar, on the eighteenth of August 1519,
the Emperor Bābur, the remarkable soldier-poet and founder of
the Turk dynasty in India who was descended in the male line
from Timur Leng and through his mother from Genghis Khan,
embarked on a raft for a picnic with some companions.

'Just where the Panjhīr-water comes in, the raft struck the
maze of a hill and began to sink. Rauh-dam, Tīngrī-qulī
and Mīr Muhammad the raftsman were thrown into the
water by the shock; Rauh-dam and Tīngrī-qulī were got on
the raft again; a China cup and a spoon and a tambour went
into the water. Lower down, the raft struck again opposite
the Sang-i-Barīda (the cut-stone), either on a branch in midstream or on a stake stuck in as a stop-water. Right over on
his back went Shāh Beg's Shāh Hasan, clutching at Mīrzā Qulī
Kūkūldāsh and making him fall too. Darwīsh-i-muhammad
Sārbān was also thrown into the water. Mīrza Qulī went over
in his own fashion! Just when he fell, he was cutting a melon
which he had in his hand; as he went over, he stuck his knife
into the mat of the raft. He swam in his *tūn aūfrāghī* (long
coat) and got out of the water without coming on the raft
again. Leaving it that night we slept at raftsmen's houses.
Darwīsh-i-muhammad *Sārbān* presented me with a seven-
coloured cup exactly like the one I lost in the water.'*

Descending stiffly from our vehicle, we drank tea on the

* The Bābur-nāma in English (*Memoirs of Bābur*), by Zahiru'd-dīn Muhammad Bābur Pādshāh Ghāzi. Trans. by A. S. Beveridge from the original
Turki. 2 vols., London, 1921.

balcony of a *chaie khana* which hung on stilts over the little
Shatul river, which came purling down into the town between
narrow banks. The tea place was beside the bridge at the junction of three roads and from its shelter we could watch the life
of the little town.

Sitting with their backs to us on the wall of the bridge five
ancient men, old Tajiks, with dyed beards, sat motionless. On
the opposite side of the river, twenty feet away from us in
another tea-house a band of Pathans, their eyes dyed with an
extract from the plant called madder, carried on an animated
conversation, passing a water pipe from hand to hand until,
feeling themselves watched, they glared at us suspiciously.

The air was full of cries, outlandish smells of smoke and
animals, dust and excitement. A bus gaily painted like a fantastic dragonfly and laden to suffocation point with passengers,
failed to make the sharp turn and became jammed at the entrance
to the bridge just at the moment when a flock of sheep, several
hundreds strong, coming from the mountains also debouched
on it. The noise was deafening as the sheep, mad with fear,
tried to nuzzle the old men over the pediment of the bridge and
into the water below, but they sat stolidly on.

There was an interval of calm while five women, saucy ghosts
in all-enveloping *chador*, with crocheted holes for faces, rode
over the bridge on horseback, each with an anxious-looking
husband trotting behind on foot.

They were succeeded by two urchins who fought strenuously
in the dust, ripping great chunks out of one another's already
ragged clothing. Then, quite suddenly, the road was deserted
and a young man appeared strutting slowly and stiffly with both
arms held straight down in front of him. He was almost goose-
stepping and he was completely naked. For some minutes
he stood in the middle of the bridge with his fingers extended,
holding up the traffic.

No one, including the five old men, took the slightest notice
of him. He went slowly up the road at the head of a small
procession of men, animals and vehicles that had been piling up,
waiting for him to make up his mind where he wanted to go,
and disappeared. Lunatic, *Darwīsh* from some strange sect, or

simply someone from the city come to take the waters of the Shatul (well known for their medicinal qualities) who had lost his bath towel, we shall never know. Even the omniscient Ghulam Naabi, who went off to interrogate the inhabitants, returned no wiser.

Just beyond Gulbahar where the mountains join the plain, east of the Panjshir, on a low and isolated ridge, is the yellow sandbank called Reg-i-Ruwan (the Running Sands) which is said to have the singular property of singing or moaning when agitated by the wind or otherwise disturbed. Among the local inhabitants opinions have always been divided; some say that it emits a sound like the beating of kettle-drums and then only ten or twelve times a year; others maintain that it only happens on Fridays; almost all agree that it is most likely to occur when the wind is strong from the north-west.

This sandbank so fascinated Lord Curzon that in 1923, when he was Foreign Secretary and in the midst of his other pre-occupations, he addressed a letter to the British Envoy Extraordinary and Minister Plenipotentiary at Kabul, Colonel Humphrys, instructing him to visit the Reg-i-Ruwan and make a report.

Colonel Humphrys duly visited the sandbank and, in an effort to drag some sound from it, he despatched bands of men to the top of the slope and made them glissade down the face of the sandbank. 'As the sand was dislodged it flowed down in parallel, rectangular streams,' says the Colonel's report, 'and emitted a rustling sound faintly audible at twenty yards.' The sort of noise that any sandbank might be expected to give out if disturbed by a body of men tramping up and down it.

It was late in the afternoon when we left Gulbahar. The road, with puddles a foot deep, mounted swiftly through a waste of banked rock and shingle brought down by the turbulence of the river in spate. Growing incongruously from these banks were a few stunted trees.

In a few minutes we came to the mouth of the Panjshir gorge from which the river raced, shooting down with little scuds of foam, brilliant in the sun. It was an exciting moment. Ahead of us the mountains rose straight up like a wall. Those on the left, towards the west, formed part of the main Hindu Kush range; those to the right, separated by fifty yards of the rushing water that had cut this gorge, were the final spurs of the great massif, itself a spur of the Hindu Kush that projects southwards from the Anjuman Pass at the head of the Panjshir Valley, forming the western marches of Nuristan in which was Mir Samir, our mountain.

I took one last look at the smiling plain behind us with its rich market gardens and the mountains to the west where the sun was beginning to sink, then we were in the cold shadow of the gorge with the river thundering about us, cold and green and white, sucking and tugging at the great boulders that lay in the stream, the noise of it reverberating from the walls thirty yards from side to side like the entrance to a tomb.   After about a mile the gorge suddenly opened out into a valley where the mountains were no longer sheer but ran back in steep banks of scree.

As we drove on we had momentary glimpses of jagged peaks. They were as dry as old bones; there was no snow or ice to be seen—that would be farther back, higher still in the Hindu Kush.

The road turned a corner and now, on the far bank of the river, infinitely secret-looking villages with watch towers built of dried mud, loop-holed and with heavily barred windows, clung to the mountainside. We turned another corner and suddenly were in paradise.

It was evening but the last of the sun drenched everything in golden light.   In a field of Indian corn women were slyly using their veils.   They no longer wore the wraithlike *chador* that we had seen in Gulbahar and Kabul.   In the small terraced fields, which fitted into one another like a jig-saw or, when they were at different levels, like some complicated toy, the wheat was being harvested by men using sickles.   From the fields donkeys moved off uphill in single file to the tomb-like villages, so loaded that they looked like heaps of wheat moved by clockwork.

But it was the river that dominated the scene.   In it boys were swimming held up by inflated skins and were swept downstream in frightening fashion until the current swirled them into deep pools near the bank before any harm could come to them; while in the shallows where the water danced on pebbles smaller children splashed and pottered. On its banks, too, life was being lived happily: a party of ladies in reds and brilliant blues walked along the opposite bank, talking gaily to one another; poplars shimmered; willows bowed in the breeze; water flowed slowly in the irrigation ditches through a hundred gardens, among apricot trees with the fruit still heavy on them, submerging the butts of the mulberries, whose owners squatted in their properties and viewed the scene with satisfaction. Old white-bearded men sat proudly on stone walls with their grandchildren, grave-looking little boys with embroidered pill-box hats and little girls of extraordinary beauty. This evening was like some golden age of human happiness, attained sometimes by children, more rarely by grown-ups, and it communicated its magic in some degree to all of us.

The road wriggled on and on. It was like driving along the back of a boa-constrictor that had just enjoyed a good meal, and equally bumpy. At Ruka, the principal town of the lower Panjshir, the main street through the bazaar was covered in with the boughs of trees to form a dark tunnel in which the shopkeepers had already lit acetylene flares. It was not yet the time for custom and the owners of the stall-like shops sat cross-legged and motionless, waiting; proprietors of *chaie khanas* with their big brass samovars boiling up behind them and shelves of massed teapots; butchers in their shops where legs of mutton, still black with the day's flies, hung from cruel-looking hooks; sellers of shoes with curly toes, rock salt in blocks, strange clothing —all ready for business. In the middle of the bazaar, chocked up on tree-trunks, without wheels stood an enormous American automobile of the thirties, the reputed property of a German who had gone prospecting over the Anjuman Pass and who had not returned.

Now that we were near our destination, Ghulam Naabi began to identify the scenes of the various mishaps that had overtaken him and Hugh on the road when they were last there in 1952. As we screeched round a particularly nasty bend with a steep drop to some water-logged fields below, it seemed likely that at least one of the disasters would be re-enacted.

"Here I was overset in a lorry with Carless Sahib."

"You never told me that," I said to Hugh.

"It was nothing. The driver lost his head. Ghulam Naabi was a bit shaken, that's all."

Another mile. We ground up a really steep piece covered with loose stones. "Here we had a puncture."

A little farther and we reached a place where the radiator had boiled over. It seemed impossible that such a short distance could encompass so many misfortunes.

At the meeting of a lesser stream, the Parandev, with the Panjshir, we got down and washed. The water was very cold. Coming from the regions of snow and ice it reminded us, as we stood there sticky and hot, of the rigours that awaited us higher up in the mountains.

"Very high the Parandev," said Hugh, "nearly 16,000, according to a book I read. We couldn't measure it, we hadn't got an aneroid, but there's snow on it from October to May."

I asked him about the passes into Nuristan.

"Probably higher. Don't mention the word Nuristan when we come to hire the drivers, otherwise they won't come. They're terrified of the place."

The road continued close along the river bank and now Ghulam Naabi began to look out for the man we had come to find, the Tajik who had accompanied Hugh on his previous journey and whom we hoped would now come with us, bringing with him two more drivers with horses.

"ABDUL GHIYAS!"

Ghulam Naabi let out a great cry that scared the driver causing him to swerve so that he nearly landed us in the river.

As we flashed past, there was a momentary vision of someone glaring up at us from the water's edge. By the time we had stopped and got out he had climbed up the bank and was coming towards us along the road. Abdul Ghiyas had been saying his prayers and had been just as frightened by Ghulam Naabi as the driver. He was dark and thin, aged about thirty-five, with a moustache and no beard. His face was deeply lined on either side of the nose towards the corners of his mouth, and his eyes were dark brown. He was wearing a *chapan*, a loose woollen cloak-like garment of white homespun with wide sleeves. On his head was an old black headcloth, tattered but clean. This was the man who had been struck on the head by a stone on the last visit to the mountain, the one I had read about in a hotel bedroom in Manchester, half a world away. It was an historic moment, but for someone who hadn't seen his one-time master for more than four years he did not manifest any great enthusiasm; rather he showed a lively apprehension.

"He doesn't seem very excited to see you," I said to Hugh, while we were parking the station wagon in a little lane that led steeply off the road and into the orchard at the back of Abdul Ghiyas's house.

"He's probably wondering how he's going to feed us all. We *are* rather a mob."

"I expect after the last time he wonders what you're planning for him. Seeing you must be rather like being handed a death warrant."

We climbed a wall of crumbling stones into a little garden that led down to the river. It was a charming place. Mulberry trees and a trellis of vines sheltered it from the heat of the day and the grass was green. Willows overhung the river, which here ran swift and deep except close into the bank where some quirk of the current made it move sluggishly upstream. Beyond the narrow road which divided it from the garden was the house, like all the other houses, a fortress of brown mud with loophole windows, wooden gutter pipes and a flat wooden roof with wide eaves. From it came the sound of giggling and there was a swirl of gaily coloured cloth on the roof as his wives gazed down on us, until he shouted something sharp at them and they vanished.

"He always was a dreadful prig about women," Hugh said and proceeded to tell him so.

From one of the loopholes half-way down the sheer wall of the house a minute girl of three or so was observing us, but as soon as she felt herself watched, she veiled herself with a scarlet cloth.

Now, with great solemnity, the greetings and introductions began. Besides Abdul Ghiyas himself there was his old father,

toothless and doddery, and a line of his relations down to a
degree when kinship must nearly have been extinct: several
sinister-looking men in skull caps, hangers-on, who were ignored,
and a host of children, all boys. All these had appeared as if
they had been expecting our arrival; as indeed they had, the
news having in some mysterious way preceded us from the
capital.

"*Salamat bashi*," droned Abdul Ghiyas, looking apprehensively
at the roof. "May you be healthy. *Khub hasti? Jur hasti?*
Are you well? Are you harmonious?"

"*Mandeh nabashi. Zendeh bashi*," we intoned. "May you
never be tired. May you live forever."

"*Salaamat bashi*," squeaked the old father and, because Hugh
had been a secretary, "*Sar Ketab*. I remember you, Head-of-the-
Book."

Meanwhile rugs and quilts had been brought out from the
house and we sat down in a half-circle with our legs drawn up.
A young man came up from the river with two big, circular
baskets, one filled with apricots, the other mulberries—the
Panjshir *tūt*—dripping with the water in which he had just washed
them.

"You have arrived for the last of the apricots but for the *tūt*
there is still time," said Abdul Ghiyas.

The apricots were good but the mulberries were delicious,
small and sweet and white with a faint purplish tinge. It was
difficult to resist them. Like a mechanical shovel, Ghulam
Naabi's hand rose and fell, scooping them from the basket and
into his mouth until I thought he would burst. As the light
failed he seemed to grow larger and larger like a white balloon.

After an hour of *tūt* eating he lay back on his quilt and languidly
gave instructions for the preparation of an evening meal, waving
a sticky hand. My spirits rose. I was hungry, too hungry to
satisfy myself with sweet mulberries however good. I noticed
that he took no part in the actual cooking, which was carried
out over a dung fire in a remote corner of the garden. Judging
by the blasphemous sounds that came out of the darkness, it was
not altogether easy but the results were satisfactory. A dish of
eggs and *nan-i-roughani*, thin, flat wheat bread fried until crisp

in clarified butter, and a pot of tea for each one of us. It was evident that if Ghulam Naabi was with us all would be well.

While we were eating a big moon rose and shone down on us through the trees, throwing a network of shadows over us. The village *Mullah* arrived, an elderly man with a full beard dyed bright red. Soon a water pipe began to circulate, passing from hand to hand. It reached me but I made it gurgle so horribly that I quickly passed it on, afraid of becoming a social disaster.

Up to now there had been no mention of the business we had come about, perhaps before dinner it would have been considered impolite. Now Abdul Ghiyas gently broached the subject.

"Last year an American came to Jangalak." (Jangalak was the name of the little hamlet where Abdul Ghiyas lived.) "I went with him to Mir Samir."

"What happened to the American," said Hugh. "How far did he get?"

"Not so far as you did, only to the glacier. But for me the journey was more pleasing. I was not hit on the head by any stones. The American had ropes. He was rich."

"All Americans are rich," said Hugh. "but they were my ropes, I lent them to him, they cost me £17 from England."

To me it seemed a lot of money for a few ropes.

"They came from England by air. The freight was terrific. They didn't come in the 'Bag'. There was some kind of mistake and I had to pay the duty. The Customs worked out the value at the bazaar rate of exchange and then charged the duty on that. It was most unsatisfactory."

With infinite slowness all was agreed. Abdul Ghiyas was to be our guide and caravan master. He was to bring his own horse and two other drivers, each with their own beasts. We were to leave the following morning. It was not considered advisable to discuss the financial arrangements before Ghulam Naabi and such a large audience, and at any rate the other two drivers would have to be present.

Now we sat for hours and hours while the *Mullah*, who had constituted himself chairman, decided who of the company should speak of the problems that afflict the world. It was obvious that we were going to be up all night. Like everyone present, the *Mullah* was a Tajik.

We were now in fact in the heart of Tajik country. As Abdul Ghiyas said proudly, later in the evening, "From the British Embassy at Bāgh-i-Bālā through Panjshir and over the Anjuman Pass to Faizabad in Badakshan all is Tajik."

He was right. The embassy at Kabul is on the northern fringe of the city. All day we had been travelling in Tajik territory. There are also Tajiks in Andarab, the parallel valley to Panjshir to the west and also around Ghazni and Herat. In the Panjshir there are, according to the *Mullah*, about 5,000 households, about 30,000 people in all. The Tajiks are the original Persian owners of the Afghan soil, conquered and dispossessed by the Pathans but still speaking Persian; pleasant, regular-featured people; agriculturists, Sunnites, intense in their religion, a far more ancient people than the Hazaras, round-headed, flat-faced Mongols who were settled in Central Afghanistan by Genghis Khan in the fourteenth century in the region he himself had depopulated, and converted to the Shiah faith in the eighteenth by Nader Shah's Persian Army.* Now like the Tajiks the Hazaras are a subject race, independent only in the fastnesses of their own country, the Hazarajat.

For hours and hours we sat there. The *Mullah* spoke of the King and how he came to hunt in the mountains just behind us.

"He comes by jeep and good horses wait him. There are ibex and panther; wolves also. In winter there are many wolves. They attack the people and take sheep."

"Do many young men come from the city to hunt?"

"They would not come to our mountain," said Abdul Ghiyas; in spite of his misfortunes on Mir Samir he still seemed proud

* The death of Muhammad, the founder of Islam, without male heirs and his omission to appoint a successor, led to the division of Islam into two sacerdotal and political factions—the Shiites and the Sunnites. The Sunnites took their name from a collection of books on traditional law called the Sunna which are received as having authority concurrent with and supplementary to the Koran. The Sunnites claim the right of nominating the prophet's successors. The Shiites recognise the divine right of succession to rest with his cousin Ali and his descendants.

of his connection with it. "The mountain needs men of hard flesh."

I shuddered, thinking of our efforts to climb Legation Hill four days before.

It was now very late, and cold too; here we were nearly 8,000 feet up. Our breath smoked in the moonlight. The river was over the banks; the effect of the glaciers melting in the midday sun was only just making itself felt. In the last hour it had risen six inches.

Hugh was telling an interminable story, something from South America, about an anaconda killing a horse. To express it in classical Persian was heavy going; judging by the look of almost hysterical concentration on the faces of his audience it was pretty difficult for them too. I was very tired and my head kept falling forward with an almost audible click. Fortunately, the story of the anaconda broke even the *Mullah*'s resistance, and soon we were left alone. We wrapped ourselves in our sleeping-bags and instantly fell asleep.

CHAPTER NINE

A Walk in the Sun

I WOKE the following morning to find Abdul Ghiyas regarding me at close range with his large haggard eyes. I had the sensation that he had been doing this for some time, perhaps trying to make up his mind by a close inspection what defects I possessed. Partly in order to reassure him, I went to swim in the river. The water was like ice. I emerged from it with chattering teeth to find that Ghulam Naabi had made tea and that the other drivers had already arrived.

While drinking our tea Hugh and I regarded them covertly. Our first reactions were not altogether favourable; judging by the hostile glances they shot at us from time to time, neither were theirs. Both of them were about our own age. One was thin, with a small foxy moustache. He wore a striped jacket that was part of a western suit, loose *shalvār* trousers, a huge, floppy turban and shoes with curly points. He looked cunning, intelligent and the antithesis of the faithful retainer. The other had a broad, stupid face, like an old-fashioned prize fighter, with a thick, trunk-like nose and a deeply lined forehead with a wart on it. On the back of his head he wore a little pill-box hat. He looked as hard as nails.

They were crouching with Abdul Ghiyas over a wooden bowl containing curds and talking with great animation while they scraped the bottom of the bowl with great hunks of bread; occasionally they would interrupt their conversation to look at us with sinister emphasis. There was no question of our accepting or rejecting them. It was Abdul Ghiyas who was hiring them.

Outside the garden, on a small strip of green by the river,

the three horses were picketed to iron pins driven into the ground.
I knew little enough about horses but these seemed very small
horses.

"Surely mules would be better.   Why don't we take mules?"

"There aren't any mules in Afghanistan.   At least I've never
seen any."

It seemed extraordinary that, after a century of guerrilla warfare on the north-west frontier, no one had succeeded in capturing
any mules from the British, but whatever the reason I never
saw a mule in Afghanistan.

Now all our gear was brought out and stacked around us in
the garden; coils of rope, boxes of rations, bags of flour, damp
things that had already squashed and our *crampons*, those metal
frames covered with sharp spikes that defied all efforts to pack
them.

The driver from the Embassy prepared to leave.   From an
inside pocket Ghulam Naabi produced a letter addressed to
Hugh which he handed to him.   His face wore an expression
of mask-like innocence.   The letter was short but to the point.
It was from his employer, the Australian.

'Sir,

I understand from my servant, Ghulam Naabi, that you
are proposing to relieve me of his services for a month, leaving
me with a sick wife, several children and no cook.   I write
to inform you that Ghulam Naabi is *not* accompanying you
on your expedition.   He will return to Kabul immediately.'

There was nothing to say to this.   It was the sort of letter
I should have written myself in similar circumstances.   With
some show of emotion Ghulam Naabi transferred his few
belongings to the station wagon.   They were so few that it
was obvious that the contents of the letter had already been
communicated to him before he had left Kabul.   Soon he was
gone in a cloud of dust.

My worst fears were realised.   I was now alone in Asia with
a companion whose attitude to food was one of undisguised con-
tempt and whose ideas were almost as austere as those of the
followers who surrounded us.

"I can't understand that Australian," said Hugh. "It's a most extraordinary attitude. Never mind, we shall probably get on much better without Ghulam Naabi. Be able to travel faster. Less of a problem."

"Yes."

"Of course, it means doing the cooking ourselves."

"Yes."

"Still, it's all in tins."

"I know."

"You're unusually quiet."

"Yes."

"Hope you're feeling all right. Nothing wrong inside?"

"Nothing like that. I just feel as though I've been sentenced to death."

There seemed little hope of leaving that day. It was not due to lack of preparation. There was very little to prepare. It was simply that the first day of a caravan was like being under starter's orders on a racecourse—only there was no starter.

Bloated with mulberries and slightly sticky, I lay on my stomach on the river bank, looking into the water. Occasionally a shaft of sunlight filtering down through the upper branches would illuminate a small fish, not more than six inches long, darting among the roots of the willows where the earth had been washed away. Out in midstream in the midday sun the river bubbled and surged past, the colour of jade rippled with dazzling silver. On the far bank sheep and goats browsed in a deep water meadow; birds Abdul Ghiyas called *Parastu*, brown banded bank-swallows, flew over the shingle without ever alighting; above the valley the mighty screes with small sunbaked patches of grass on them swept up and up; beyond the road the house simmered in the heat, its brown mud walls baking harder and harder. There was no sign of Abdul Ghiyas or the other drivers.

I was joined by Hugh. He buried his head in the river and drank.

"Is that a good thing?" I asked.

"Excellent water. Comes from the high glaciers. You shouldn't drink it when you're hot, of course."

Remembering the affair of the ice-cream that had all but destroyed my wife, and the *qanat* water in north Persia, I was suspicious. The water certainly looked delicious; besides, there was so much of it. Surely such a volume would nullify all but the most urban germs.

"What about the villages higher up?"

"There's nothing large enough to infect it," he said. "Besides, you have to accustom yourself to this kind of thing. The most important thing is never to drink unless you absolutely have to. I never do," he added.

So I drank some too.

By three-thirty in the afternoon all hope of leaving seemed to have gone. Drivers and animals were locked in lassitude and indifference. Neither wanted to leave at the fag-end of the day —and they were right; to venture into the oven-like landscape beyond the garden seemed to them suicide. Only by shouting at them and appealing to Abdul Ghiyas were the drivers finally prevailed upon to load their horses.

It was a long job. All the stuff had to be slung in nets made from a special reed and hooked to the pack saddles. Soon everything was ungetatable: the rations in their fibre boxes, everything else in sacks as a protection against the battering it would receive from the rocks. It was obvious that unless one started the day with the gear one required, one would never see it till the evening.

Unwisely, we decided to carry loaded rucksacks. "To toughen ourselves up," as we optimistically put it.

"About forty pounds should be enough," Hugh said, "so that we can press on."

Our drivers were aghast. It was difficult to persuade Abdul Ghiyas that we were not out of our minds. With the temperature around 110°, carrying our forty-pound loads and twirling our ice-axes, we set off from Jangalak.

It was good to be on the road; it stretched ahead of us full of ruts, following the river. On both sides the mountains rose steeply. Looking back we could see Abdul Ghiyas in the orchard at Jangalak where he was making the last adjustments, putting off his departure to the last possible moment.

At first we congratulated ourselves on seeing more of the countryside on foot. What we had not taken into account was the diminished social status that was accorded to a couple of Europeans plodding through Asia with heavy loads on their backs. It was after a long mile, when we met two wild-looking crop-headed mountaineers coming down from above by a rough track, that we first realised that nobody admired us for what we were doing. They themselves were carrying immense loads of rock salt in conical baskets. We waved cheerfully but they uttered such angry cries and made such threatening gestures that we passed hurriedly on. They turned to shout after us. It was always the same word.

"What's a *sag*?"

"It's a dog."

"Is it rude in Persian?"

"Very, they think we should be on horseback."

The road followed the west bank of the river through mulberry orchards and fields of wheat and Indian corn. At this time of day all were deserted. After two miles we reached the village of Mala Asp. From here the road became impassable for vehicles. At the stop beyond the village the evening bus stood up to its axles in a deep puddle. That we should have walked here heavily laden when we might quite easily have travelled by bus seemed to make us even more ludicrous figures. As we left a nasty old man screamed at us from the top of a rock, "*Xar, Xar*, Donkeys! Why don't you ride?"

To which we replied, in fury, "—— off!"

The two miles we had covered since Jangalak had wrought great changes in us. We no longer chatted gaily. In the cool garden it had been difficult to realise how hot it really was. Soon we were suffering all the agonies of heat, thirst and fatigue, accelerated by our poor condition. Our legs felt like melting butter.

So that Hugh could give me a piece of chewing-gum, we

halted for a moment in the shade of a solitary tree. Already our mouths were full of a thick, elastic scum, which with the chewing gum became like a gigantic gobstopper. Our rucksacks with their forty-pound loads seemed to weigh a hundredweight; nevertheless we both agreed that whatever else happened we should carry them for today. I was wearing a new pair of Italian boots that had been specially constructed for me in Italy. In the whole of England I had not been able to find, in the short time at my disposal, a pair of climbing boots that would fit me (my old boots had collapsed during the visit to Wales). As the Italian bootmaker at Brescia said, with a simplicity that robbed his words of offence:

"*Signore, non sono piedi d'uomo, sono piedi di scimmia.*" "Sir, these are not the feet of a man, but of a monkey."

The boots had arrived by air in Tehran on the morning we left for Meshed and, apart from our short outing on Legation Hill, I had not tried them. Now, in the hot afternoon, they became agonising. Apart from a pair of gym shoes they were the only foot covering I possessed, my walking shoes having failed to arrive from England, where they too had had to be made.

We were now travelling what, before the motor road had been constructed over the Hindu Kush by the Shibar Pass, had been the main caravan route to Northern Afghanistan, Badakshan and the crossing of the Oxus. Coming down towards us we met a variety of travellers. First a band of Tajiks mounted on donkeys who were on their way from Jurm in Badakshan more than 150 miles to the north-east to buy teapots and tea at Gulbahar; they had been twelve days on the road and the skin around their eyes was all shrivelled by the sun. Then there were some Pathan camel drivers who had come over from Andarab with wheat, their beasts swaying down like great galleons under a press of sail. Going up were caravans of donkeys with cotton goods from the mill at Gulbahar. All the people we met who were travelling the road were more friendly than the householders we had so far encountered.

"How is your condition?" "Are you well?" "Are you strong?" "Where are you going?" To which we replied, invariably. "Up" or "*Parian mirim*. To Parian", the upper part of the Panjshir Valley; vague enough, yet it seemed to satisfy them. All soon became a bore. For our part we did not speak to one another; we had no moisture to spare.

At six o'clock, when the heat had gone, we reached a place where the road passed close to the river at its junction with a torrent coming from a big valley to the east. This was the Darra Hazara, where some 400 families of Hazaras live who have become Sunnites as the price of living in peace among the Tajiks.

It was an eerie place. Behind us the sun was lost in clouds of yellow dust raised by the wind that had got up suddenly, howling across the valley as the sun went down and lashing the river so that it smoked.

On the left of the track, already in cold shadow, were a number of tombs on a hillock; piles of stones decked with tattered flags that fluttered sadly in the wind and ibex horns decorated with twists of coloured paper. According to Hugh it was a *ziarat*, a shrine, and the tomb decorated with ibex horns that of a *Mirgun*—a matchlock man, or master hunter.

On the Hazara side there was a fort. Marz Robat, the Fort of the Frontier. It was about a hundred feet square, built of mud brick and defended at the four corners by towers that tapered thickly to their bases.

"One way into Nuristan," Hugh said as we plodded past the Darra Hazara. "Two days over the pass and you'd be on the head-waters of the Alishang river, but you'd still only be on the outskirts of Nuristan. You'd have to cross the Alishang Pass into the Alingar Valley and then you'd only be in the lower part. I want to get to the upper part."

It sounded very complicated.

As we covered the last awful mile into the village that takes its name from the fort but is called by the locals 'Omarz', two fit-looking men came steaming up behind us. The taller of the two, a fine-looking fellow with a black beard, turned out to be of the same profession as the one under the pile of stones, a *Mirgun*.

I was too far gone to really care what a *Mirgun* was but Hugh,

with a perversity that I had already remarked in him, proceeded
to tell me at great length, translating, sentence by sentence, as
the man spoke.

From beneath an immense *chapan* the *Mirgun* produced a
muzzle-loading rifle fired by a percussion cap. It looked quite
new. Everything this man had about him was robust and
strongly constructed for the hard life he lived on the mountainside.

"From *Englestan*," he said. "I have not had it long."

While I was trying to imagine some small factory in Birmingham still turning out muzzle-loaders for *Mirgun*, he
added, "I have buried my other in an orchard. When I killed
a thousand Ibex I became a *Mirgun*. Then I buried the gun
with which I slew them. It is the custom. I buried it secretly
in my orchard. Then the young men from the village came to
seek for it. He who finds it can buy the gun."

"Why should he wish to do so?"

"Because with it he too will slay a thousand ibex and himself
in turn become *Mirgun*."

At six-thirty we arrived at the village of Marz Robat itself.
We had been on the road for three hours and during this time
had covered perhaps ten miles but, nevertheless, I felt utterly
exhausted. By the look on Hugh's face he was experiencing
somewhat similar sensations.

Outstripped by the *Mirgun* and his companion, whose opinions
of our powers of locomotion were plain enough, we followed
them into a narrow enclosure on the right of the road and sank
down on the scruffy grass.

"You know," said Hugh, "I feel rather done up, I can't think
why."

"It must be the change of air."

We were in a little garden high above the river, on the outskirts of the village, which belonged to a *chaie khana* across the
road. The *chaie khana* was really only a hole in a wall with a
sagging roof of dead vegetation strung on some long poles.
Standing in a wooden cradle, looking like a mediaeval siege

mortar and equally defunct, was a Russian samovar made of copper and decorated with the Imperial eagles. It was splendid but unfortunately it was not working. Deciding that it would take a long time to get up a head of steam in a thing of this size, I closed my eyes in a coma of fatigue.

When I next opened them I was covered with a thick blanket of flies. They were somnolent in the cool of the evening and, when I thumped myself, squashing dozens of them, they simply rose a foot in the air and fell back on me with an audible 'plop', closing the ranks left by the slaughtered like well-drilled infantry.

Now the samovar was belching steam, jumping up and down on its wooden cradle in its eagerness to deliver the goods. It no longer resembled a cannon; it was more like an engine emerging from its shed anxious to be off up the line and away.

Bending over us was the proprietor, a curious-looking giant in a long brown cloak reaching to his feet, which stuck out coyly from under it. He was an object of nightmare but he brought with him all the apparatus of tea.

My teeth were chattering like castanets and without a word the giant took off his verminous cloak and wrapped me in it, leaving himself in a thin cotton shift. Another cloak was brought for Hugh. Here, when the sun went down, it was cold.

Regarding us silently from the walls of the little garden there was an immense audience. The male population of Marz Robat, all but the bedridden, come to view these extraordinary beings who to them must have had all the strangeness of visitors from outer space. To appreciate their point of view one would have to imagine a Tajik stretched out in a garden in Wimbledon.

It was green tea and delicious but the cups were too small; pretty things of fine porcelain. After we had each drunk two entire pots we still had need of more liquid. Ours was not a thirst that proceeded from dry throats but a deep internal need to replace what had been sucked out of us in our unfit state by the power of the sun.

"I shouldn't do that," Hugh croaked, as I demanded water. "You'll be sorry."

My powers of restraint, never great, had been broken. Now our roles were reversed.

"I thought you wanted me to drink it."

"Not when you're tired. It's too cold."

He was too late; the giant had already sent down to the river for a *chatti* of water. Somewhere I had read that salt was the thing for a person suffering from dehydration, so I called for salt too; a rock of it was produced and I put it in the pot, sluiced it round and drank deep. It was a nasty mixture but at least I felt that in some way I was justifying my lack of self-control.

All this time the crowd had been quietly slipping down off the wall and closing in on us; now they were all round us gorging with their eyes. We were the cynosure. Hugh was the first to crack.

"——!" He got up and stalked to the far end of the garden, tripping over his *chapan*. The crowd followed him but he barked at them so violently that they sheered off and settled on me.

With the intention of splitting them, I made for the only available corner (the other was occupied by the *Mirgun* and his friend), but as soon as I started to walk I found that there was something very wrong with my feet inside the Italian boots. It was as if a tram had gone over them. I sat down hastily, took the boots off and found that my socks were full of blood.

It seemed impossible that such damage could have been done in the space of three hours and some ten miles. My feet looked as though they had been flayed, as indeed they had.

How it had happened was a mystery; the boots were not tight, rather there was an excess of living-room inside them. The real trouble was that they were slightly pointed, whether because pointed shoes were the current Italian fashion and the designers thought that the appearance was improved or whether to facilitate rock climbing was not clear. What was certain was that for me pointed boots were excruciatingly painful.

Hugh tottered over to look and the villagers made little whistling sounds when they saw the extent of the damage. All of them knew the value of feet in the Hindu Kush. For some time Hugh said nothing. There was nothing to say and nothing to be done until Abdul Ghiyas arrived with the horses and the medicine chest.

"They're very bad," he said at last. "What do you want to do, go back to Kabul?"

To return to Kabul was useless; yet to go on seemed madness.

There was no question of my feet healing, the daily quota of miles would ensure that. I thought of all the difficulties we had overcome to get even as far as Marz Robat: the children uprooted from school; our flat let; my job gone; the money that Hugh and myself had expended; his own dotty dream of climbing Mir Samir to be frustrated at the last moment; my own dream, equally balmy, of becoming an explorer in the same way going up in smoke. I thought of the old inhabitant at Kabul. "They're always setting off," he had chuckled, "that's as far as they get." Were we to join this select body who had travelled only in their cups? There seemed to be no alternative but to go on. The fact that there was none rallied me considerably.

"We might be able to get you a horse," Hugh said.

He could not have said anything better. I am completely ignorant of horses. The last time I had attempted to mount one I faced the wrong way when putting my foot in the stirrup and found myself in the saddle facing the creature's tail. Worse, being nervous of horses, I emanate a smell of death when close to them so that, sniffing it, they take fright themselves and attempt to destroy me. A horse would certainly have destroyed me on the road we had traversed that afternoon. At some places it had been only a couple of feet wide with a sheer drop to the river below.

"I think I'll carry on as I am. Another horse means another driver."

"It would be *your* horse. We wouldn't need another driver."

"If I walk they may harden up." It was a phrase that I was to use constantly from now on.

It was fortunate that Abdul Ghiyas chose this moment to arrive with the rest of the party. Drivers and horses came lurching into the garden, all our gear banging against the stone walls in an alarming way. If this was what had been happening all along the road at the narrow places, most of it must have been shattered long ago.

All three were in a filthy temper, having been uprooted from their afternoon siesta and made to travel in the heat of the day. In an instant they cleared the garden of the crowds that milled about us and began to unload the horses, banging the boxes down like disgruntled housemaids and mumbling to themselves with averted eyes. It was not a propitious beginning to our life together.

"Are they always like this?" Watching this display of temperament I expressed my fears to Hugh.

"We haven't discussed terms with them yet. They're building themselves up for a good set-to about how much they're going to be paid. Then they'll quieten down a lot."

"They're rather like *vendeuses*. Can't we put them out of their misery?"

"You can't hurry things in this part of the world. They'll do it in their own way. Besides we don't want an audience. Wait until it gets dark. I should get on with dressing your feet."

As it grew dark Abdul Ghiyas moved all the equipment of the expedition close-in around us, hedging us with boxes and bundles so that we resembled ambushed settlers making a last stand. "For fear of robbers," as he put it. Within this enclosure we ate stewed apricots with lots of sugar, the only food that we could stomach in our debilitated condition. Almost at once, as Hugh had prophesied, we started to wrangle over wages.

"For the journey we offer thirty Afghanis a day. Also we will provide the food for your horses." Hugh managed to make the part about the food sound like a benediction. At the bazaar rate of exchange thirty Afghanis is about four shillings.

The larger of the two drivers, whose name was Shir Muhammad, a surly-looking brute, said nothing but spat on the ground. To dispose of him at this delicate moment in the negotiations Hugh sent him to get sugar.

"Sugar, what do you want with sugar? If you come to our country why don't you live like us," he mumbled, throwing the bag down in an ungracious way. "This is a country of poor men."

"What a noble animal is the horse," said Abdul Ghiyas, striving to inject a more lofty note into a conversation that was in imminent danger of degenerating into an affair of mutual recrimination. "The way is stony and hard for our horses. No man will take you to this mountain for thirty Afghanis a day."

". . . and food for the men," said Hugh.

"That is the custom.   Besides, who knows what perils Carless *Seb* will lead us into.   Where will he take us after the mountain? Mir Samir is very close to Nuristan."

"Thirty-five Afghanis."   Abdul Ghiyas had struck a subject that neither of us wanted to discuss at this stage.   It was a shrewd thrust.

The silence that followed was so long that I began to think the discussion had lapsed completely.

"The horse is the friend of man," he said at last.   "The road is a difficult one.   There are many perils on it, robbers and evil men.   We are all married men.   I am married, Shir Muhammad is married, Badar Khan is married . . ." he indicated the smaller driver, the one with a thin moustache, who began to giggle.

"He looks like a pansy to me," said Hugh in English.   "Forty Afghanis.   Not one more."

"Our children are numerous," Shir Muhammad leered horribly. "Who is to look after them when we are gone?"

"This is your own country.   Surely you're not afraid of Tajiks."

"There are Hazaras, heathen Shias . . ."

"But the Hazaras of the Darra Hazara are your brothers, Sunnites."   This was one up to Hugh but Abdul Ghiyas ignored it.

"I have heard from the *mullah* at Jangalak," he went on, "that only two days ago a Nuristani going down to Kabul to stay with his brother in the army was robbed of everything, his cloak too, by the Gujaras."

I asked who the Gujaras were.

"Hill shepherds; partly nomad, from the Frontier, originally from the Punjab.   There are some in Nuristan.   They're semi-criminal—forty-five Afghanis."

Finally, we settled for fifty Afghanis.   Hugh grumbled a lot, "don't know what the country's coming to," but to me it seemed remarkable that we had secured the services of three able-bodied men and their wiry little horses for the equivalent of six and eightpence each.

Now that all was concluded satisfactorily, the water pipe was circulated and Shir Muhammad heaped the fire with the fuel that the horses were producing at a greater rate than it could be consumed, an unusual experience for anyone used to living in Britain.

All night I was racked with pains in the stomach, the result of drinking water that was both ice-cold and dirty. Hugh, of course, was completely unaffected. Each time I got up I encountered Abdul Ghiyas. He was not asleep but squatting in the moonlight, ghostly in his white *chapan*, brooding over the kit, listening to the roar of the river.

CHAPTER TEN

Finding our Feet

ABDUL GHIYAS was first up the next morning (not that I think he had ever been to bed) harrying and chivvying us like a nurse in a superior household. "We should have started at the third hour," he said, but Shir Muhammad and Badar Khan were not of the same opinion. It was, at any rate, the fault of their masters, who lay in their bags waiting for the tea that never arrived, growing more and more bad-tempered because each knew that he was behaving badly and storing up trouble for the rest of the day.

It was a quarter to six before we finally moved off. For the Panjshir Valley the day was already far advanced. Beyond the village we crossed a torrent that boiled out of a defile. Once across it, out of the shade of the village, the sun was hot and growing stronger every minute. We travelled packless and this time in step with the others to avoid the comments from the roof-tops.

The valley was the scene of ceaseless activity; in the groves of mulberry trees close to the road, beyond the crumbling walls, the Tajiks were gathering the fruit. Like apprentices up in the rigging, the boys were shaking the branches while underneath, like charming firewomen waiting to catch someone from a burning building, their beautiful sisters held striped homespun blankets extended at each end by a bow-shaped wooden stretcher. The mulberries descended in an endless shower and the air was full of a soft pattering. There were mulberries everywhere; round every tree there was a depression scooped out to receive them and the ground was swept clean with brooms for the windfalls. They were on the road too, little drifts of them

120

like newly-fallen hail. They were on the roofs of the houses, spread out to dry in the sun, alternating with piles of apricots, a staple food to be exported out of the valley or else stored for the winter, much appreciated in a place where sugar is a luxury that is rarely available and never used in tea.

A strong wind began to blow, curling the Panjshir back on itself where it flowed less violently in these wide reaches between banks of shingle that were littered with broken trees and rounded boulders, the debris of the river in spate. Here the valley was perhaps a mile wide. The fields rose in terraces as far as the screes of fallen stones that streamed off the steep sides of the valley. Even these high fields, several hundred feet above the river, were irrigated by water drawn off from the Panjshir many miles higher up and carried along the hillside by brilliant engineering, a silver ribbon glittering in the sun.

In the fields the harvest was far advanced; whole families worked happily together threshing the wheat, the chaff rising on the wind in ragged clouds; children in charge of the bullocks which plodded blindfolded round and round the threshing floor; men in waistcoats worn over white shirts, and wide trousers, wearing on their heads turbans of black or white or navy blue; girls beautiful but unforthcoming, drawing their head cloths tightly across their faces and turning their backs as we approached in such a manner that we began to feel ourselves the vanguard of a whole cohort of sexual maniacs come to this paradise to violate and destroy. Perhaps one of the most disagreeable features of fanatic Islam is its ability to make people of other faiths feel impure in thought, word and deed.

There were no large villages: only an occasional hamlet or a solitary farm standing in its own fields of wheat or Indian corn, ten feet high—enchanted forests in which little children played hide and seek; fields of barley, maize, bright fields of clover, creeping vetch, beans and tobacco. There were compact orchards of apples and magnificent groves of walnut and clumps of poplars, the wind sighing in their high tops. Here in the middle part of the valley the houses were of stone, sometimes faced with mud. At the mouths of the valleys that descended from the frontiers of Nuristan there were watch towers with

farms clustered about them. The few bridges were crazy cantilevers of tree-trunks and turf.

The first of these valleys, Darra Ghuzu, was reached after an
hour on the road from Omarz. Sitting by the side of the track,
looking up it, was an old man dressed in a long coloured cloak
of striped material and a close skull cap. Seeing our interest he
pointed to a peak, a snow-covered pinnacle that must have been
well over 18,000 feet high, glowing pink where the sun was now
reaching it.

"Ghuzu," he said, "under it there is a great river of ice."

He asked us where we were going.

"Kuh-i-Mir Samir. We are going to climb it."

"Ghuzu," he said, pointing to the impressive pinnacle, "is
nothing but a child. Kuh-i-Mir Samir is a great mountain. It
is quite vertical. No man can reach the summit."

For some time we plodded on in silence while I digested this
unpalatable information.

"If it's worse than Ghuzu he's probably right."

"It's higher, that's all. We'll do it somehow," said Hugh.
Somehow his confidence was infectious.

"We'll do it all right," I said.

Another two hours and we were in Khinj, a shady place where
the men were building a mud wall, happily puddling the stuff
like schoolboys. Beyond the village the road was full of people:
shepherds coming down out of Badakshan with big flocks of
fat-tailed sheep, a thousand at a time, following the track nose
to tail, all trying to edge us over the precipice; mountaineers
out of Andarab; wild-looking Pathan traders; men loaded with
blocks of brownish rock salt. To all, except the sheep, we
mumbled the obligatory greetings and replies that by now, as
the morning advanced, had become almost an incantation.

"Mandeh nabashi."

"Salamat bashi."

"Khush amadid."

"Khub hasti."

"Jur hasti."

"Che hal dari."

More rarely we received voluntary invitations to rest and

refresh ourselves, *"mehrbani kho"* and *"nush i jan ko"*: all in Kabuli Persian which resembles the dialect of Khurasan, the Meshed province, rather archaic and with some Turki expressions.

After four hours on the road, we came to the village of Safed Jir. Here the doorways of the houses were high with pointed arches, the wooden doors decorated with fretted work and painted cabalistic signs. We rested on a low wall and were soon surrounded by a horde of old men and children. Some of the children had blue eyes. Not all the women veiled themselves and some giggled archly, like girls inviting attention in a high street. But all this pleasantry came to an end when Abdul Ghiyas arrived, shouting to them to veil themselves in the presence of idolatrous unbelievers, and we were known for what we were, unrighteous, ungodly men.

"Sometimes I could strangle Abdul Ghiyas," Hugh said. "He's worse than a *mullah*. When he gets out of the Panjshir into the summer pastures he spends most of his time in the nomad camps with the women, but he takes good care that I don't see any. He's what you might call a religious man."

"You surprise me. He seems more like a nanny to me."

"He's more like Rasputin."

For whatever other reason the women giggled, our appearance alone would have given them good cause. On his head Hugh wore a Chitrali cap, not itself in this region an object of mirth but worn flat like a pancake, together with a khaki bush-jacket and trousers, the dress of an officer of the Eighth Army, rather more bizarre. He still carried his ice-axe, whereas I had long ago consigned mine to the baggage train. He had, too, a certain straight-backed rigidity of movement as he passed on always a few yards ahead of me. I, too, contrived to look ridiculous with a hat from Bond Street which was a sort of Anglicised version of something from Kitzbühel, blue jeans from Petticoat Lane and a camera slung round my neck with an attendant host of supplementary lenses, exposure meters and filters of varying degrees of intensity. I also carried a large notebook—already I was being introduced to the people we met on the road as *Motakhasses Seb*, 'The Specialist'.

By eleven o'clock we were really done in. All the fires of hell seemed concentrated in my monstrous feet. At every small rill we washed our faces and rinsed our mouths but it was no good. We sucked gum drops but they only filled our mouths again with thick, lime-flavoured mud.

We had outstripped the horses. It was difficult to gear ourselves to their leisurely progression.

On the right of the road an orchard sloped gently to the river. Like men about to commit a felony we crept into it, took off our boots and steaming socks and shamelessly drank the water that a young man brought us unasked. There we lay like dead men until the drivers came up and passed us by, Shir Muhammad looking down on us with a lack of respect that even in our ruined state was nonetheless extremely disagreeable.

"Last time I was in the Panjshir with Dreesen we did forty miles the first day, Marz Robat to the upper Valley," Hugh said as once again we took the road. He looked dreadful. I asked him what was wrong.

"Diarrhoea. It's most unusual."

"I'm not a bit surprised. It's all this filthy water we're drinking."

"There's nothing wrong with the water."

"Perhaps we're not strong enough for it."

"You have to get used to it."

"Like old women drinking meths?"

In spite of the halts that became more and more frequent, we overtook the men.

"*Vagt i tup.* The gun has sounded," said Abdul Ghiyas spitefully. In Tajik parlance this meant that it was noon and we should by now have arrived at our destination.

"How far to the next *chaie khana*?"

"One and a half *kro*."*

"What's a *kro*?" I could see that the heat and our conversation about water had made Hugh testy. The fact that it was he who had to do most of the interrogation was already driving him into a state of despair.

"One *kro* equals half an Iranian *farsak*."

* Kuruh.

It was some time before I was able to pluck up courage to ask what an Iranian *farsak* was.

"The distance a man travels over flat ground in an hour—about three and a half miles. And, quite frankly, I think you should have made more progress with your Persian by now."

In Panjshir each bay of cultivation is succeeded by a great bluff up which the track winds, sometimes leaving the river a thousand feet below in the gorges, overhanging it in hair-raising fashion. Now, when we had been going for five hours we made the worst crossing so far. On this bluff there were no trees, there was no vegetation and, therefore, no shade; the earth was red and burning hot and the dust swirled about us. The sun seemed to fill the entire sky like a great brass shield. In the gorge below us the river was a dirty, turgid yellow. Frequently Hugh had to stop, consumed by stomach trouble, to take what solace he could on the barren hillside. Fortunately there were no other travellers. Our men were far behind; all others had long since taken refuge from the heat of the day.

The descent from the col was long and slow. It was like walking on red-hot corrugated iron. In exactly an hour and a half, as Abdul Ghiyas had predicted, we rounded a bend and there was a village, close to the river, green, cool and inviting. Dasht-i-Rewat, 'The Plain of the Fort', the last village before the gorges leading to Parian. Better still, even at a distance, we could make out two samovars belching steam.

In the village we collapsed in front of the wrong samovar, one that was not patronised by our drivers, so that when they arrived we had to get up and totter bootless to the next establishment. There we spent the rest of the day in the shade of a huge walnut tree, the horses tethered round us.

It was a charming spot, like something from a painting by Claude Lorraine. We were in a natural amphitheatre of green grass deeply shaded by mulberries and walnuts. At the far end there were some curiously eroded cliffs over which a waterfall came bouncing down. At the foot there was a spring where the water bubbled up through silver sand into a little natural basin. The only sounds in this paradise of rock, water and green turf came from superabundant nature: the roar of the distant

river, the splashing of the waterfall, the chattering of the little
stream that led down from it, the buzzing of flies, the noise made
by Abdul Ghiyas's stallion as it tried to mate with Badar Khan's
little mare, and the clucking of the hens that had gathered about
us attracted by the bread crumbs.

We bathed in a pool below a mill. It was very deep and cold.
Out in the main river the stream was running at twenty knots.
Above us at least a hundred men and boys watched us silently
from the cliff. Presently some of the boys came in, too, swimming with a curious dog-paddle-cum-breast stroke.

Feeling infinitely better, we returned to the walnut tree,
trailing behind us a whole tribe of schoolboys. At first they
surrounded me whilst I went through the grisly ritual of dressing
my feet, but the smaller ones got clipped on the ear by older,
hairier schoolboys, who were themselves clipped by Shir Muhammad, leaving only a half-circle of nosey men, the minimum
audience that we were resigned to playing to wherever we went.
We were hourly thinking more highly of Shir Muhammad;
already, sure sign of popularity, he had received a nickname
Sar-i-Sargin, 'Head of Horse Dung', from the immense amount
of this material which he accumulated whenever we lit a fire on
the way.

Again we slept hemmed in by our belongings. Some time
after midnight I woke up. A great moon was shining down on
the road. As I lay there, a number of men, closely wrapped
in dark cloaks, went by silently and quickly on horses, going up
in the direction that we were following.

We left early the next morning and it was still dark when we
took the road. By five o'clock we had left the last houses in
the lower valley behind and were beginning the long climb from
the lower to the upper Panjshir. Soon we were abreast of the
Darra Rewat, away to the east over the river, leading to a pass
of that name into Nuristan.

"We're coming to the last samovar before Parian," said Hugh.

But he was wrong. When we reached the top of the pass,
really the crest of a big bluff, there was nothing; only some
forgotten fields and what Hugh had remembered as a *chaie khana*
which was now ruined and deserted. Far below, scarcely

moving, was the river, covered with a thick green scum, confined between high cliffs of eroded sàndstone, choked with rocks at the lower end and only escaping through a narrow sluice into the broad cultivated valley of Dasht-i-Rewat.

"Why did they have a *chaie khana* here anyway?"

"It's a junction," Hugh said. "Up there"—he pointed up the hillside to the north-west—"is the way to the Til Pass into Andarab. The country's drying up. The glaciers are receding every year." He pointed to the ruined fields. "Four years ago there were beans growing there. All the earth's dropping into the river, blowing away in dust. That's why they're abandoned. Nobody will live here any more."

Two Tajiks appeared, driving before them a herd of goats. They offered us dried mulberries made into a cake with walnuts, which they called *talkhan*. They themselves took green snuff, placing it under the tongue.

"You know," Hugh said, "for the first time since we left England I'm beginning to feel fit. I can actually feel my legs under me."

It was true. In spite of the fearful liberties we had been taking with our insides, we were undoubtedly becoming stronger.

"I can feel my legs all right," I said. "The only trouble is I can feel my feet, too."

By this time Abdul Ghiyas had come up, closely followed by the others.

"How long is the gorge?"

"Twelve kro."

"That's about twenty-one miles on flat ground."

"That's right," said Hugh.

"But is it flat?"

"Not a bit."

"Golly!"

"More than twice a *farsakh-i-ghurg*, a wolf's farsakh," said Abdul Ghiyas with relish.

The road swooped downhill to the river. Soon the horses were battling across a deep torrent, which swept at right angles into the main river.

Waiting for us on the far bank, as we emerged dripping from

the torrent, was a band of Pathans going down to Dasht-i-Rewat; father, mother, two sons and a sulky-looking girl on a pony, an evil-looking bunch, the men armed with rifles. As we went past they mumbled something to Abdul Ghiyas.

"What did they say?" Hugh asked him when we were clear of them.

"That there are robbers on the road between here and Parian who have just taken everything from a man travelling."

A couple more miles and we came to a place where the river swirled round the base of a cliff and another torrent came racing down from the left to join it.

"*Ao Khawak*," said Abdul Ghiyas, "the meeting of the waters; where it comes in from the Khawak Pass. The way of Timur Leng."

This was the place where Timur Leng's wild cavalry crossed the Hindu Kush on their way from the Oxus to India in 1398.

The bridge over the Khawak consisted of two parallel tree-trunks, one higher than the other, with the gap between filled with rocks and turf. The trunks were loose and as we trod on them they rolled apart and chunks of rock and turf crashed into the torrent below.

The fording of the river itself was not easy for the horses. They staggered through the torrent with their drivers perched on top of the loads, but it was nothing to what they were to be called on to do later.

Beyond the river we found the traveller who had had everything taken from him. He was a young man of about twenty and he was lying face downwards in the shadow of a boulder with his skull smashed to pulp. Whoever had done it had probably struck him down from behind while someone else had engaged him in conversation. The instrument was lying some yards away—a long splinter of rock with blood on it. He was only very recently dead.

"What do you think we should do?" Hugh asked Abdul Ghiyas. His suggestion was so eminently suitable that we adopted it.

"Let us leave immediately," he said.

Above our heads hovered a large bearded vulture, a lammer-

15. The top.

16. The camp on the ibex trail. Hideous awakening.

7. The way to Nuristan. The col on the Chamar Pass marked by cairns.

18. Nuristanis on their way to see two Englishmen.

19. Aruk, one of the butter carriers of the Ramguli Katirs, on his way from the high pastures to Pushal,

20. Early visitor to Nuristan? Colonel Alexander Gardner.

21. Pushal, capital of the Ramguli Katirs.

22. Crossing the Chamar in Nuristan. The bridges are unsuitable for horses.

23. Young men of Pushal.

24. Ramguli baby.

25. Young man of Pushal on his way to a funeral.

26. Butter carrier in the Ramgul.

27. Author with attendants.

geier, a whitish bird with brown wing markings. As we stood there it was joined by another.

"We call them 'the burnt ones'," said Abdul Ghiyas.

After placing a large flat stone over the head of the corpse we went on our way.

Now the road became even more desolate, the gorge narrower still, filled with a wild chaos of granite blocks. We could see the flood level of the river, thirty feet above its present course. High on the cliffs above where there were slabs of limestone, we could see the mouths of dark caves. Higher still granite cliffs overhung the track and from time to time a slab of granite would detach itself and fall with a clang into the gorge. It was no place to linger.

Yet down by the water's edge, wheat was growing in minute fields hemmed in by rocks, and the water sparkled as it ran swiftly in the irrigation ditches. There were many birds; rollers, black and white Asian magpies and a beautiful bird whose feathers had a blue or green sheen according to the way the light fell on them. It was hot but the wind was blowing down the gorge, bringing with it a cool green smell of water. In spite of its air of solitude, the track was well used. In the dust beneath our feet beetles were at work cutting up and carting away newly-dropped horse dung to some private storehouse. On the steep eastern side of the valley 400 feet above us an irrigation channel slowly descended, flowing in the opposite direction to the river and giving the curious illusion of flowing uphill. Perhaps it was flowing uphill. In this place anything seemed possible.

Finally after two hours' march, during which we constantly drank from the river and bathed our faces in it, we came out of the gorge. The valley broadened out; to the east the hills rolled back, covered in mustard-coloured grass like grass which has had snow on it. Beyond these hills a range of big jagged snow peaks rose up shimmering in the sun.

"Parian," said Hugh. "This is the upper valley and those peaks are the outriders of Mir Samir. Tomorrow we'll see it at last."

CHAPTER ELEVEN

Western Approaches

IN a few minutes we came to a hamlet of rude houses, the ragged inhabitants of which were strangely at variance with the clean air of the valley itself. This was Shahnaiz: the place Hugh and Dreesen had reached on their first day's march, forty miles from Omarz.

Beyond it the road climbed again high up the side of the hills, but we kept to the banks of the river, in the water-meadows of soft spongy grass. After the confined close air of the gorge it was good to be in the open with a cool breeze fanning us. Soon the water-meadows ended at the bottom of a crumbling cliff.

The river was quite shallow but running very fast. We decided to cross it. It was a hazardous operation. The water was only thigh deep but the current was immensely strong and the bottom was formed of stones the size of footballs slippery with weeds. Half-way across we were forced to abandon the attempt; if a man slipped in such a place he would be gone for good. We should have known better than to attempt a short cut.

We splashed back through the meadow by the way we had come and ascended the side of the hill where we met our drivers who had been watching our efforts with some amusement.

"In Panjshir and in Parian there is only one way and that is the way of the road," remarked Abdul Ghiyas. "The roads were made long ago; if there were another way we should use it."

Together we went on until we came to a suicide bridge with a village beyond it, the houses nothing more than heaps of stones, but down by the river there was a grove of poplars, an ideal camping place, at which we looked lovingly.

By now we were both a little tired of one another's company. Hugh continued along the west bank and I, following the road as Abdul Ghiyas had advised, crossed the bridge with the horses and scrambled up through a labyrinth of alleys into the village which was more primitive than anything I had yet seen. It seemed deserted; the doors of every house were padlocked with half a handcuff, made I was glad to see in Birmingham. The alleys were blocked by great boulders over which the horses were moved with the greatest difficulty. Outside the village we floundered ankle-deep in a maze of water lanes which wound round the fields.

A mile away, now far ahead of us striding out stiffly high above the river, I could see Hugh. He looked very solitary marching through Asia without attendants. But it was already clear that he had quite literally chosen the path of wisdom. As for the rest of us, at times we seemed to be making progress but then the track, which was nothing more than a morass between stone walls, would wind round the property of some landowner and land us back where we had started. Nor was there anyone to guide us; like the village the fields, too, were completely deserted.

"Everyone is at the *Aylaq*," said Abdul Ghiyas, "gone to the summer pastures."

In two hours we reached a camping place at the mouth of the Darra Samir. It was a grove of poplars near the river. Hugh was already there. "In Parian there is only one way and that is the way of the road," he said meaningly to Abdul Ghiyas, who blushed.

Too tired to be hungry we forced ourselves to eat the noxious bread that Badar Khan had got from Shahnaiz and between us ate a tin of jam from the compo. ration boxes that we had now broached. The rations were a bit of a shock: all four boxes were the same. They were of a particularly rare kind, without biscuits. Most of the tins contained Irish stew. The future that stretched before us looked unrosy.

Although far from the next village, Kaujan, we had already been smelled out, in the mysterious Asian manner, by a number of elderly inhabitants who were too decrepit to make the ascent with the others to the high pastures, some of which were as high as 14,000 feet, but were ready for a good jaw.

Here, in Parian, a valley twenty-five miles long extending to the Anjuman Pass on the main divide of the Hindu Kush, the people were still Tajiks but with flatter, heavier faces, due perhaps to a mixture of Uzbeg blood from the north. They were poorer and more primitive than the people in the lower valley, living a semi-nomad existence, taking their sheep, goats, cattle and ponies (for they are fond of horse coping) up to the high valleys in the spring and staying there until the first snows in September. In Parian there is no fruit and few trees except poplars and willows and these only close to the river. From their fields these people get beans, barley and corn; from the high pastures milk and butter.

As the sun set it became very cold with a nasty draught blowing down the Darra Samir, 'The breath of Mir Samir', as one of the old men picturesquely described it. It made us huddle over the fire which, in addition to dung, was now fed with a sweet smelling root called *buta*, and we talked of Panjshir Tajiks and the mountain. One of the old men opened the conversation.

"Panjshir," he piped, "is *sarhadd*, the frontier."

"The frontier of what?"

"The *Jadidi* and of the country to the north. The Panjshir road is the road to Turkestan."

"Ah," everyone said, nodding, "that is what we call it, 'The Road to Turkestan'."

"Who are the *Jadidi*?"

"The *Jadidi* are the Nuristanis. Until the great Emir (he meant Abdur Rahman) converted them by the sword they were pagans and great robbers."

"They still are," said someone.

"We Tajiks had five leaders to defend the valley. They were the *panj shir*, the five tigers, holding the eastern passes against the *Jadidi*; the way to Turkestan (he meant the Anjuman Pass) against the Badakhshanis, the Khawak and the Salang against the Turkis (Uzbegs) of Andarab and the Jabal us Siraj (at the southern end of the Panjshir) against the Shi'a Hazaras. That is the meaning of Panjshir."

"Not so," said Abdul Ghiyas, who had been listening with rising impatience. "Shir is 'tiger'; in the old times there were many tigers in the valley. Even now on the summit of the Til, going into Andarab, there is a tiger. People have seen it."

"But the great Amir says that Panjshir is called after the tombs of five saints of Islam." This from Hugh.

"Where are the tombs?"

"I don't know." At this all the old men grunted. This was not a subject to be discussed by a stripling of thirty-five, an unbeliever, from outside the valley.

"But it has also been said that *Panj-sher* are the five lion sons of Pandu," he went on.

"Who says this?" they all asked.

"The Hindus of Hind. I have read it in a book of an *Amrikai*." *

"An Amrikai!" It was obvious that this was acceptable to no one. "And the people of Hind, what do they know of Panjshir? Those that have made the journey to it have perished by the sword."

"It is none of these things. It is from *shirmahi*, the tiger fish that is in the river," said another.

"Pah," everyone said.

But about the name Mir Samir no one had any idea at all.

"No man has been there," was all they could say, "even the *bozi kuhi*, the ibex, has only once trodden there. That was in the time of Tufan-i Nūh, when Noah's Flood covered the earth. Then the waters rushed up the valley destroying everything, and so up the *Darra* to *Kuh-i-Mir Samir* itself. And there the last ibex took refuge on the very top. And the water followed up to the very belly of the ibex. Then it rose no more and after a while began to sink; ever since that time the belly of the ibex has been white. This is how it came to be."

A mist had risen from the river enveloping us like smoke. The old men rose to go. One of them was the water bailiff, *the Mirab*, 'Lord of the Waters'. On his way home he opened the sluices in the higher fields, so that by three o'clock we all woke to find ourselves lying in a puddle, the whole wood swimming

* The American traveller Charles Masson. *Narrative of Various Journeys*, etc., London, 1842.

in water. Later still there was a terrific crashing outside the wood where a wild pig had got into a field of Indian corn and was churning it up. All night the horses were restless, pawing and snorting. I had dreadful dreams.

After the horrors of the night the dawn had an almost mocking beauty, the mist had risen, a gentle wind blew and the tops of the poplars waved gently against an apple-green sky. At six we set off.

The mouth of the Darra Samir was very narrow and the path by the torrent blocked by boulders the size of a small house. Twice the horses had to swim the river with the lower part of our gear underwater; Shir Muhammad's grey cut one of its forelegs badly, an inauspicious beginning to the day.

Once past this bottleneck the valley rose steeply, flanked by gigantic hills, with little terraced fields of barley, blue vetch and clover half-hidden among the rocks. Here the irrigation ditches were of a beautiful complexity and I thought how my children would have liked them; the water running swift and silent until it reached a place where the dyke had been deliberately broken by the 'Lord of the Waters', allowing it to gurgle through into some small property and continue its journey downhill on a lower level as a subsidiary of the main stream.

The track followed the line of the main ditch, never more than two feet wide. Along the dykes there were beds of thick green moss, sedge, golden *ranunculus*, and bushes of wild pink and yellow roses were growing, all now, in the early morning, thickly covered in dew. Strung between the bushes the webs made by a very large sort of spider were as complex as wire entanglements and, when the sun rose over the hill ahead, they glistened like thick white cords. Only the limp and dying wild rhubarb that covered the lower slopes of the hill, like the flags of the losing side after a battle, imparted an air of melancholy to the scene.

In an hour and a half of hard climbing we came to a collection of round stone huts, like bothies in the Hebrides but roofed with earth and wild rhubarb stems. Among the rocks on the hillside on the far side of the torrent they were almost invisible, only the smoke that hung over them in the still air showed that they were human habitations. The fuel for the fires was spread out on flat rocks to dry in the sun, pieces of dung the size and shape of soup plates at which Shir Muhammad looked longingly.

Down by the water a large herd of black and white cattle, smallish beasts with humps, were feeding on the grass that grew in round pincushions among the stones. There were also flocks of fat-tailed sheep high up on the hillsides and some angry-looking goats.

"The *aylaq* of the Kaujan people," said Abdul Ghiyas. This was the summer pasture of the people of the village whose elders we had entertained the previous night. Without another word all three drivers drove their long iron pins into the ground, picketed the horses and sat down crosslegged in the excruciating position that Hugh found second-nature and that I was still only able to endure for minutes at a time.

"One of the great advantages of travelling in this part of the world is that, if you wait long enough, something happens," said Hugh, after we had been sitting for ten minutes without anything happening at all. "You can't imagine doing this in England, squatting down, outside a village. You'd starve to death."

"I can't see much point in doing it here."

But I was soon to be confounded. Gradually, our arrival began to cause a disturbance. Women and children came to the doors of their houses, making gay splashes of colour in the sombre landscape and uttering long, wailing cries that were taken up and echoed by men, up to now unseen, high up on the mountainside. There was a sudden baying of dogs and a wild stream of curs and hounds came leaping from rock to rock across the river and up towards us, ravening for flesh and blood, to be beaten off with volleys of stones and appalling blasphemy. They were followed by two men; one short and stocky, the other taller, with brown eyes, strong neat beard, a straight nose, a man with an air of dignity. Abdul Ghiyas seemed to know him, for he embraced him warmly. His name was Abdul Rahim.

They had brought with them an earthenware pot containing *dugh*,* boiled and watered milk, some *qaimac* in a wooden bowl, the thick yellowish crust that forms on cream, and some bread to mop it up. Our drivers tucked in with gusto. For us it was no time to be stand-offish, it was vanishing down their gullets far too quickly for that; we joined them. The *dugh* was cool, slightly sour and very refreshing; the *qaimac*, mopped up with bread that was still hot from the oven, was delicious.

We went on our way, Abdul Rahim accompanying us. The going was really hard now, very steep over landslides of flat slab lying loose on the mountain, now almost red hot in the sun. Abdul Rahim led, picking his way easily, while far behind the expedition wallowed and hesitated. The air was full of the sounds of slithering as the horses struggled up, and the sounds of walloping and awful curses. All of us had eaten and drunk unwisely at the *aylaq* and now we burped unhappily, like windy babies, as we toiled upwards.

We were crossing the head of a deep defile. Above us the mountains swept back in screes of the same slab on which we were making such heavy weather. Above these screes were great bulbous outcrops of what looked like limestone and behind them, seen through clefts, were pinnacles shining with ice and snow. Every now and then one of the slabs underfoot would start to move, gain momentum and slither downhill like a toboggan, over the precipice and into the invisible river.

Finally, at half-past nine, we rounded the last bend, climbed a steep wall of debris and saw at the end of a long, straight valley, an enormous mountain.

"Mir Samir," said Hugh.

It was about six miles off, and seeing it from the west against the morning sun and at this distance, it was an indistinct brown pyramid, flecked with white, veiled in haze, the base in deep shadow.

It was an exciting moment, but it was not the mountain, but the prospect immediately before us, so enchanting was it, that held our attention.

We were in a great meadow of level green grass, springy under-

* Pronounced *oog* not *ugh*.

foot and wonderfully restful to my battered feet. Winding through it was the river, no longer a torrent but peaceful between grassy banks, with a maze of backwaters forming narrow promontories and islands, all coming together in a small lake at the foot of which we were now standing. A cool breeze was blowing, rippling the water. It was a place to linger, making the programme ahead seem even more unattractive than usual.

The valley was full of magnificent horses, the joint property of the people in the *aylaq* and some Pathan nomads, still higher up. Now, terrified, they went thundering away in single file, weaving through the maze of channels and up on to the mountainside, manes streaming in the breeze.

This meadow was succeeded by a second in which the Pathan nomads were camped in black goatskin tents, an altogether fiercer, tougher bunch than the Tajiks and more mobile.

The third and highest had the same beautiful grass, and the same labyrinth of watercourses. At the far end, by the foot of a *moraine* that poured down into the meadow in a petrified cascade of stone, there was a large rock, covered with orange lichen, which offered some slight shade from the heat of the sun. Here we unloaded our horses. In the chronicles of any well-conducted expedition this would have been called the 'base camp'.

All through the afternoon we lay close in under the rock, our heads and shoulders in shadow, the rest of our bodies baking in the sun. In the intervals of dozing we studied the mountain through Hugh's massive telescope, which he normally carried slung in a leather case and which gave him a certain period flavour. From where we were at the foot of the *moraine* that ended a hundred yards away, it was obvious that there was a lot of what the military call, often with only too great a regard for accuracy, 'dead ground' between ourselves and the actual base of the mountain. We were in fact in almost the same position as we had been on the *Milestone Buttress*: at the 'start' but not at the 'beginning'.

What I could see was awe-inspiring enough. Mir Samir, seen from the west, was a triangle with a sheer face. It was obvious, even to someone as ignorant as I was, that at such an altitude not even the men whose kit reposed in the 'Everest Room' back in Caernarvonshire would be able to make much of the western˙wall. The same objections seemed to apply to a sheer gable-end directly facing us, which we had already christened with that deadly nomenclature that has a death-grip on mountaineers, the *North-West Buttress*. More possible seemed another more distant ridge of the mountain that appeared to lead to the summit from a more easterly direction.

"That's our great hope," Hugh said. "You can't see it from here but out of sight under the buttress there's a glacier running down from a rock wall that joins up with the buttress itself. That's the west glacier. This *moraine* comes from it." He indicated the labyrinth in front of us. "On the other side of the wall is the east glacier under the east ridge. My idea is to get up on the wall and either down on to the east glacier or round the edge of the buttress and up on to the ridge that way. It's difficult to explain when you can't see it," he added.

"It's impossible."

What I *could* see was a continuous jagged ridge like a wall running from Mir Samir itself directly across our front and curling round to form the head of the valley.

"*Pesar ha ye Mir Samir*, the sons of Mir Samir," was how Abdul Rahim picturesquely described the outriders of this formidable rock. He had promised to accompany us to the high part the next morning, though not to climb. Now he started to talk as any squire might of the hunting and shooting.

"When I was a young man I could run through the snow as fast as an ibex and caught three with my bare hands. The winter, when the snow is deep, is the best; then the partridge and the ibex are driven into the valleys and with dogs and men we can drive them against a rock wall or into the drifts. But now I am old (he was thirty-two) and have grey hairs in my beard and sometimes my heart hurts like a needle. I have been many things. I was two years a soldier and when there was the uprising of the Safis I fought against them." *

He went on to tell us about his married life. "I have had

---

* This little-known campaign against the Safi tribes of the Kunar Valley took place sometime between 1945 and 1947.

three wives. The first two were barren but the third had
three children. They were suffocated because she slept on them
each in turn. She is a heavy woman. I would like to take
another but they cost 9,000 Afghanis (at the official rate of
exchange 50 to the pound about £150 in our money; at the
bazaar rate of 150, about £50). That is in money. In kind,
two horses, five cows and forty sheep. After the wedding perhaps three hundred people come for a whole week of feasting.
They must be given rice; so you see it is not cheap."

It was time for the evening prayer and the four men made
their devotions, orientated, I thought, rather inaccurately towards
Mecca.

"I expect Abdul Ghiyas will be saying a few extra ones this
evening," Hugh said as the ceremony, moving in its simplicity,
came to an end. "I've asked him to come with us as far as the
rock wall tomorrow."

For the first time I noticed that planted in the meadow in front
of Abdul Ghiyas where he had been saying his prayers was an
ice-axe.

As the sun went down, the wind began to blow, dark clouds
formed behind the mountain and the whole west face was bathed
in a ghastly yellow light that in the southern oceans would be
the presager of a great gale. The heat of the day had rendered the
mountain remote, almost unreal; now suddenly the air was
bitterly cold and I tried to imagine what it could be like up
there on the summit at this moment. We issued the windproof
suits. Shir Muhammad rejected his, as did Badar Khan and
Abdul Rahim; only Abdul Ghiyas accepted one.

The sun was setting behind the Khawak Pass. At this time
I should have been leaving Grosvenor Street after a day under
the chandeliers. Instead we were cooking up some rather nasty
tinned steak over a fire that was producing more smoke than heat.
The smell of burning dung, the moaning of the wind, the restless
horses, the thought of Abdul Ghiyas saying his prayers, dedicating
his ice-axe, and above all the mountain itself with its summit
now covered in swirling black cloud, all combined to remind
me that this was Central Asia. I had wanted it and I had got it.

When it was quite dark the noises began.

"Ibex," said Hugh.

"I think it's damn great rockfalls."

"In the spring a panther took three lambs from this place," said Abdul Rahim.

"Brr."

We got up at four and huddled grey and drawn over a miserable fire of dung and the miracle root, *buta*, at this hour not readily combustible, and which never got going. The arrival of two barefooted Pathans, one wearing nothing but a shirt and cotton trousers, the other an ancient tottery man of eighty, a walking rag-bag, did nothing to make us feel warmer. Abdul Ghiyas was a fantastic sight in a rather mucky turban he had slept in all night, a windproof suit in the original war department camouflage and unlaced Italian climbing boots. He no longer looked like a nurse, more like a mad sergeant.

After drinking filthy tea and eating some stewed fruit, we set off, leaving Badar Khan to look after the horses. It would be tedious to enumerate the equipment we took with us; it was much the same as anyone else would have taken in similar circumstances: there was certainly less of it than any other expedition I have ever heard of. Each of us carried about forty pounds, all except Shir Muhammad who had a large white sheet with all the ropes and ironmongery in it slung across his shoulder. In the grey light we looked for all the world as though we were setting off for an exhumation. Even our ice-axes looked more like picks. I wished Hyde-Clarke could have seen us now.

"I wonder what the Royal Geographical Society would think of this lot?" said Hugh, as we splashed through some swampy ground in 'Indian file'.

"Doesn't matter what they think, does it? We're not costing them anything."

"They've lent us an altimeter."

"It's nice to think they've got an interest in the expedition."

Beyond the meadow that wetted our feet nicely for the rest of the day, we reached the *moraine*, grey glacial debris up which we picked our way gingerly. Above us the long ridges were already brilliant in the rising sun. We were three-quarters of an hour to the head of the *moraine*. Here we rested. Abdul

Ghiyas had a splitting headache brought on by the altitude; his face was ash-grey.

By seven the sun was blinding on the snow peaks. We were off the *moraine* now and on sticky mud where the torrents spilled over the edge of the plateau. Higher up, in the pockets of earth between the rocks, Abdul Rahim showed us fresh tracks of ibex and wolf. Then, suddenly, there was a terrific fluttering as birds got up in front of us and Abdul Rahim was off, dropping his rucksack, his *chapan* looped up, running like a stag at over 15,000 feet and disappearing over the edge of the hill.

There was an interval, then he reappeared half a mile away. Originally there had been five birds; now there were only two but he was on the trail of one flying ten yards ahead of him, going towards a lake which it splashed into. Whether he wanted to or not his impetus carried him into the water in a flurry of spray and he scooped the bird up.

Very soon he came loping towards us, the bird under his arm. "*Kauk i darri*," "I'm going to tame it," he said. It was a white snow cock, half grown. It seemed completely unafraid, nestling close to him. It was a remarkable achievement, particularly for one who had only the night before been telling us that he suffered from a weak heart.

Shir Muhammad chose this moment to unsling his sheet full of ironmongery and drop it with a great clang on the stony ground. Like a child out shopping with its mother, bored with the conversation over the baskets, he too was fed-up with standing around at 15,000 feet doing nothing in particular; *kauk i darri* taken by any means were commonplace to him. His action settled our camping place. It was as suitable as any other.

CHAPTER TWELVE

Round 1

WE were in an impressive and beautiful situation on a rocky plateau. It was too high for grass, there was very little earth and the place was littered with boulders, but the whole plateau was covered with a thick carpet of mauve primulas. There were countless thousands of them, delicate flowers on thick green stems. Before us was the brilliant green lake, a quarter of a mile long, and in the shallows and in the streams that spilled over from it the primulas grew in clumps and perfect circles.

The lake water came from the glacier of which Hugh had spoken; we were in fact in the 'dead ground' that I had been trying hard to visualise during our telescope reconnaissance. From the rock wall that was our immediate destination, the glacier rolled down towards us from the east (to be accurate E.N.E.) like a tidal wave, stopping short a mile from where we were in a confusion of *moraine* rocks thrown up by its own movement, like gigantic shingle thrown up by the sea.

The cliff at the head which divided it, according to Hugh, from a similar larger glacier flowing down in the opposite direction, looked at this distance, about two miles, like the Great Wall of China; while above it, like a colossal peak in the Dolomites but based at a far higher altitude, the mountain itself zoomed straight up into the air to its first bastion, the pinnacle of the north-west buttress. Above the buttress there was a dip, then a second ridge climbing to another pinnacle, twin to the first, then another ridge that seemed to lead to the summit itself.

The cliff joined the buttress low down on its sheer face. Vast slopes of snow or ice (in my untutored state there was no way of

knowing the difference) reached high up its sides. To more
skilful operators they might have offered an easy beginning;
no one could have found the rock above anything but daunting.

For some time we considered our task in silence.

"It's nothing but a rock climb, really."

"I can see that."

"Just a question of technique."

"What I don't see is, how do we get on to it."

"That's what we've got to find out."

The west wall that had filled me with such awe when the sun
set on it was now scarcely to be seen at all; only the apex of that
fearful triangle was visible with a light powder of snow on it,
far less than I had imagined.

The lower part was obscured by *pesar ha ye Mir Samir*, 'one
of the sons', a mountain loosely chained to the parent at a great
height. 18,000 feet high, rising from the pediment of snow
slopes above the glacier and running parallel with it across our
front. From the valley it had seemed a continuous ridge but
immediately beyond the lake it broke in a gap a mile wide, then
rose again but not to the same heights. Between these two
ridges there seemed to be the entrance to a deep valley, the far
side rising in a fiendish-looking unscaleable ridge, serrated with
sharp pinnacles, like a mouth full of filed teeth.

Hugh was full of excitement.

"That's the way to the foot of the west wall."

"That's the place I was hit on the head by a great stone with
Carless *Seb*." This from Abdul Ghiyas who was looking
extremely unwell; I was not feeling so good myself, having now
rejoined Hugh in his troubles; inheritance of the deadly drinking
habits we had cultivated in the Panjshir.

We set up our little tent. It was impossible to drive in pegs,
there was too little earth. They simply folded up on themselves;
instead we used boulders. With its sewn-in ground sheet and
storm-proof doors it was like an oven. From it we emerged
dripping with perspiration.

Abdul Rahim and Shir Muhammad now withdrew, having
first bade us farewell in their different ways. There were tears
in Abdul Rahim's eyes as he clasped our hands. I was as deeply

affected as he was. I respected his judgement in mountain matters and this demonstration of emotion I took as a confession that he did not expect to see us again. Nothing could shake that man of iron, Shir Muhammad; he set off down the mountain without a word and without a backward glance. He was negotiating with one of the Pathan nomads to buy a lamb and was anxious to resume business.

It was half-past seven; already the day seemed to have lasted unduly long. Hugh was already laying out the gear.

"The sooner we get to the top, the sooner we can leave; this is no place to linger," he said.

For once I agreed with him. Before we left I slipped behind a rock (no remarkable thing now that both of us were doing this anything up to a dozen times a day) and quickly studied the section of the pamphlet on the ascent of glaciers. It was rather like last-minute revision while waiting for the doors of the examination room to open, and equally futile.

We set off at a quarter to eight. All three of us were now dressed alike in windproof suits, Italian boots and dark goggles. On our heads we wore our own personal headgear. It was essential to wear something as the heat of the sun was already terrific. Our faces were smeared with glacial cream and our lips with a strange-tasting pink unguent of Austrian manufacture. We looked like head-hunters.

At first the way led over solid rock which shone like lead, polished by the friction of thousands of tons of ice passing over it. It was only a surface colour; chipped, it showed lighter underneath, like the rest of the mountain, a sort of unstable granite. To the left was another lake, smaller than the lower one but more beautiful, the water bright blue, rippled by the wind, inviting us to abandon this folly. At last we reached the terminal *moraine*, the rock brought down by the glacier now locked across the foot of it in confusion. It was as if a band of giants had been playing cards with slabs of rock, leaving them heaped sixty feet high. Through this mess we picked our way like ants. From the depths of the *moraine* came the whirring of

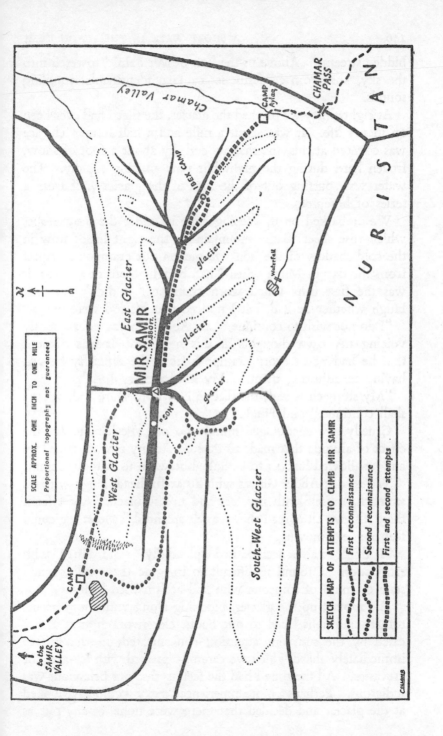

SKETCH MAP OF ATTEMPTS TO CLIMB MIR SAMIR

First reconnaissance	
Second reconnaissance	
First and second attempts	

SCALE APPROX. ONE INCH TO ONE MILE

Proportional topography not guaranteed

N

to the
SAMIR VALLEY

CAMP

West Glacier

South-West Glacier

MIR SAMIR
19,880 FT.

East Glacier

glacier

glacier

glacier

Waterfall

IBEX CAMP

CAMP
Aylaq

Chamar Valley

CHAMAR
PASS

N U R I S T A N

hidden streams. Above us the 'son of Mir Samir' towered into the sky, and from its fastnesses came unidentifiable rumbling sounds.

At eight-thirty we reached the glacier, the first I had ever been on in my life. It was about a mile and a half long. The ice was covered at this, the shallow end, by about a foot of snow, frozen hard during the night but now melting rapidly. The water was spurting out of the foot of the glacier as if from a series of hosepipes.

We embarked on it, keeping close in under the snow slopes which rose sheer to the mountain on the right hand; now in the cold shadow of the 'son' we put on our crampons. Apart from the day in Milan when I had bought them in a hurry, it was the first time I had worn crampons. I didn't dare ask Hugh whether he had, but I noticed that his too were new.

"I do not wish to continue," said Abdul Ghiyas, courageously voicing my own thoughts at this moment. It was obvious that he had never worn crampons from the difficulty he was having in adjusting them. "My head is very bad."

"My stomach is bad; the feet of Newby *Seb* are bad, yet we shall continue," said Hugh.

Cruelly, we encouraged him to go on. Perhaps it was the effect of altitude that made us do so. At any rate we roped up and he allowed himself to be linked between us without demur.

We set off; Abdul Ghiyas with his awful head, Hugh with his stomach, myself with my feet and my stomach. Apart from these ills, we all agreed that we felt splendid, at least we could feel our legs moving.

"I think we've acclimatised splendidly," said Hugh with satisfaction. I found it difficult to imagine the condition and state of mind of someone who had acclimatised badly.

We moved up the glacier, plodding along with the unaccustomed crampons laced to our boots, clockwork figures, desiccated by the sun, our attention concentrated on the surface immediately ahead which we carefully probed with ice-axes for crevasses. All the time I had the feeling that our behaviour was ludicrous. Perhaps a more experienced party would have looked at the glacier and decided that there were none, at any rate as low down as this.   But in the absence of any qualified person to ask it seemed better to continue as we were.

The light was very trying; even with goggles it was like driving into someone else's headlights.   We were thirsty and all around us was running water.   It was difficult to resist the temptation to scoop up a mouthful but the state of our insides was sufficient warning for us not to do so.

Now the angle of the glacier increased as we began to climb towards the head.   Here the snow was deep and I began to cut steps.   At first unnecessarily large but, as I got better, smaller ones.   The rock wall was looming up now above us but running round the head of the glacier between us and the wall was something that looked like an anti-tank ditch.

"*Bergschrund*," said Hugh.

"What's that?"

"A sort of crevasse.   This one's only five feet deep."

"How do you know?"   We were in a rather unsuitable place for a prolonged discussion.

"The year I was with Dreesen I slipped coming down and fell in it."

"Did you have crampons?"

"No.   Get on."

I went on, marvelling.   Even with crampons it seemed difficult enough but, of course, we were all wearing rubber soles.   With nails it would have been more feasible; but then Hugh had not been wearing nailed boots in 1952 either.

Slowly we gained height until we were close under the overhang of the rock wall which was in cold shadow with great slivers of ice reaching down to impale us.   Here the *bergschrund* gave out and we crossed it and began to traverse across the top of it on snow that was so hard and shiny as to be almost ice.   It was not possible to see into the *bergschrund*; only the opening was visible.   For all I knew it might have been a hundred and fifty feet deep.

Traversing this steep slope was far more difficult than the direct ascent we had been making up to now.   For the novice crampons are both a blessing and a disaster and I was continually catching the points in my opposite trouser leg.   For some time we had been belaying and moving in pitches in the correct manner taught us by the Doctor.

Finally at ten-thirty we hauled ourselves wearily up a few feet of easy rock and on to the top of the wall. We had only been travelling for two hours but at this altitude it was sufficient for mountaineers of our calibre. At this point the wall was about fifteen feet wide; below us to the east it fell away in a sheer drop of two hundred feet to the head of the other glacier, the twin of the one we had just ascended. It was a much larger twin, tumbling away to the east in an immense field of white. Above it the north face of the east ridge swept up 3,000 feet from the glacier in fearful snow slopes, like something out of the pamphlet illustrating the dangers of avalanche, with overhangs of black rock and a really deep-looking *bergschrund* high up, under them.

"What about *rappelling* down on to it?" said Hugh.

"How do you propose to get back if we do?"

"It would be difficult," he admitted.

Somewhere above us was the summit but it was invisible, masked by the north-west buttress, smooth and unclimbable from the point where it was joined by the wall we were perched on. The wall itself was crowned with pinnacles of rock thirty feet high; at this moment we were in a dip between two of them.

Far away beyond the east glacier and a labyrinth of lesser mountains was a great mass of peaks, all snow-covered; one of them like an upturned cornet.

"That's Point 5953, the one we're going to climb if we have time after this one," Hugh said.*

The whole thing was on such a vast scale; I felt a pigmy, powerless.

"Just what I thought," Hugh said. "It just confirms what Dreesen and I decided last time. Too much for us."

I smothered an overwhelming impulse to ask him why we had come this far to find out something he already knew, but it was no place for irony; besides, the view was magnificent.

"I'd like to see the other side of that ridge," he went on,

* A spot height in metres in the N. Hindu Kush shown in map 1/1000000, Geographical Section, General Staff N 1-42.

indicating the east ridge. "If we fail on this side we'll try it, there'll be less snow."

"But more rock."

"It's only three days' march. We've got to go there in any case. It's the way into Nuristan."

The retreat began. I was end man. The feeling of relief that I experienced when I knew that we were to go no farther, coupled with the belief that the *bergschrund* was only five feet deep, had induced in me a light-headed sense of freedom from care; what the Americans call euphoria, a state of mind not consonant with my present responsibilities. It was no place for playing about. The snow was as hard as ice; none of us knew how to make an ice-axe belay on such a surface.

It was all right when I was controlling Abdul Ghiyas's descent. He was behaving splendidly anyway and, probably from an innate appreciation of what to do in such a situation, he was handling the tools with which he had been issued admirably. It was only when I was descending myself that I felt irresponsible. Twice I caught my crampons in my trousers and slipped, giggling, fortunately in places where the snow was deep and soft.

Finally Abdul Ghiyas shouted to Hugh, who immediately halted.

"He says you're trying to kill us all," he bellowed up at me. "Are you mad?"

"We're over the worst."

"I don't care a —— what we're over. Watch what you're doing."

I was sobered.

By now all three of us were tired. The journey over the glacier was a test of endurance. Our goggles were steamed up; we moved infinitely slowly. As we neared the end of the glacier, my horizon dropped more and more until it took in nothing but the loop of rope between myself and Abdul Ghiyas and the ice immediately underfoot. In the ice were mysterious holes eight inches deep and perhaps an inch wide. It was as though they had been made with a drill or else as though a plug had been removed. At the bottom there was sometimes a little earth or

a single stone. The glacier was now in full melt: from beneath
it came the whirring of invisible streams and when we reached
the foot the water roared from it like a mill race in flood.

We reached our camp at half-past one. The exhilaration
we had felt perched high on the wall seemed a dream, something
we had never experienced. Now all the disadvantages of the
place we had chosen as 'Camp I' were apparent. The sun was
high overhead and there was no shade; the tent was like a small
oven. It was not constructed for this sort of thing; it was
intended for 'the final assault' and lacked a fly sheet which would
have reduced the temperature inside to a bearable level for at
least one of the party. 'The tent for the approach march',
fitted with all the aids of comfort that any explorer could desire,
ventilators, fly screens, ridge poles and extensions, had been a
non-starter. It was an excellent tent but it had been obvious,
when we had erected it in a garden in Kabul, that if we took it
with us we should be spending most of our waking hours putting
it up and dismantling it.

Tentless, we rigged up our sleeping-bag covers on the ends
of our ice-axes and cowered behind them, too tired to do anything but drink tea and nibble a little mint cake.

Hugh looked green. "As well as that other trouble, I've got
a splitting head," he said.

"At least your head's not bleeding." I was carrying out my
twice-daily dressing on my feet; each time the operation became
more and more gruesome. I was wondering whether there
would be enough lint to last the whole journey. "And I've
got an inside, too."

Abdul Ghiyas said he proposed to give up climbing altogether.
"I have a headache. Also, I have a numerous family," he remarked. I sympathised with him. Similar thoughts had been
occurring to me constantly throughout the morning.

With the general lack of amenity and conversation resembling
that of three elderly hypochondriacs, I found it impossible to
sleep. All through the afternoon I trudged miles over the
plateau. I even revisited the higher lake and lay down on my
stomach half-tempted to drink. The shallows were a ledge of
rock two feet wide; beyond they plunged into green, icy depths,

in which strange fish, like little brown sticks fitted with furry stoles, shrugged themselves along.

Besides the primulas which were growing everywhere, there were golden *ranunculus* and *pontentilla*, blue *nepeta* and yellow and red rose root; there were bees and small ivory butterflies with grey wing markings; high above the plateau choughs with ragged wings cawed sadly; also I saw numbers of small speckled birds rather like thrushes and, wheeling about the crags near the *Son of Mir Samir*, one solitary great eagle.

By seven o'clock the sun had gone from the plateau and once again clouds swirled about the mountain. After a good dinner of soup, chocolate, jam and coffee we got into the tent. It was a very tiny tent so Abdul Ghiyas slept in the open. Wrapped in an Arctic sleeping-bag with a hood fitted to it so that he looked like some fantastic insect at the chrysalis stage, he was really better off than we were.

Before retiring into it he made us arm ourselves with knives and ice-axes.

"Against the wolves."

"It seems silly," I said to Hugh.

"It's all right for us. We're inside."

Like all the other nights I ever passed with Hugh it was a disturbed one. The tent fitted us like a tight overcoat and it was difficult to avoid waking one another on the journeys to the outside that we were forced to make with increasing frequency as the night wore on. Every time one or other of us emerged Abdul Ghiyas would start up brandishing his ice-axe. Exposed on the mountainside in the wind, everything crackling cold around us, Abdul Ghiyas's night terrors seemed more tangible.

Yet in the morning Hugh seemed surprised when I complained that I had had a bad night.

"Whenever I got up you were sound asleep."

"I wasn't. That was to avoid hurting your feelings. I pretended to be asleep. *You* were asleep when I got up. I heard you snoring."

"But I didn't sleep *at all*."

Whether because of too little sleep or too much we all got up far too late in the morning and it was half-past five before we left. We should have started an hour earlier. From what we had experienced the previous day, it was obvious that it was going to be far too hot to beat about investigating routes up the mountain much after eleven o'clock. Abdul Ghiyas remained behind. But it was difficult to envy him his solitary vigil, exposed to the sun on this beautiful yet awful plateau.

Our destination was the south-west side of Mir Samir—if such a side did in fact exist, which was by no means certain. We hoped to reach it through the break in the rock wall beyond the lake.

Inside, beyond the break, the valley was a fearsome place choked with vast boulders that rocked underfoot at the lightest touch; from far under them came the sound of distant streams. To the left the inner walls of *The Son* rose sheer above us; to the right the smooth icy wall from which Abdul Ghiyas's great stone had descended on him. Ahead the *moraine* was so steep that the mountain itself was invisible.

At the top we came to a wall of rock with a trail scooped out of it by ibex, up which we got easily enough, roped together, and found ourselves in a vast box with three sides, shut in under the west wall, with the 'Son' towering above us on the left. It was a dark fearsome place at this hour, full of swirling mist which obscured the summit, with black rock underfoot in which were pools of water still covered with thick ice from the night frost. To the right Abdul Ghiyas's stone-falling wall died out, and there was a defile between the end of it and the mountain which rose in a vast buttress to a false summit. Up one side of this buttress there was a possible way to the false summit, starting with steep snow, but there was no way of knowing whether one could reach the summit itself from it other than by going to see, which neither of us was anxious to do. The foot of the buttress was littered with fragments of rock that had only fallen quite recently. As we moved gingerly round the base, other small pieces came whistling down, none of them larger than a penny but heavy and quite lethal, like falling shrapnel.

"I wish those climbing waitresses from the inn were here," said Hugh. He voiced a thought that I had been about to express myself. "They'd be worth their weight in gold."

Quite suddenly we found ourselves looking on to another glacier. The part we could see was about two miles long and on the far side was the ridge we had been looking for, the south-west ridge, a jagged reef a thousand feet high, curving round at the head of the glacier and joining on to the mountain itself in much the same way as the wall on the other glacier but far higher and longer; like a saw with teeth, sixty feet high.

The glacier was a strange place. Here there was no sound of rushing water. There was an immense silence except for the occasional rumble of falling rock.

We sat down on some curious flat boulders supported on stalks of ice, phenomena of glacial action, and considered what to do next.

"If we can get on to the ridge, we might do it," Hugh said.

"How do you propose to get on to the ridge?"

"From the end. We can work our way along it."

I thought of the pinnacles ; negotiating these might take us days. With no porters to back us it seemed impossible. I produced these objections.

"All right, let's try the backside of this buttress; at least it's near."

We were about two-thirds of the way up the glacier; the backside of the buttress led to the false peak we had admired from the other side in the three-sided box earlier on.

Hugh led. The rock was a sort of demoralised granite which came to pieces in the hands. After two pitches I had been hit on the head twice by fragments the size of a ping-pong ball, but when pieces as large as cannon balls began to fall I called on him to stop. On this front the whole thing was falling to pieces. It was suicide.

By now it was intensely hot. The sun was sucking the strength out of us like a gigantic sponge. Because of this, the time of day and our own lack of guts, we gave up. I am ashamed to write it but we did.

Back in the box we tried the other side of the buttress, climbing the first steep ice slope. By now the mist had cleared and the way ahead shone clearly. Both of us were convinced that the way led nowhere that would advance us to the top.

"Down?"

"Damn! Yes."

We made our way to the head of the wall where the ibex trail was, coming to it too far to the left where it was really steep. Now with the same recklessness born of fatigue that I had shown the previous day, Hugh raced ahead and began to descend it unroped.

All the way down to the camp with Hugh far ahead of me, I nursed this grievance, treasuring up all the disagreeable things I was going to say to him. I even hoped he would fall and break his ankle so that I could say 'I told you so'.

It was in this unhealthy frame of mind that I tottered into the camp but he, himself, was so exhausted and so obviously pleased to see me that I forgot these insane thoughts. Abdul Ghiyas had already made tea and rose to meet me with a steaming bowl the size of a small chamber pot. Unfortunately he had damaged my airbed by dragging it over the rocks and sitting on it with no air in it.

"I suggest we try another day's reconnaissance," Hugh croaked, as we lay side by side on the rock, like a couple of herrings grilling steadily. "I think we should try the south-west ridge, in spite of what you said up on the glacier."

"It's crazy."

We wrangled on for some time; such an altitude is not conducive to mildness. Finally Hugh said, "The only alternative is to try the other side of the mountain, the south side of that ridge which we saw from the rock wall yesterday."

"How far?"

"Three days' march—the state we're in at the moment. If we leave at once we can be at Kaujan tonight, half-way up the Chamar Valley by tomorrow night and under the mountain the day after tomorrow."

When we sorted out the gear, I discovered that I had left a karabiner and a nylon sling at the foot of the glacier when we had unroped after the attempt of the day before. It says something for the state of mind induced by altitudes even as moderate as this that I immediately decided to go and fetch them.

"Where the devil are you going?" I was putting on my boots.

"Going to fetch the karabiner and the sling."

"Don't worry.   It's not worth it.   We've got quite enough."

All would now have been well but he added in a rather school-masterish way, "The only thing is don't make a practice of it."

"I knew you'd say that, that's why I'm going to fetch them."

"You must be mad," said Hugh.

I was mad.   I went up past the lake that invited me to drink from it or bathe in it or drown in it, all by turns; over the *moraine* by a different route.   I reached the glacier, here a mile wide, and by an unbelievable stroke of fortune struck the exact place where I had left the karabiner lying on a flat rock.

I turned back feeling virtuous.   But not for long; this time the lake was too much for me.   It twinkled and beckoned in the sunshine, stirred by the gentle breeze.   I thought how agreeable it would be to plunge my head under water, if only for a moment. The next instant I did so.   Before I realized what I was doing I was drinking deeply from the warmer shallows.   Having done so I felt exactly as though I had participated in some loathsome crime, like cannibalism, a crime against humanity that turns all men's hands against one.   Actually, it was only a crime against my own person but the feeling of defection from moral standards was the same.

I reached the camp at a quarter to one, exactly two hours after I had quitted it.   It was no longer a camp, just a slab of rock with my pack resting on it, strapped up, waiting for me; somehow it accentuated the loneliness of the place.

Apart from the sound of rushing water and the occasional boom of falling rock there was not a sound.   I stayed there for ten minutes, enjoying the experience of being alone in this great amphitheatre of mountains and at the same time not doing anything.   Then I started off with my load.   For the descent the loads had been divided among the three of us, so the shares were larger than they had been going up.

By now my powers of concentration were seriously impaired. Instead of following the main torrent down to the meadow, I started to come off the mountain too far to the north and found myself in the middle of the moraine that descended to the meadow a thousand feet below.

The descent was a nightmare. It was only a thousand feet but the rocks were balanced insecurely on top of one another, making it impossible to hurry. I could see the rock of our 'base camp' below, the horses, our men crouched over the fire, the green grass, but none of these things seemed to get any closer. I was nearly in tears from vexation.

Finally I got down and stumbled over the blessed grass and the few yards to the shadow of the rock. For the moment shade was all I required. An hour later we left for Kaujan in the valley below. The mountain had won—at least for the moment.

CHAPTER THIRTEEN

Coming Round the Mountain

AT the bottom of the third meadow, sitting cross-legged on the thick green grass beside the river, Abdul Rahim was waiting for us. He had already been down to the *aylaq* and returned, and we wondered what had brought him back to meet us half-way up again. He had been waiting for several hours, news of our failure on the mountain having reached him by the mysterious system of communication, part telegraphy, part telepathy that operates all over Asia. With him he had brought a loaf of bread for each of us. It had been cooked in butter and was just sufficiently burnt to make it delicious, far better than the awful stodges produced by our drivers.

"I baked it for you myself," he said, and waited politely for us to finish it before telling us what he had come about.

"There has been an accident. This morning, while it was still dark, Muhammed Nain, my brother's son, went out from the *aylaq* with his rifle to shoot marmot. He was high on the mountain waiting in *kamingah* (ambush) on a needle of rock. At the fifth hour I heard a shot and looking up saw Mani (this was how Abdul Rahim contracted his name) fall from the top. Like an ibex I ran up the hill and found him lying like a dead man. I carried him on my back to the *aylaq*. He is badly hurt; I fear that he will die. Only you with your medicine can save him."

Abdul Rahim had seen Hugh dressing the deep cut on the foreleg of Shir Muhammad's horse; also the saddle sores which that feckless and brutal man had allowed to develop by neglect. Watching Hugh as he had applied ointment and lint, gently as though to a sick child, he had commented drily:

"If Shir Muhammad was ill he would never receive such treatment as his horse does today."

We set off at a tremendous pace, pains in feet and stomachs forgotten, to catch up with the drivers who were an hour's march ahead and prevent them going on down to the Parian Valley with the medicines. Soon we came to the rock wilderness where Abdul Rahim, who had up to now been travelling barefooted with his shoes slung round his neck, stopped to put them on. I could see no difference in the going, most of the way the track itself had been equally rough. Perhaps like Irish peasants who are reputed to carry their boots to the church door, he sensed that he was nearing civilisation.

At this point I was forced to a halt by an overwhelming necessity and the other two pressed on ahead without me. Thence I had to follow the trail of Abdul Rahim's shoes in the dust. Soled with American motor tyres they left the imprint 'Town 'n Country' in reverse—yrtnuoC n' nwoT, yrtnouC n' nwoT. On and on it went until by repetition it acquired an almost mystic quality, Town 'n Country, Town 'n Country, Town 'n Country, and I became bemused by it like a Buddhist saying *om mani padme hum om mani padme hum*, as he tonks along the road to the holy places. As a result I lost myself high above the main track at a dead-end fit for ibex only with a descent as difficult as the descent from the glacier had been a few hours before.

I was tired and the track seemed to go down and down for ever; past the defile where we had had such difficulty with the horses on the way up; past nomad tents that had not been there three days previously; past a woman who crouched like a scared rabbit by the side of the track, face averted until I passed; past mountain men, Tajik and Pathan, who clasped my hand silently but in a friendly way; down until I reached the *aylaq* where I found Hugh with the horses all unloaded and the medicine spread over the path blocking the way.

He was in a filthy temper. "Couldn't find the —— medicine chest; had to unload every —— horse before I could find it. Never realised we had so many packets of soup in my life. Do you know where it was? In the last box, on the last —— one."

"Should I have given him morphia?" he asked anxiously.

Hugh's attitude to medicine was always a little vague, reflected in the curious collection of drugs he had assembled for this journey.

"What have you done up to now?"

"Cold compresses, washed the cuts I could get at."

"You haven't told me what's wrong with him yet."

"I've seen him," Hugh said. He was calmer now. "I went with Abdul Rahim. He was lying in one of the bothies under a pile of quilts. It was very dark, difficult to see anything inside and the place was crowded with people. He must be about sixteen; his moustache was just beginning to grow. I could only see his face. It was covered with flies. His nose and his lips were so swollen he looked like a negro. The women had shaved his scalp; it was all bruised and covered with bloody patches. He was very restless, moving under the quilts and groaning."

"Lucky you didn't give him morphia: he's probably got concussion. It would have finished him off."

"I didn't. His eyes were sealed up with congealed blood. We washed his head and face. Gradually he managed to open one eye and part of his lips. He groaned a lot. Then everyone began to shake him. 'Mani, Mani, can you hear us?' they began to shout but he couldn't answer. Then the most extraordinary thing happened. The time had come to dress his other wounds. Abdul Rahim pulled the quilt back and uncovered his arms and chest. It was the most devilish thing I have ever seen. *The boy had the body of a goat.* He was completely encased in a thick black goatskin. It fitted close up under his arms and sticking up above his chest were two grey nipples. I asked Abdul Rahim what was the meaning of it."

"When our people are sick," he said, "we always put them in this goatskin. Its heat draws the poison out of the body and into the skin."

It was a strange story. Was Mani's goatskin a last vestige of the kingdom of the goat-god Pan who, having been driven from the meadows by the sword of Islam, still retained some influence in the sick room of the nomad peoples?

Back in the poplar grove at Kaujan we were too tired to eat much. Abdul Ghiyas and his men cooked the lamb they had bought from the Pathans in the top meadow, boiling it for an hour and a half in a big iron pot with salt, pepper and the fat of the tail until it was ready to eat. The meat was rather tasteless and peppery, but the smell of fat was almost unendurable after such a day. We had been on the go since half-past four, climbed to 17,000 feet and had now come down to 9,000. Thinking to please me, for I had kept my views about the tail of *ovis aries* to myself, Abdul Ghiyas dug into the wooden bowl from which we were eating communally and fished out the most esteemed gobbets of fat which he presented to me. Not daring to hurl them away, I chewed them with grunts of appreciation for some minutes and then, when no one was looking, put them inside my shirt to be disposed of later.

During the night the *Lord of the Waters* played his joke with the dykes for the second time and once again we were flooded out. I woke to find myself in an attitude of prayer, completely lost, having forgotten which way round I was sleeping.

The next morning we lay around after breakfast but apart from repairing our punctured airbeds and taking pills for bad stomachs we did very little. In the compo. boxes I found several bottles of water-sterilising tablets and made a solemn vow that I would not drink a drop of water that had not first been treated with them. Sterilising water is tedious work: from now on, I was a more than usually remarkable sight on the march as I swung my water bottle like an Indian club in an effort to dissolve the tablets, which were as hard as lead shot and far less appetising. There was another little pill that was supposed to take away the bad taste but sometimes this failed to operate and I was left with an Imperial pint (the contents appropriately enough of my water bottle) of something that reeked of operating theatres.

But it was not until late the following afternoon that we summoned enough energy to set off.

To get to the south side of Mir Samir we had to go right round the base of it. At Kaujan we crossed the river by a wooden bridge. Ahead of us going through the village were a band of Pathan nomads on the way up to their tents, members of the Rustam Khel, a tribe who spend the winter in Laghman, what they call the *garmsir* (warm place) near Jalalabad, kinsmen of the tented nomads we had met in the Samir Valley.

The eyes of the young men were coloured with madder. Some of them carried sickles made from old motor-car springs. With the tribe there was an old blind woman and when they crossed at the next bridge, a single pole over the river, she went over hanging on to the tail of a donkey.

We were accompanied up the Chamar Valley by a Tajik to whom some strange mutation had given pink eyes and a blond moustache. With this Albino, the *Thanador* (literally the Keeper of Nothingness) of the Nawak Pass, the keeper of the Pass retained at a salary of 500 Afghanis a year to over-see it, we never got on good terms. He came at his own request, 'to protect us from brigands' as he put it. How he was to do this unarmed without recourse to bribery was not clear.

His name was Abdullah, *The Slave of God* (it was unseemly, as he backfired like an early motor-car all the way up the valley). Shir Muhammad and Badar Khan ragged him unmercifully at the frequent halts he insisted on making at the nomad encampments to eat *mast*, for he was a greedy man.

"Look at his face."

"Look at his hair."

"Look at his eyebrows." He had no eyebrows.

"Like a bastard German."

"O, Abdullah, who was your father?"

And so on.

Abdul Ghiyas took little part in these pleasantries. He was in his element. Down by the river the Pathan women, beautiful savage-looking creatures, were washing clothes. Now as Hugh had predicted he vanished into the tents on one pretext or another, ostensibly to gather information, having first warned the laundresses to veil themselves.

The Chamar was a wide glen, more colourful than the Darra Samir, with grass of many different shades of green and full of tall hollyhocks in flower. The nomad tents were everywhere and there were sheep high on the mountains. At seven we rested at a small hamlet of bothies, Dal Liazi. Behind us, above Parian, we could see the way to the Nawak Pass with Orsaqao, the big brown mountain which it crossed, with a serpent of snow wriggling across it.

It was an interrupted journey. At the instigation of Abdullah we had stopped at seven, at eight we stopped again and this time everyone disappeared into the tents for half an hour, leaving Hugh and myself outside with the horses, fuming and sizzling in the heat. But when he wanted to stop at nine, even Abdul Ghiyas protested.

"O thou German," said the drivers.

"My mother was a Kafir."

"Ha!"

Like small boys at prep school, they mocked him. From now on he sulked.

As we climbed, the country became more and more wild, the tents of the Chanzai Pathans, in which the drivers had been assuaging themselves, less frequent. From the rocks on either side marmots whistled at us officiously like ginger-headed referees. Here the horses stopped continuously to eat worm-wood, *artemisia absinthium*, a root for which they had a morbid craving.

After five hours on the road we came to the mouth of a great cloud-filled glen stretching to the west.

"East glacier," said Hugh, "we're nearly there. Pity about the cloud."

As we stood there peering, it began to lift. Soon we could see most of the north face of the mountain as far as the rock wall, and the summit, a snow-covered cone with what seemed a possible route along the ridge to it. Our spirits rose. "If we can only get to the ridge we can make it," we said.

With the cloud breaking up and lifting fast, the whole mountain seemed on fire; the cloud swirled like smoke about the lower slopes and drove over the ridge clinging to the pinnacles. From out of the glen came a chill wind and the rumble of falling rock. It was like a battlefield stripped of corpses by Valkyries. In spite of the heat of the valley we shivered.

"If the south face is no good we can always come back and

try here," said Hugh. As always he seemed unconscious of the effect he created by such a remark.

Ahead of us in the main valley, a waterfall tumbled down over a landslide of rocks; climbing up beside it we rounded the easternmost bastion of the mountain and entered the upper valley of the Chamar.

We felt like dwarfs. On our right the whole southern aspect of Mir Samir revealed itself: the east ridge like a high garden wall topped with broken glass; the snow-covered summit; the glaciers receding far up under the base of the mountain in the summer heat; and below them the *moraines*, wildernesses of rock pouring down to the first pasture, with the river running through it, a wide shallow stream fed by innumerable rivulets. To the east the mountains rose straight up to a level 17,000 feet, then, rising and falling like a great dipper, encircled the head of the valley, forming the final wall of the south-west glacier where we had made our unsuccessful effort among the ice toadstools on the other side only two days before.

"On the other side of that," said Hugh, pointing to the sheer wall with patches of snow on it to the east, "is Nuristan."

It was a lonely place; the last nomad tents were far down the valley in the meadow below the waterfall. Here there was only one solitary *aylaq*, a wall of stones built against an overhanging rock and roofed over with turf, the property of the headman of Shahr i Boland, a Tajik village we had passed in Parian on the way to the Chamar. The shepherd was the headman's son. As we came, more dead than alive with our tongues lolling, to the camping place on a stretch of turf hemmed in by square boulders, he appeared with a bowl of *mast*, wearing long robes and a skull cap, the image of Alec Guinness disguised as a Cardinal.

It was midday. The light was blinding. To escape it we crawled into clefts in the rocks and lay there in shadow, each at a different level, in our own little boxes, like a chest of drawers.

As soon as he had eaten, the *Thanador* of the Nawak Pass went off without a word to anyone.

"What's wrong with him?"

"He's in a huff because they kept calling him a German."

"Well, it is rather insulting. I wouldn't like it myself."

"But he was a bore."

All through the afternoon we rested, moving from rock to rock to escape the sun as it spied us out. Hugh read *The Hound of the Baskervilles*; I studied a grammar of the Kafir language. Apart from the pamphlets on mountaineering, this was the only serious book the expedition possessed. (Put to other uses our library was disappearing at an alarming rate.) Both of us had already read all John Buchan, who in the circumstances in which we found ourselves had been found wanting, the mock-modesty of his heroes becoming only too apparent, the temptation to transport them in the imagination to the Hindu Kush too great to resist. Remarks something like "Though I say it who shouldn't, I'm a pretty good mountaineer, but this was the hardest graft I ever remember," cut very little ice with people in our position about to embark on a similar venture with no qualifications at all.

Notes on the Bashgalī (Kāfir) Language, by Colonel J. Davidson of the Indian Staff Corps, Calcutta, 1901, had been assembled by the author after a two-year sojourn in Chitral with the assistance of two Kafirs of the Bashgali tribe and consisted of a grammar of the language and a collection of sentences. I had not shown this book to Hugh. He had been pretty scathing about my attempts to learn Persian, no easy matter in my thirty-sixth year, confronted by Tajiks who at any rate had their own ideas on how it should be spoken.

I had schemed to memorise a number of expressions in the Kafir language and surprise Hugh when we met up with the people, but, in the midst of all our other preoccupations, the book had been lost in one of the innumerable sacks; now with Nuristan just over the mountain, it was discovered in the bottom of the rice sack, where it had been ever since I had visited the market in Kabul.

Reading the 1,744 sentences with their English equivalents, I began to form a disturbing impression of the waking life of the Bashgali Kafirs.

"*Shtal latta wōs bā padrē ū prētt tū nashtontī mrlosh*. Do you know what that is?"

It was too late to surprise Hugh with a sudden knowledge of the language.

"What?"

"In Bashgali it's 'If you have had diarrhoea many days you will surely die'."

"That's not much use," he said. He wanted to get on with Conan Doyle.

"What about this then? *Bilugh âo na pī: n'pā bilosh.* It means, 'Don't drink much water; otherwise you won't be able to travel.'"

"I want to get on with my book."

Wishing that Hyde-Clarke had been there to share my felicity I continued to mouth phrases aloud until Hugh moved away to another rock, unable to concentrate. Some of the opening gambits the Bashgalis allowed themselves in the conversation game were quite shattering. *Inī ash ptul p'mich ē manchī mrisht wariā'm.* 'I saw a corpse in a field this morning', and *Tū chi sē biss gur bītī?* 'How long have you had a goitre?', or even *Iā jŭk noi bazisnā prēlom.* 'My girl is a bride.'

Even the most casual remarks let drop by this remarkable people had the impact of a sledgehammer. *Tū tōtt baglo piltiā.* 'Thy father fell into the river.' *Ī non angur ai; tū tā duts angur ai.* 'I have nine fingers; you have ten.' *Ōr manchī aiyo; buri aīsh kutt.* 'A dwarf has come to ask food.' And *Iā chitt bitto tū jārlom,* 'I have an intention to kill you', to which the reply came pat, *Tū bilugh lē bidiwā manchī assish,* 'You are a very kind-hearted man.'

Their country seemed a place where the elements had an almost supernatural fury: *Dum allangitī atsitī ī sundī basnâ brā.* 'A gust of wind came and took away all my clothes', and where nature was implacable and cruel: *Zhī marē badist tā wō ayō kakkok damītī gwā.* 'A lammergeier came down from the sky and took off my cock.' Perhaps it was such misfortunes that had made the inhabitants so petulant: *Tū biluk wari walal manchī assish.* 'You are a very jabbering man.' *Tū kai dugā iā ushpē pâ vich: tū pâ vilom.* 'Why do you kick my horse? I will kick you.' *Tū iā kai dugā oren vich? Tū iā oren vichibâ ō tū jārlam.* 'Why are you pushing me? If you push me I will do for you.'

A race difficult to ingratiate oneself with by small talk: *Tŏ'st kazhīr krūi p'ptī tā chuk zhi prots asht?* 'How many black spots are there on your white dog's back?' was the friendly enquiry to which came the chilling reply: *Iā krūi brobar adr rang azzā: shtring na ass.* 'He is a yellow dog all over, and not spotted.'

Perhaps the best part was the appendix which referred to other books dealing with the Kafir languages. One passage extracted from a book* by a Russian savant, a M. Terentief, gave a translation of what he said was the Lord's Prayer in the language of the Bolors or Siah-Posh Kafirs:

Babo vetu osezulvini. Malipatve egobunkvele egamalako. Ubukumkani bako mabuphike. Intando yako mayenzibe. Emkhlya beni, nyengokuba isenziva egulvini. Sipe namglya nye ukutiya kvetu kvemikhla igemikhla. Usikcolele izono zetu, nyengokuba nati siksolela abo basonaio tina. Unga singekisi ekulingveli zusisindise enkokhlakalveni, ngokuba bubobako ubukumkhani namandkhla nobungkvalisa, kude kube igunapakade. Amene.

'It does not agree with the Waigul or Bashgalī dialect as recorded in any book which I have seen,' the Colonel wrote rather plaintively. 'There are no diacritical marks.'

But later in a supplementary appendix he was able to add a dry footnote to the effect that since writing the above a copy of the translation had been submitted by Dr. Grierson, the distinguished editor of the Linguistic Survey of India, to Professor Kuhn of Munich who pronounced that it was an incorrect copy of the version of the Lord's Prayer in the language of the Amazulla Kaffirs of South Africa.

* M. A. Terentief, *Russia and England in Asia*, 1875. Transl. by Dankes, Calcutta, 1876.

CHAPTER FOURTEEN

Round 2

THE two of us left at five o'clock the next morning to find a way to the east ridge. Abdul Ghiyas, still wearing his windproof suit and labouring under the delusion that he was a sergeant, produced green tea for us brewed as strong as the army sort, and very nasty it was. We both harboured a determination to reach the ridge and, if possible, the summit that in retrospect I find unbelievable. Our drivers watched us go sadly and Abdul Ghiyas asked us what he should do if we failed to return. (All our impulses were to tell him to head a search party but this seemed unfair.) Apart from telling him to go home, it was difficult to know what to say. The air was full of the promise of disaster. I had not felt it so strongly since the day I embarked on what was to prove my last voyage in a submarine and the wardroom orderly had come running down the mole waving my unpaid bill.

After an interminable climb through a wilderness of black rock we reached the *moraine* at the foot of the glacier. A few minutes on the *moraine* convinced us that we would be better on the black rock, however unstable, and we moved back on to it close under the ridge, leaping from plate to plate as they see-sawed underfoot. Here we met our first snowfields, so tiny that it seemed hardly worth while putting on crampons, but they were frozen hard and we fell several times, hurting ourselves badly, so we roped ourselves instead.

At 17,000 feet we were high up on the approaches to the ridge, following a narrow ledge. Above our heads a sheer wall rose a thousand feet to the ridge itself, below it fell away five hundred to the head of the glacier. It was a charming spot;

The wall overhung the ledge in a bulge and under it there was a little earth in which giant primulas were growing. Farther under still, in perpetual shade, columns of ice and hard snow stretched from roof to floor.

But this was something seen only as we clumped by; soon we were out in the sun again, which was now very hot, and were crossing another snowfield, no bigger than a football pitch, that some strange action of wind or weather had forced up in stalks four feet high set together, like a forest of fossil trees, through which we battled our way sweating and swearing horribly.

Up another ledge, this time less friendly than the first and up to now the property of the ibex whose droppings littered it, and we were on bare rock with streams of melting snow pouring over it. It was not a particularly impressive face but there were hardly any projections to belay to, the handholds either sloped downwards or else were full of grit, a sort of shiny mica that poured ceaselessly down from above and had to be picked out of each handhold in turn, as lethal for the the fingers as powdered glass.

I had never seen such a mountain. It was nothing like anything we had seen in Wales. To someone like myself, completely unversed in geological expressions, it seemed to be made from a sort of shattered granite; 'demoralised' was the word that rose continually to my lips while, as the thaw continued and progressively larger rocks bounded past us on their way to the glacier, the childish 'it isn't fair' was only repressed with difficulty.

To cheer one another in this hour, when the first intimations of fatigue were creeping up on us and while whoever was leader was scrabbling awfully with his feet for a possible foot-hold where none existed, we pretended to be Damon Runyon characters trying to climb a mountain. Hugh was Harry the Horse. "Dose Afghans soitinly build lousy mountains" was what he said, as a particularly large boulder went bouncing past us over the edge and on to the glacier below with a satisfying crash.

At eleven we reached the foot of a gully and, with the help of the pamphlet, which we consulted unashamedly in moments of crisis, ascended it.

By this time, by the application of common sense and without the help of the book, we had evolved a far swifter method of roped climbing than we had ever practised before. Previously if Hugh led he had waited for me to come up to the place where he was belayed and, when I had hooked myself on, repeated the whole ghastly process. Now, instead of halting, I went straight on up to the full extent of the rope; in this way we moved much faster. Like Red Indians made cunning by suffering, we were learning by experience. That what we were doing is common mountaineering practice is a measure of our ignorance.

In this way we ascended this nasty gully, the head of which was jammed with loose rocks, all ready to fall, and at eleven-thirty came out on to snow on top of the east ridge.

It was a tremendous moment. We had reached it too low down and further progress towards the top was made impossible by a monster pinnacle of extreme instability. Nevertheless, the summit looked deceptively close. The altimeter after a good deal of cuffing read 18,000 feet.

"That's about right," Hugh said. "Splendid, isn't it!"

"I'm glad I came."

"Are you really?" he said. He sounded delighted.

"I wouldn't have missed it for anything." And I really meant it.

Two thousand feet below us, like an enormous new frying-pan sizzling in the sun, was the east glacier. Away to the east the view was blocked by a bend in the ridge in which we sat, but to the south the mountains seemed to surge on for ever.

Hugh was full of plans. "In some ways I'm sorry we didn't try that," he said, pointing to the impossible slopes that swept down to the east glacier, "but perhaps it's all for the best. What we've got to do now," he went on, "is to put a camp on that second ibex ledge, just below the smooth rock, at about seventeen thousand with enough food for two nights. Then we must hit the ridge farther up, beyond this pinnacle. Unless there's something extraordinary between here and the top, we ought to be able to make it in one day."

"What about dead ground?" I said. It was my stock objection but only put up half-heartedly. At 18,000 feet in the rarified atmosphere Hugh's enthusiasm was infectious. Like him, I could now think of nothing else but getting to the top.

"We've been six and a half hours from the valley to the ridge but only an hour and a half from the ibex ledge. It shouldn't take us much more than that to reach the ridge beyond the pinnacle. It's just a matter of choosing another *couloir*.* From there it can't possibly be more than three hours to the summit, but make it five and a half at the outside—that's seven hours. If we leave at four in the morning, we'll be on the top at eleven o'clock. It can't take us longer to come down. We'll be at the ibex camp before dark."

"We're really going to do it this time," I said: both of us were entranced by this nonsensical dream of planning.

After drinking some coffee and munching Kendal mint cake that seemed the most delicious thing we had ever tasted, we began the descent. Going down was a good deal more horrible than going up and I regretted that so much of our meagre formative training had been concerned with getting to the top and then walking down.

Two hours later we were once again shoving our way through the snow forest; four hours later, very tired and cross, we dragged ourselves into the camp, surprising Abdul Ghiyas, who was lying on his back watching the ridge through the telescope and giving a kind of running commentary on our progress to Shir Muhammad and Badar Khan. They all seemed pleased to see us.

While we were waiting, flat out, for tea to arrive, Hugh held his hands towards me.

"Look at these," was all he could croak. They were raw, red and bleeding and looked like some little-known cut of meat displayed in a *charcuterie*. The rock of Mir Samir is granite long past its best that comes away in great chunks with points as sharp as needles and edges that tear the fingers to shreds.† For today's climb I had worn wash leather mitts. They were already worn out. Hugh had been bare-handed. I set to work to

* *Couloir*—gully.
† Geologically, I believe it consists of plutonic rocks; gneiss, hornblende, microschists.

bandage his hands. Before I was finished he looked as though he were wearing boxing gloves.

"How the hell do you expect me to climb like this?" he said gloomily.

"They'll be better tomorrow."

"No they won't."

"I'll cook," I said, feeling heroic. Each night, unless we were eating Irish stew, we took it in turn to prepare some primitive delicacy. It was really Hugh's night. This evening I chose Welsh rarebit.

Fascinated by this dish that was outside their experience, the drivers gathered round me whilst I assembled the ingredients, opened the tins of cheese and started the primus. Soon, just as the mixture was turning from liquid to the required consistency, the stove went out. It had been snuffing out all the time in the wind but this time it went out for good because it had run out of fuel. Abdul Ghiyas rushed off and returned with a can of what I soon found, when he started to pour it into the stove, to be water and Badar Khan, on this the only recorded time during the entire journey that he ever did anything that was not in his contract, produced another containing methylated spirits that would have blown us all to glory. Faced with the failure of the Welsh rarebit and the rapidly cooling stove I got up to find the paraffin can myself, caught the trousers of my windproof suit in the handle of the frying-pan and shot the whole lot over the rocks.

At this moment, looking sleek and clean, Hugh returned from the stream where he had combed his hair and put on a clean shirt and thick sweater.

"Ready?" he asked pleasantly.

"It —— well isn't."

"Taking a long time."

Was it possible that he couldn't see us all trying to scrape it off the rocks?

"You'll have to wait a long time for this one. I should go to bed."

Both of us were temporarily done in. The effort that we had made to put ourselves on the ridge had cost a lot in terms of energy; other more experienced climbers would have done the

same expending less. This, and the mental effort of probing
and finding a way on an unknown rock face, had been as much as
we could take in one day.

As the sun went down behind Mir Samir in a final blinding
blaze of light, the wind rose and howled down on us from the
screes. But in spite of it, huddled together over the smoky fire
chewing Abdul Ghiyas's abominable bread, speaking of pil-
grimages to Mecca and similar things, we began to feel better.
Although there had been no Welsh rarebit, inside us was the
best part of a packet of Swiss pea soup, a tinned apple pudding
and a pound of strawberry jam eaten straight from the tin with
spoons.

CHAPTER FIFTEEN

Knock-Out

TO make certain that there was no easy walk to the top used by elderly Nuristanis on Sunday afternoons, I set off the following morning to explore the valley towards its head, while Hugh with Abdul Ghiyas and Shir Muhammad, whom he had dragooned into this service, staggered off uphill towards the ibex ledge, each carrying appalling loads. As always Badar Khan contrived to remain in his passive role, looking after the horses which were all extremely frisky, possibly due to some aphrodisiac quality possessed by the root *absinthium* on which they continued to gorge themselves. He was also in charge of a sheep the three of them had bought as a syndicate (with our help) for 200 Afghanis from the cardinal in the *aylaq* who, in successfully demanding such an outrageous sum, showed a financial acumen that would not have disgraced a prince of the church.

Higher up the valley, the meadow grew narrower as the rock closed in on it on either side and a thousand tiny streams purled down to the parent one. Finally the grass came to an end under some high cliffs at the foot of which a bunch of wild horses drummed up and down the slopes in a frenzy as I drew near them.

From the top a waterfall roared down 200 feet in a deep gorge it had cut for itself, throwing off broken arches of rainbow as it plunged down, and finally crashing into a deep pool. The last leap where it bounced off a great black rock took it so far out from the cliff that it was possible to stand right underneath it, deafened by the noise, in cold shadow among frozen stalactites and stalagmites and look through the falling water that was like a window of molten glass shimmering and dissolving against the sunlight.

Out in the sun among the rocks and in the water, there were flowers; in the watermeadows primulas; in the drier earth small flowers with gold petals and green buttons for centres; and in the crevices among the rocks pointed flowers with the furry texture of edelweiss and the shape of rabbits' ears.

At the head of the falls there was no more grass, only a little earth, still more primulas and a little lake full of clear water, a brilliant green, that fed the falls below. Beyond it to the right was Mir Samir, from here exactly resembling a crouching lion; its head the summit, a long plume of snow the mane. For the purpose of our climb this approach seemed useless, its sides were sheer, the ridges dividing the three small glaciers from one another steep and unwelcoming. Once again I had the delightful experience of being absolutely alone, but this time, on the eve of our attempt, its imminence gave the scene an air of unreality, like a stage set on which a piece is about to be enacted—as indeed it was. I only hoped it would be comedy.

Back at our camping place there was no sign of Badar Khan; judging by the noise that was coming from the bothy he was inside. After eating a gorgeous mess of condensed milk, sugar and a little snow I had brought back from the foot of the waterfall, a mixture that would have made me vomit in more civilised circumstances, I set off from the ibex ledge with my own load.

In two hours I reached the ledge; before leaving I had dressed my feet and I went up like a rocket. Hugh was waiting for me but there was no sign of Abdul Ghiyas and Shir Muhammad.

"They must have passed you down in the black rock," he said. "It took us four hours to get here. Half-way up Abdul Ghiyas wanted to go back. I practically had to kick him up. I think he's unnerved."

"I expect it was watching me falling about on the other glacier. He has my sympathy."

I asked about Shir Muhammad.

"He was splendid. He just plodded on and on and didn't

say anything. When he got here, he dropped his load, growled goodbye and started off down. He was in a hurry because he's got to cook the sheep for the *Id-i-Qorban** tonight."

"It'll take him hours. We'd better start cooking something ourselves, otherwise it'll be dark."

It was five o'clock; although the ledge on which we were now perched with all our gear was in deep shadow, directly overhead the sky was still a deep cobalt, while lower down to the east beyond the Chamar Valley and the ridge dividing us from Nuristan, it was a golden colour like honey.

Soon the wind began coming from the north-west, bitterly cold, battering against the ridge above and streaming over it and down into our camp, extinguishing the stoves and sending us scuttling into our sleeping-bags, to continue cooking using our bodies as windbreaks.

In this hour before everything froze solid, the mountain began to disintegrate; dislodged by the wind, the rocks fell about us in earnest. Lying as close as possible to the face on a bed of shattered stones which had only recently fallen, waiting for my stove to deliver the goods, I could see five hundred feet above us a vast rock the size of an omnibus poised delicately on the spine of the east ridge.

"This is a fatheaded place to choose for a camp," I said grumpily. "That thing's bang overhead."

"It's probably been there for centuries. Think of the grant you're going to get from the Everest Foundation."

"I distinctly saw it move. If that thing comes down there won't be anything left of us to give a grant to."

But our immediate preoccupation was with what was actually descending rather than with potential missiles. Fifty feet above our heads nature had provided a projection so that bigger boulders bouncing down the mountain hit it and leaped out beyond us into space and on to the glacier below. But, in spite of this shield, a continuous shower of stones fell about us the size of large hailstones but more lethal.

Against them, in the fatuous hope of breaking the shock of impact and also to shut out the noise, we muffled our heads and

* A religious feast. The Feast of the Sacrifice.

ate our dinner, the replica of the previous night's and our current favourite; pea soup, tinned apple pudding and strawberry jam.

As it grew dark the wind fell slightly and, as the mountain froze, the awful bombardment ceased, except for an occasional fall of rock so heavy that freezing could not arrest it. Apart from an unidentifiable roaring, like the sound that comes from a sea-shell pressed against the ear, there was a great silence.

But not for long. Soon something like a distant artillery bombardment began in the direction of Nuristan and distant peaks were illuminated by tremendous flashes.

"North India," Hugh said, with the tremendous authority that I had learned to mistrust. "Pakistan. Electric storm, possibly monsoon. Must be a hundred miles away. Lucky; if it reached here we'd be in a nasty spot."

"This is a nasty spot."

"I read somewhere," said Hugh, "that an electric storm is only dangerous on a mountain when you can hear a noise like bees swarming. But I don't think there's anything for us to worry about. The monsoon doesn't extend this far."

"Who said it was the monsoon?"

Until midnight the lightning flashed, illuminating vast mushroom-shaped clouds.* Neither of us slept well; it was difficult to breathe and our boots, which we were nursing in our sleeping-bags to keep them malleable for the early start, kept on riding up, so that at one moment I found myself with the toe-cap rammed into my Adam's apple, sucking a leather bootlace like a long black strip of liquorice.

At two I got up to light the stove. The storm had ceased: the mountain was very cold and dark and still. I was happy doing anything to bring to an end a night as awful as this one. It took three-quarters of an hour for the water to boil for tea and whilst I waited the morning star rose.

We left at half-past four, when it was just growing light. With us we took two ropes, some slings, karabiners, a hammer, an assortment of ironmongery, a thermos of iced coffee, some

---

* Later we learned that the storm had not been over Pakistan but over Nuristan, some fifteen miles away.

Italian nougat, the aneroid, and two cameras, one a miniature, the other a little box.

This time we followed the edge of a precipice above the glacier and made for the foot of a deep gully filled with snow that led eventually by way of a T junction to the ridge at its highest visible point, where we could see a prominent peak the shape and size of a castle.

At first we made slow progress across a bowl of loose scree. From a distance it had seemed the size of a small back garden; in reality it was more like a forty-acre field. Once across it we reached the rock. Everything was still freezing hard and the air seemed to crackle as we breathed it.

The rock face was covered all over with a thin glaze of ice. On its surface, our noses close to it as we felt our way slowly up-wards, time ceased to have any meaning at all. Only the coming of the sun, at first warm, then hot on our backs and the swift melting of the ice so that suddenly we were like a pair of water beetles crawling up a steep weir, told us that it was ebbing fast.

We came to the snow high up at the T junction we had planned to reach. Here, exposed every day to the full heat of the sun, it had melted and frozen so many times that it was more like ice.

"What do you think we should do now?"

It was a ridiculous question which we both asked simul-taneously. The only possible answer was to go up, but the angle was more than seventy degrees—never had either of us seen anything so unpleasant.

"Let's have a look at the book."

In it there was a picture of someone cutting steps in an almost vertical ice face—much worse than the thing we were on. Encouraged by this I began to cut steps; there was nothing else to do. It was far harder work than I had imagined and the heat was terrific; almost at once my goggles steamed up, making it difficult to see anything. I pushed them up on my forehead and was blinded by the reflected light and flying chips of ice.

After thirty feet I realised that I couldn't go farther. I was not worried by the height; it was simply that the feeling of instability was getting me down, this was nothing like the rigging of a ship. It was imperative that I make a belay so that Hugh could come up but there seemed nothing to make fast to. Tentatively I tried what the pamphlet had called 'an ice-axe belay on hard ice' but this convinced me that it would be murder and suicide to try and hold anyone with such an inadequate anchor. From below Hugh was watching anxiously.

"Put in an ice piton."

"You've got the hammer and the pitons are in my rucksack. I can't get at them. I'm going to try and reach that rock."

Projecting from the ice about fifteen feet above me was a small rock. Unfortunately there was no way of telling whether it was part of the mountain or merely a large fragment embedded in the ice. I took a fearful risk, reached it and sat on it facing outwards, jamming my crampons into the ice. The rock held.

"Come up."

With this insufficient belay Hugh came up and went straight on. It was no place to linger.

Still higher the slope became steeper but it also became softer; finally, just below the ridge, it became real snow. At the ridge there was an unpleasant crested overhang but Hugh went up the side of it, while I waited nervously below in a similar position to that which he had occupied lower down on the ice, to see whether he would start an avalanche and annihilate me. At last he disappeared over the top and a few moments later I was on the ridge beside him, breathing like a landed fish. It was nine-thirty; we were just below the great castle; the top was still invisible and we had taken five hours to get there instead of two.

"We're late," Hugh said.

"We'll do it."

"Nougat or mint cake?"

It was not a place for extended conversation.

"Keep the nougat for the top."

"How high are we?"

Hugh produced the aneroid. In its way it was as massive testimonial to Victorian engineering as a cast-iron cistern. "I'd say 18,500," he said finally after he had hit it several times. "I hope for our sakes it's right."

We crossed the ridge and once again the whole of the east and most of the west glacier was visible. And the top came into view with a long final ridge running to the foot of it.

First we tackled the castle-like knob to our left, going up the north side. It had all the attributes of an exposed face, together with a truly awe-inspiring drop of three thousand feet to the east glacier, and it was bitterly cold; like everywhere else we had so far been on this aggravating mountain there were no good belays. Up to now in the most difficult circumstances we had managed a few grim little jokes, but now on the face of this abominable castle our capacity for humour finally deserted us.

From the top of the castle there was the choice of the north side which was cold and grim or the south, a labyrinthine chaos of rock, fitted with clefts and chimneys too narrow to admit the human frame without pain. In one of these clefts that split a great boulder twenty feet long, we both became wedged and only extricated ourselves with difficulty. Sometimes exasperated with this lunatic place we would force a way over the ridge through the soft snow only to find ourselves, with no way of going on, forced to return by the way we had come.

But as we advanced, the ridge became more and more narrow and eventually we emerged on to a perfect knife edge. Ahead, but separated from us by two formidable buttresses, was the summit, a simple cone of snow as high as Box Hill.

We dug ourselves a hole in the snow and considered our position. The view was colossal. Below us on every side mountains surged away it seemed for ever; we looked down on glaciers and snow-covered peaks that perhaps no one has ever seen before, except from the air. To the west and north we could see the great axis of the Hindu Kush and its southward curve, from the Anjuman Pass around the northern marches of Nuristan. Away to the east-north-east was the great snow-covered mountain we had seen from the wall of the east glacier, Tirich Mir, the 25,000 foot giant on the Chitral border, and to the south-west the mountains that separated Nuristan from Paryshir.

Our own immediate situation was no less impressive. A stone dropped from one hand would have landed on one of the upper glaciers of the Chamar Valley, while from the other it

would have landed on the east glacier.   Hugh, having determined
the altitude to be 19,100 feet, now gave a practical demonstration
of this by dropping the aneroid, which fell with only one bounce
into the Chamar Valley.

"Bloody thing," said Hugh gloomily.   "I don't think it was
much use anyway."   Above us choughs circled uttering melancholy croaking noises.   "We've got to make a decision about
going on," he said.   "And we've got to be absolutely certain
it's the right one, because our lives are going to depend on it."

Anywhere else such a remark would have sounded over-
dramatic.   Here it seemed no more than an accurate statement
of fact.

"How long do you think it will take to get to the top?"

"All of four hours and then only if we don't go any slower."
It was now one-thirty; we had been climbing for nine hours.

"That means four-thirty at the summit.   Going down, four
hours at least to the Castle, and then twenty minutes to the *col*
on the ridge.   It'll be nine o'clock.   Then there's the ice slope.
Do you think we can manage the *col* to the camp in the dark?"

"The only alternative is to sleep on the ridge.   We haven't
got any sleeping-bags.   I'm afraid we wouldn't last out.   We
can try if you like."

For a moment we were dotty enough to consider going on.
It was a terrific temptation: we were only 700 feet below the
summit.   Then we decided to give up.   Both of us were
nearly in tears.   Sadly we ate our nougat and drank our cold
coffee.

The descent was terrible.   With the stimulus of the summit
gone, we suddenly realised how tired we were.   But, although
our strength and morale were ebbing, we both agreed to take
every possible precaution.   There was no mountain rescue
service on this mountain.   If anything happened to one of us, a
bad sprain would be enough, it would be the end for both.   As
we went down I found myself mumbling to myself again and
again, "One man's death diminishes mee, one man's death
diminishes mee."

Yet, though we were exhausted, we felt an immense sense of
companionship.   At this difficult moment the sense of depend-

ence on one another, engendered perhaps by the fact that we were roped together and had one another's lives in our hands, produced in me a feeling of great affection for Hugh, this tiresome character who had led me to such a spot.

At six we were at the *col* below the castle, exactly as he had prophesied. The conditions were very bad. All the way down from the castle a tremendous wind had been blowing and the mountain-side was flooded in a ghastly yellow light as the sun went down. As the clouds came up the wind became a blizzard, a howling gale with hail and snow battering us. We had come down from the castle without crampons. Now to cross the head of the *col* in this wind on the frozen snow, we had to put them on again. Still wearing them, we lowered ourselves one by one over the overhanging crust into a gully on the south face.

The south face was a grey desolation and the gully was the wrong one. It was too wide for an easy descent and was smooth ice the whole way for two hundred feet.

Twice we had to take off and put on our crampons, almost blubbering with fatigue and vexation, as the straps were frozen and adjusting them seemed to take an eternity. Worst of all the wind on the ridge was blowing snow into the gully, half-blinding us and sending down big chunks of rock. One of these hit Hugh on the shoulder, hurting him badly, and I thought he was going to faint. The gully was succeeded by a minute chimney full of ice, down which I glissaded on my behind for twenty feet until Hugh pulled me up. Very stupidly I was wearing my crampons attached to a sling round my middle and I sat on them for the full distance, so that they went in to the full length of the spikes, scarring me for life in a most interesting manner.

By now it was quite dark. We had an hour on the rocks, now covered with a fresh sheet of ice, that I shall remember for the rest of my life. Then we were home. 'Home' was just the ledge with the two sleeping-bags, some food and the stoves, but we had thought of nothing else for hours.

As we stumbled on to it, a great dark shape rose up and struck a match, illuminating an ugly, well-known face with a wart on its forehead. It was Shir Muhammad, most feckless and brutal of drivers, come up to find us.

"I was worried about you," he said simply, "so I came."

It was nine o'clock; we had been climbing for seventeen hours.

By now we were beyond speech. After a long hour the contents of both cooking-pots boiled simultaneously, so we drank tea and ate tomato soup at the same time. It was a disagreeable mixture, which we followed with a pot of neat jam and two formidable-looking sleeping-pills that from their size seemed more suitable for horses than human beings.

"I don't approve of drugs," were Hugh's last words before we both sank into a coma, "but I think that under the circumstances we're justified."

We woke at five. My first thought as I came to was that I had been operated on, an illusion heightened by the sight of Hugh's bloody bandaged hands gripping the mouth of his sleeping-bag. Mine were now in the same condition as Hugh's had been two days previously; his were worse than ever.

It took us both a long time to dress and Shir Muhammad had to button our trousers, which was a difficult operation for some one who had never had fly buttons of his own. It was the only time I ever saw him laugh. Then he laced our boots.

As soon as I started to move I realised that my feet were beyond boots, so I decided to wear rubber shoes.

By the time we left the platform it was like a hot plate. Shir Muhammad went first, skipping downhill like a goat bearing a great load. Soon he became impatient with our funereal progress and left us far behind.

At the head of the glacier Hugh stopped and took off his pack.

"What's the matter?"

"Rope," he croaked. "Left a rope. Got to go back."

"Don't be an ass."

"Might need it . . . another try."

"Not this year."

It was useless to argue with him. He was already crawling uphill. My return to fetch the karabiner on the other glacier had created an impossible precedent.

The glare on the small snowfield was appalling. My goggles

were somewhere in my rucksack, but I had not the will power to stop and look for them. Soon I developed a splitting headache. With my rubber shoes on I fell continuously. I found myself becoming very grumpy.

At the top of the *moraine* Abdul Ghiyas was waiting for us. He had passed Shir Muhammad without seeing him, somewhere in the labyrinth on the lower slopes of this provoking mountain, and was clucking to himself anxiously.

"Where is Carless *Seb*?"

"Up."

"He is dead?"

"No, he is coming."

"You have climbed the mountain?"

"No."

"Why is Carless *Seb* not with you?"

It was only after much pantomime that I was able to convince him that Hugh was not dead, sacrificed to my own ambition, and he consented to follow me down, carrying my load.

But at the camp we waited an hour, two hours for Hugh; there was no sign of him. I began to be worried and reproached myself for not having waited. The three drivers, huddled over the fire preparing a great secret mess in honour of our arrival, were mumbling, "Carless *Seb*, Carless *Seb*, where is Carless *Seb*?" droning on and on.

Finally Hugh appeared. With his beard full of glacial cream and his cracked lips, he looked like what he in fact was, the survivor of a spectacular disaster.

"Where have you been? We've been worried stiff."

"I got the rope," he said, "then I went to sleep under a rock."

CHAPTER SIXTEEN

Over the Top

BACK at the camping place in the Chamar after our failure
on the mountain both Hugh and myself would have welcomed the attentions of the administrative officer, who to me
had seemed such a figure of fun when Hugh had proposed his
inclusion in the expedition. We would also have welcomed a·
cook and supplies of invalid food, meat essences, biscuits and thin
soups, instead of the robust fare which was all we had to look
forward to. I was glad to notice that even Hugh was becoming
tired of Irish stew; but I still wondered what we should have
lived on if I hadn't insisted on bringing the compo. rations.

The need for the administrative officer made itself particularly apparent when it came to discussing the next part of our
journey with the drivers: instead of having a well-earned rest,
Hugh was forced to spend half the night persuading them to
accompany us into Nuristan.

Against the journey Abdul Ghiyas and Badar Khan had
advanced every possible objection: that the way was impossible
for the horses; that the inhabitants were idolatrous unbelievers
who would murder us all; that we had no written permission
to enter the country; and that if we did manage to reach it there
would be no food for man or beast. Only Shir Muhammad,
that unpredictable man, said nothing. In some ways he was
much more Citizen of the World than the others; perhaps, too,
he thought himself the equal of any Nuristani he was likely to
encounter.

Finally, after the argument had gone on for some hours and
still showed no sign of coming to a satisfactory conclusion, Hugh
lost his temper.

"Go back then!" he said. "Go back to Jangalak and tell your people that Newby *Seb* and I have gone to Nuristan alone—and that you let us go alone! They will call you women."

As soon as he had said this it was abundantly clear that both Abdul Ghiyas and Badar Khan were prepared to let us do just this very thing. Hugh was forced to try a more subtle approach.

". . . that you would not come with us to Nuristan because the way is hard and because you are faint-hearted I can perhaps forgive, but that you should call the Nuristanis who are your brothers 'idolatrous unbelievers', they who have only recently been converted to Islam and need your prayers—Sunnites like yourselves, and probably better ones—*that is another matter*."

Here Hugh paused, glaring frightfully. After allowing his words to sink in he resumed: "When I return *from Nuristan* (masterly stroke) I shall demand audience of General Ubaidullah Khan and tell him what you said about 'idolatrous unbelievers'. General Ubaidullah Khan is a man of importance and," Hugh added with the final touch of genius, "he is also a Nuristani."

The effect of this was remarkable. At once all opposition ceased. Before we finally fell asleep long after midnight I asked Hugh who General Ubaidullah Khan was.

"So far as I know," he said, "he doesn't exist. I just invented him; but I think he's going to be a very useful man to know."

At five o'clock the following morning the valley was full of white cloud. Whereas waking on the ibex ledge had been like coming-to from an operation, waking to find oneself wrapped in cloud was like being dead and in heaven.

After Shir Muhammad and Badar Khan had done up our buttons and laced our boots, just when the main body of the expedition was moving off, I went to try to photograph the *aylaq* and, if possible, the occupants. I would not have considered doing so for a moment, if the girls who lived in the bothy with the cardinal had not betrayed such a lively interest in our affairs. But all the previous afternoon, when neither Hugh nor I had been fit to take any active interest in anything, they had stood on the roof unveiled, laughing and shrieking, even waving at us; in fact behaving in a fashion that would have been unthinkable at a lower altitude and in a less remote place. But, as I expected, when I reached the *aylaq* there was no sign of anybody.

Taking a photograph with a complex modern camera when one's hands are done up in bandages is like trying to eat asparagus with boxing gloves on. As I struggled with the apparatus Abdul Ghiyas intervened—in fact he emerged from the bothy to do so.

"*Seb*, it is a bad thing," he said sombrely, "it is against the religion."

In the face of such opposition, I abandoned the attempt to photograph even the pile of stones that was the *aylaq* and after saying goodbye to the cardinal, who had come to the door with Abdul Ghiyas, together we followed the others who had already set off in the direction of the Chamar Pass.

By now the clouds had rolled away and as we crossed the Chamar river the water danced and sparkled in the sunlight. Although the water was extremely shallow, the drivers made a great business of fording it. They were being forced to go to Nuristan against their wills and they were not going to make it easy for us to get there.

Beyond the stream the trail was difficult to follow, only showing itself where the rock was scratched and by an occasional footprint in the patches of earth where a strange plant grew, with a furry cap on it like a mauve bearskin.

As we went on the signs became fainter and I began to be anxious. Finally they became so indistinct that it required an act of faith to recognise them at all; and we were left plodding over an expanse of black rock exactly the same as the rest of the hillside. In front of us the mountain that divided us from Nuristan rose up like a wall topped with spikes. It seemed impossible that we could find a way up it, let alone with the horses.

"Do you think this is the right way?" I asked Hugh, who was striding doggedly towards the foot of the cliff.

"I hope so. If we make a bog of it the first time and don't hit the track to the top, the men will give up."

All of a sudden we came on a small pile of horse droppings. It was as if under different circumstances we had found a bag of gold.

"That's encouraging," Hugh said, as Shir Muhammad whisked them into a bag which he carried for the purpose. "If only there were more of them. If only they weren't so old."

We came to a muddy green lake. Around the edge of it there were footmarks showing the usual impressions of motor tyres. There were chips of wood lying about. Whoever owned the feet had been whittling a stick. We were back on the road.

We began to climb in earnest. The sun was high and the heat was awful; it beat down on the leaden rocks and reflected back at us in a dull glare.

The track went up the mountainside in steps, a series of sharp diagonals marked here and there by cairns formed by two or three stones piled on top of one another. The horses hated it; they shied, lurched forward a few steps, then slipped back with their hooves screeching. All the time Abdul Ghiyas and Badar Khan were talking to them in undertones. I wondered what they were saying; perhaps they were telling them to take it easy. Abdul Ghiyas was beginning to look triumphant. Shir Muhammad did nothing. The fate of the expedition hung in the balance.

"If the horses can't do it, there's only one thing to do. Unload them and hump the stuff over ourselves."

Fortunately at the very moment that Hugh made this inhuman proposal Badar Khan raised a cry of ibex, pointing high up the mountain that rose a thousand feet above us.

"*Bozi kuhi*, there he goes!"

"There he goes, the *bozi kuhi*!" from Shir Muhammad.

"Ah, the *bozi kuhi*!" said Abdul Ghiyas.

All three of them were shielding their eyes against the glare and moving their fingers from right to left following the *bozi kuhi*.

All I could see was acres and acres of black rock.

"There he is," said Hugh. He pointed a bandaged hand at the mountain; with his incipient beard he looked like a minor prophet.

"Can you really see him?"

"I think so. Yes. Now I can. There." He took my finger and guided it. I could still see nothing.

"There!"

"Where?"

"There! No, not there! There! You must be blind!"

At last I lost patience.

"There he goes," I said. "I can see him now."

"He's not moving," said Hugh.

"I can see two *bozi kuhi*," said Shir Muhammad.

In the excitement of seeing the ibex, the air or torpor that hung like a cloud over our little party was dispelled. Thumping and bellowing, the drivers urged the wretched horses round the hairpins and up the slabs. Subsequently there were many halts whilst we pushed and pulled, but at least there was no longer any question of unloading them and carrying the gear bit by bit a thousand feet to the top—a prospect that was almost impossible to contemplate in our present condition. In just over two and a half hours from the *aylaq* we reached the top and halted in the shade just below the *col* itself. It was an extremely high pass. Without the aneroid it was impossible to be sure but, by a comparison with heights we already knew on Mir Samir, it must have been between 16,000 and 16,500 feet. Mir Samir itself was about three miles distant as the crow flies and we could see the whole south side of the mountain right up to the head of the Chamar Valley. We could see the ibex ledge where our camp had been, the Castle buttress and the whole of the east ridge. For the first time we really understood how very close we had been to getting to the top.

The crest of the ridge now immediately above our heads was like a harbour breakwater built by convict labour, a wild confusion of loose blocks heaped one on top of the other. The way through it was narrow, like the neck of a bottle, so that it was only by pushing and shoving that the horses were popped through to the other side like corks.

"*Kotal-i-Chamar*," said the drivers.

It was the *col*; we were beyond the great divide; we were in Nuristan.

One more step and we would have fallen straight into it. We were huddled together, men and animals, on the edge of a cliff at the head of a desolate valley that stretched away downhill, a wilderness of bleak, brown scree with here and there a drift of dirty, speckled snow, until it was lost in haze. The mountains that rose above it to the north and east now concealed the fields of snow and ice we had seen from Mir Samir and were a uniform khaki brown. It was all a little disappointing.

The first part of the descent needed two men to each horse; one to lead, the other with a tight grip on the tail to brake hard at the bends; but once we were off the ridge Hugh and I pressed on alone.

For an hour and a half we followed the valley down and down. All the time it grew hotter; a little vegetation began to appear, pincushions of tough grass. Finally we came out into a deep valley that ran north and south, at right angles to our own. It was green and open with a river running through it and on the meadow grass cows, sheep and horses grazed placidly. Standing alone in the green sward was a solitary *aylaq*, a bothy and some stone cattle pens open to the sky. It seemed deserted; in the whole valley there was no sign of anyone.

After the miles of scree we had descended the grass was like a carpet into which our feet sank; after the still airlessness of the upper valley the breeze that blew was as refreshing as a cool drink. Apart from the sighing of the wind and the sound of the river, a huge silence hung over the place.

Men and horses were far behind. Feeling slightly nervous we began to cross towards the *aylaq*.

We were a hundred yards from it when there was a shout and we saw our first Nuristanis.

They came pouring out of the bothy and raced over the grass towards us at a tremendous pace, dozens of them. It seemed impossible that such a small building could have contained so many men. As they came bounding up they gave an extraordinary impression of being out of the past. They were all extraordinary because they were all different, no two alike. They were tall and short, light-skinned and dark-skinned, brown-eyed and grey-eyed; some, with long straight noses, might have

passed for Serbs or Croats; others, with flashing eyes, hooked
noses and black hair, might have been Jews. There were men
like gypsies with a lock of hair brought forward in ringlets on
either side of the forehead. There were men with great bushy
beards and moustaches that made them look like Arctic explorers.
There were others like early Mormons with a fuzz of beard
round their faces but without moustaches. Some of the tallest
(well over six feet), broken-nosed, clean-shaven giants, were like
guardsmen in a painting by Kennington. Those who were
hatless had cropped hair and the younger ones, especially those
with rudimentary beards, looked as strange and dated as the
existentialists of St. Germain des Prés; while those whose beards
were still in embryo were as contemporary as the clients of a
Café Espresso and would have been accepted as such without
question almost anywhere in the Western World.

They were extraordinary and their clothes were extraordinary
too. All but those who were bare-headed wore the same flat
Chitrali cap that Hugh had worn ever since we had left Kabul,
only theirs were larger and more floppy, and the colour of
porridge. Worn on the back of the head the effect was
Chaucerian.

They wore drab brown, collarless shirts, like the Army issue,
and over them loose waistcoats or else a sort of surcoat—a waist-
coat without buttons. Their trousers were brown homespun,
like baggy unbuckled plus-fours. They reached to the middle
of the calf and flapped loosely as their wearers pounded up the
meadow. They seemed to wear some kind of loose puttee
around the lower leg, and some of the younger men wore
coloured scarves knotted loosely around their necks. All were
barefooted.

"It's like being back in the Middle Ages."

It was the only coherent remark Hugh had time for. The
next moment they were on us, uttering strange cries. Before
we knew what was happening we were being borne towards
the *aylaq* with our feet barely touching the ground, each the
centre of a mob, like distinguished visitors to a university.

I had a blurred vision of a heap of ibex horns and a row of
distended skins hanging on the wall of the bothy (inside out they

looked like long-dead dogs), then I received a terrific crack on the head as we hurtled in through the low opening—we were inside.

The floor was bare earth but on it were spread several very old rugs made of something that looked like felt, with a pattern of black and orange diamonds on them, brought up here to end their days at the *aylaq*. In the centre of the floor there was a shallow depression in which a dung fire smouldered. Over it, balanced on two rocks, was a cauldron in which some great mess was seething. There was no chimney or opening of any kind and the walls were blackened with smoke.

We were made to sit on the floor and our hosts (for that was what they turned out to be—up to now it had not been apparent what their attitude was) brought in two round wooden pots full of milk which they set before us, together with a couple of large ladles. The pots held about half a gallon each, and seemed to be made from hollowed-out tree-trunks. They were decorated with the same diamond pattern I had noticed on the rugs. Both vessels and cutlery were of heroic proportions, fit for giants.

We were extremely thirsty. Hugh was already dipping into his pot.

"Do you think it's all right?" I asked him. "They may have T.B."

"Who?"

"The cows."

"If we're going to get T.B. we've already got it," he said. "Besides, it's not cows' milk. I think it's goats' and sheep's mixed."

The bothy was crammed to the point of suffocation with people all jabbering an unknown tongue. I wondered if it were Bashguli. It was certainly unlike any other language I had ever heard but, as the Colonel's Grammar was once again somewhere hidden away in the baggage train, there was no way of discovering what it was.

After drinking nearly a quart of icy milk (the pots had just come out of the river), I felt as if I were going to burst. I put down my tree-trunk. Sitting next to me was one of the hairless

Espresso boys. He picked up the ladle. "Biloogh ow," he grunted (at least that was what it sounded like) and began to forcibly feed me as though I were senile.

One of the older, full bearded men, who seemed to have some sort of authority over the mob, addressed Hugh in Persian. Suddenly he pointed to the north.

"Nikolai!" he said.

"Nikolai, Nikolai," everyone said.

"Inghiliz, Inghiliz," said Hugh.

"Nikolai, Nikolai."

"Damn it. They think we're Russians," he said. He was very upset.

The halting conversation continued. It appeared that we were the first Europeans ever to come over the Pass.* The Russians they had heard of; but the British were something new, outside their experience.

We were in the summer pastures of the Ramguli Katirs, a tribe of the Black-robed *Siah-Posh*. We were still in the Chamar, the valley and river on both sides of the watershed having the same name.

Here in the summer months, men of the tribe lived without their women, looking after the flocks and cattle, making curds and butter to store for the winter and for trade with the outside world and every so often sending down some of their number to the valleys far below with the heavy goatskins I had seen hanging outside—a journey of from one to five days according to the destination—a sort of grim compassionate leave.

All the time this recital was going on we were being ransacked. I could feel inquisitive fingers prying about my person, opening button flaps, groping in my pockets for my handkerchief, scrabbling at my watch-strap.

We had already passed round several packets of cigarettes and a fight had developed for the empty packets. It was the silver paper they wanted. But what they really longed for were binoculars. They loved my camera, until they discovered that it was not a pair of binoculars, but they soon found Hugh's telescope and took it outside to try it.

*I don't believe this.

28. Young girl of the Ramguli Katirs.

29. The village of Lustagam, south of Pushal.

30. Beauty observed in Nuristan.

31. Lake Mundul, looking north into the Ramgul Valley.

32. Sang Nevcshteh. The rock of Timur Leng.

33. The *Mullah* leads the way into his village, Gadval.

34. Shir Muhammad setting off to steal mulberries.

35. Bridge near Lake Mundul.

36. Nomad boy near the Arayu.

37. The way to the Arayu.

38. The col
on the
Arayu

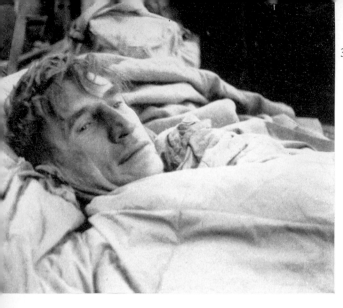

39. Wilfred Thesiger

40. Portrait of two failures.

In a world that has lost the capacity for wonderment, I found it very agreeable to meet people to whom it was possible to give pleasure so simply. Thinking to ingratiate myself still further with them, I handed over my watch. It was the pride of my heart (I, too, am easily pleased)—a brand-new Rolex that I had got in Geneva on the way out from England and reputed proof against every kind of ill-treatment.

"Tell the headman," I said to Hugh, "that it will work under water."

"He doesn't believe it."

"All right. Tell him it will even work in that," pointing to the cauldron which was giving off steam and gloggling noises.

Hugh told him. The headman said a few words to the young existentialist who had the watch. Before I could stop him he dropped it into the pot.

"He says he doesn't believe you," said Hugh.

"Well, tell him to take it out! I don't believe it myself." By now I was hanging over the thing, frantically fishing with the ladle.

"It's no good," I said. "They'll have to empty it."

This time Hugh spoke somewhat more urgently to the headman.

"He says they don't want to. It's their dinner."

At last somebody hooked it and brought it to the surface, covered with a sort of brown slime. Whatever it was for dinner had an extraordinarily nasty appearance. The rescuer held it in the ladle. Though too hot to touch, it was still going. This made an immense impression on everyone, myself included. Unfortunately, it made such an impression on the man himself that he refused to be parted from it and left the bothy.

"Where's he going?"

"He's going to try it in the river."

At this moment excited shouts and cries rose from outside. Our drivers had arrived. Everyone rushed out to greet them.

They were a melancholy little group, huddled together at the foot of the rocks, gazing apprehensively towards the bothy in the same way as we had half an hour previously: all except Shir

Muhammad who, apparently bored stiff, was looking in the opposite direction.

Only when they were offered tree-trunks full of milk did they relax a little. Even then Abdul Ghiyas refused to allow his men to enter the *aylaq*.

"It is better to go on," he said. "These men are robbers and murderers. We must make our camp far away."

"They want us to stay the night," Hugh told him. "They say there will be dancing and singing."

But it was no good. He refused absolutely.

"They are very treacherous men. We shall all be slain whilst we sleep." I had never seen him so determined.

"Perhaps it's better," said Hugh. "They want us to unpack all our gear."

The thought of such a mob let loose among our belongings was too appalling to contemplate. We agreed that it was better to go—and as soon as possible.

When the time came to leave there was no sign of Hugh's telescope or my watch.

"I want my telescope," Hugh told the headman.

"What about my watch?" I asked, when his telescope was finally produced from somewhere round the corner.

"He says the man who had it has gone away."

"Well, tell him that he must bring him back."

There was a further brief parley.

"He says the man wants to keep it." Somehow Hugh contrived to make this sound a reasonable request.

"WELL, HE CAN'T! GET IT BACK FOR ME! MAKE AN EFFORT!"

"It's *you* who should make the effort. It's really too much having to do your work *all* the time."

I could have struck him at this moment.

"Damn it, you can hardly understand the man yourself and you speak fluent Persian. How the devil do you expect me to make him understand anything?"

Just then I saw the man who had taken my watch skulking behind one of the walls of the *aylaq*. I went round the building the other way and came up behind him, and took hold of his wrists. Although he was without any apparent muscle, he was immensely strong: He radiated a kind of electric energy.

"*Tok-tok*," I said. At the same time I looked down at my own wrist and nodded my head violently.

He began to laugh. I looked into his eyes; they were strange and mad. He had about him an air of scarcely controlled violence that I had noticed in some of the others inside the hut. An air of being able to commit the most atrocious crimes and then sit down to a hearty meal without giving them a further thought. The man was a homicidal maniac. Perhaps they were all homicidal maniacs.

I saw that his right hand was clenched and I forced it open. Inside was my beautiful watch. He had washed it in the river. It was still going and it continued to do so.

As we left the *aylaq* three more Nuristanis came running up the valley, moving over the ground in short steps but with unbelievable swiftness. All three had full brown beards, they wore short fringed overcoats of a very dark brown—almost black, perhaps the last vestiges of the glory of the Black-robed Kafirs; on their backs were slung empty pack-frames.

"They have come up from the Ramgul to take the place of those who will go down with butter tomorrow morning," said Abdul Ghiyas.

No one said goodbye to us. Some of the Nuristanis had already gone loping up the mountainside towards the flocks; the rest had retired into the bothy. It was a characteristic of these people that their interest in strangers was exhausted almost as quickly as it was born.

CHAPTER SEVENTEEN

Going Down !

BELOW the *aylaq* the valley widened out until there was an expanse of grass a quarter of a mile wide on either side of the river, which here no longer raced over shallows, as it had higher up, but flowed deep and silent, winding through the meadow between high earthy banks. On the far bank a big herd of black cattle, calves and bullocks were slowly grazing their way up the valley.

Presently two men came up riding upon bullocks, urging them forward with prods from the forked sticks they both carried. Neither of these men took the slightest notice of us.

"It is time, let us make the camp," said Abdul Ghiyas. No one had the strength to disagree with him.

"So long as there are sufficient rocks for each of us to have one when we need it, I don't care where we camp," said Hugh.

He looked like I felt, wan and exhausted. The last few days had been extremely trying: our reverses on the mountain; the crossing that morning of a pass more than 16,000 feet high, followed immediately by the awful party in the *aylaq*; all these, in conjunction with our wounds and the ills we had contracted en route, had been almost too much for us. Like dreadnoughts that had received the full force of an enemy salvo, until we could drop anchor in some haven and have time to clear up some of the damage, we were temporarily out of action.

Having decided to camp, Abdul Ghiyas laid down all sorts of stringent conditions for the choice of a suitable site, mostly of a strategical nature and dictated by his distrust of the Nuristanis, an apprehension I was beginning to share with him.

Eventually he found a grassy isthmus formed by a double bend in the river that was hemmed in by water on three sides. On it there stood a large rock that offered some protection 'against being struck down from behind' as he vividly put it; while on the landward side a fall of boulders from the mountains above provided plenty of the sort of dead ground that interested Hugh and myself far more than questions of defence against an enemy.

While we were lying on the grass trying to summon up energy to unpack, two men appeared on a grey horse, one riding pillion behind the other. They both carried long wands that looked like lances. The man riding pillion wore a red skull-cap; the other, one of the large floppy sort. Seen against the background of the green meadow with the river between us the feeling of having been transported into the Middle Ages was overwhelming. With some monks in the foreground fishing for carp it could have been an illustration in a pictorial history of England. For a moment I felt homesick.

They moved along the far bank, staring rudely over their shoulders at us, until they reached a place where some boulders out in the stream made it possible to cross. There they dismounted and, after tethering their horse, crossed the river, leaping from rock to rock, using their sticks to steady themselves, and came down the bank towards us.

Close-to these two men made a most disagreeable impression on all of us. The one with the skull-cap looked nothing more than an assassin. As well as his willow wand he carried a rifle slung across his shoulder. There was nothing mediaeval about the rifle, a ·45 Martini-Henry that, although almost eighty years old, could still blow the daylights out of anything, nor about the bandolier of ammunition he wore under his shirt.

"That's a nasty-looking man," said Hugh. "He'd be better dead."

"He's thinking the same about us. But look at the other one. What a great conk he's got!"

The other was really sinister. In London in a dark suit and wearing a carnation he would have been unremarkable as a promoter of shady companies with an office in Park Lane. Here, dressed in the local costume, he was terrific.

He had very long teeth, almond-shaped eyes that swivelled and a nose like a huge beak. He wore a white and red striped shirt and the same baggy trousers as the men at the *aylaq* but made of cotton the colour of faded denim. The trousers were secured below the calf with brown puttees wrapped round and fastened with red and white woven strings which terminated in red pom-poms. He wore short ankle boots with cowhide soles and goatskin uppers dyed red, tied with coloured laces. Round his neck were slung a pair of Zeiss binoculars.

This man never looked at us except when he thought he was unobserved. Instead he sat close to Abdul Ghiyas, himself a strange figure in his windproof suit from which he refused to be parted, and from time to time hissed something in his ear.

"I'm sure he's a spy," said Hugh. "The question is who's he spying for?"

"I should have thought in your business you would have some way of recognising a spy. Don't you have some kind of sign, like Masons have? Or a badge?

"They don't issue badges."

Whether he was a spy or not there was nothing I could do about it. Besides I thought him ill-mannered. I fell asleep, and slept for four hours.

When next I woke, the sun was behind clouds, the air was soft and the grass without the glare was a darker green. The two men had moved away and were now sitting a hundred yards up the valley talking to one another. They had both put on their dark coats and at this distance they looked like seminarists out for the afternoon. With the soft air and the greenery we might have been in Ireland.

Hugh had also been asleep.

"I don't like that man with the nose at all," he said when he woke. "Abdul Ghiyas told me that he wanted to know where we were going to sleep tonight."

We set off to bathe in the river but abandoned the idea when we found out how cold it was. When we came back the men had mounted their horse and were riding away down the valley.

"Abdul Ghiyas says that we should post sentries for the night," said Hugh when it grew dark.

"Do you want to be a sentry?"

"No. I'd rather be murdered in bed."

"So would I."

"Abdul Ghiyas! No sentries!"

Here at around 13,000 feet it was cold. In the night I woke to find that we were in the clouds. Everything was soaking. On the other side of the river I could hear horses drumming up and down in the mist. Our own horses were restless and the stallion was pawing the ground, like a small, thin Rosinante.

Very early, when it was just growing light, a man appeared at a swift trot from the direction of the *aylaq*. He was barefooted and on his back he carried a skin full of butter.

"*Mandeh nabashi*. May you never be tired," said everyone, as he came up to us and unslung his load. "May you live for ever." To which he replied, "*Ayershah*."

He was a youngish man, about twenty-five, with a brown beard and a moustache. He spoke some Persian. His name, he said, was Aruk. He had been three weeks at a still higher *aylaq* than the one we had visited, somewhere on the way to the Anjuman Pass. He was a handsome man but, like most of the people we had so far seen, with the same mad look of barely-controlled savagery. Across his nose there was a shiny white scar. "A man did it with a sword," was all he would say about it.

When he was offered tea, he produced his own cup. It was beautifully made of thin porcelain decorated with a pattern of flowers. It was a Russian cup, made before the Revolution at the factory of the Englishman, Gardener, at St. Petersburg.

"There are many such in the Ramgul," he said.

I lifted his pack. It must have weighed well over sixty pounds. The frame was made of two forked pieces of willow with the fork ends lashed together and the four uprights stretched open to admit the goatskin, a horrid-looking thing, inside-out with the legs sewn up, so that the stumps, like the body, were distended with butter. The carrying straps for this contrivance were two thin cords of plaited goats' hair. Worn with nothing but a shirt between them and the shoulders they would have been excruciatingly painful, but across his shoulders he wore his fringed coat rolled up as padding. On top of the pack he carried a pair of *chamus*—the same red boots the other man had worn but faded pink with age—and a smaller skin which contained dried wild onions.

He now offered to accompany us to Pushal, the capital of the Ramguli Katirs.

Whilst the drivers were making the last adjustment to the loads I tried Colonel Davidson's Bashguli Grammar on him, reading from the book and pointing to the objects I wanted to identify.

"*Wetzâ?*" I said, pointing to his *chamus*.

"*Utzar!*" he said.

This was encouraging. I picked up his fringed coat. "*Budzun?*"

"*Bezih!*"

I pointed at myself. "*Manchī?*"

"*Manchī!*"

Girl. I made conventional curves in the air. "*Jūk?*"

"*Jug!*" he smiled.

Valley was *gōl*. The Chamar Valley, *Chamar b'gōl*. But in Bashguli bread was *yashī* and here it was *anjih*. There was no doubt the languages had something in common.

All this took a long time. Finally Hugh tried a sentence, taken straight from the book. 'The Kafir language is very sweet', "*Katõ wari bilugh aruzwā essā.*"

Aruk shook his head. "*Katõ dīz bilugh aruzwā essā,*" he said.

With Aruk leading we set off downhill at a terrific pace. At the foot of this valley the grass came to an end and we passed through a narrow funnel-shaped defile and came out at the top of a desolate, cloud-filled glen with big mountain peaks rising through the clouds and shining in the sun. Here Aruk put on his boots and plunged on again faster than ever. But after a while he stopped.

"Apparently his heart is hurting him," said Hugh.

"It isn't really surprising." Nevertheless we were disappointed to find him an unsuper superman. From now on he stopped regularly every ten minutes. For us with our various defects this was agony. On the move they were forgotten, but we were not carrying four Kabuli *Seer*.

After two hours the valley narrowed and became a gorge filled with rocks, the most difficult place we had yet been in on the whole journey and terrible for the poor horses. Sometimes the track descended to the level of the river, at others it twisted steeply over bluffs. Here we saw the first trees, a few birch and juniper growing close down to the river, and some shattered stumps of what looked like pines.

From now on the track was often blocked with tree-trunks and twisted bushes brought down by the river in flood. Here large junipers grew close to the river with willows and flowering tamarisk, blackcurrants and bushes of orange-coloured Persian roses. There was no air and the red cliffs reflected the heat down on to us. We stopped frequently to drink at the cool springs which issued from the walls of the gorge.

On the way we passed a rock with a hole in it standing in a clearing. We asked our mad-looking guide about it.

"When the Amir Abdur Rahman came with the Mussulmans, the *Siah-Posh* were brought here. Their heads were put in the hole and they were asked if they would be of the Faithful."

"And if they wouldn't?"

"Their heads were struck off with a great sword."

"What happened if their heads were too big for the hole?"

"My father had a big head but he became a Mussulman."

In 1895 the happy existence of the Kafirs as robbers, murderers of Muslims, drinkers of prodigious quantities of wine, keepers of slaves, worshippers of Imra the Creator, Moni the Prophet, Gish the War God and the whole Kafir pantheon with its sixteen principal deities, came to an end when Abdur Rahman sent his armies under the command of his gigantic Commander-in-Chief, Ghulam Haider Khan, on a *jehad* against the infidel and converted them to Islam by the sword; probably the last time in history that such a conversion has taken place.

According to his own admission, Abdur Rahman was thoroughly fed up with the Kafirs. He had invited their chiefs to visit him in Kabul and sent them back to their country loaded with rupees. With the money they immediately bought rifles from the Russians which they used to slaughter more Afghans. (It is difficult to believe that Abdur Rahman imagined that they would do otherwise.) A further source of friction arose over the sale of Kafir girls to the Afghans in exchange for cows and the subsequent disputes over their relative values. He himself says that the chief reasons that caused him to invade Kafiristan were the aggravation caused by having a semi-hostile country at his back and also the fear that the Russians might annex it.

Besides these statesmanlike considerations there were others. He longed to convert the Kafirs and win an apostle's reward and also to keep open the Kunar Valley trade route between Jalalabad and Badakshan, which their really intolerable behaviour made extremely difficult.

The campaign opened in the winter of 1895, the idea being to avoid the Kafirs escaping to Russian territory and also to keep casualties as low as possible. Whilst irritated by the Kafirs, the Amir seems to have recognised that they would be more use to him alive. Each man in the three armies that invaded Kafiristan was paid twenty rupees a day to stop him looting which, in such terrain as Kafiristan in mid-winter, would have condemned the inhabitants to death at any rate. The taking of women for private delectation was also forbidden. It was all highly respectable.

The three armies attacked simultaneously, that which Ghulam Haider Khan commanded in person consisting of eight infantry regiments, one cavalry regiment and one battery of artillery, marched by way of the Kunar Valley and attacked the *Safed-Posh* Kafirs at Kamdesh, defeating them in one decisive battle; the Afghan losses being given officially as seventy, those of the Kafirs as between four and five hundred. The army of Kohistan attacked from the south, probably by way of the Alingar river, and the army of Badakshan, 'several battalions of well trained troops from Panjshir, Andarab and Laghman', attacked from the north and west. The Kafirs gave up without much fight, all except the *Siah-Posh* Kafirs of the Ramgul Valley who fought a house-to-house and village-to-village struggle, particularly distinguishing themselves at a place called Sheshpoos. The invaders were ordered to take the Kafirs alive (a somewhat novel order in this part of the world) but it was difficult to implement it as the defence was so vigorous and the Kafirs suffered heavy losses from artillery fire, many hundreds dying in the flames when they put their own villages to the torch. From these operations, which they had conducted with the most primitive weapons, swords, bows and arrows and a few old rifles, the survivors were taken captives to the plains around Laghman in the Kabul Valley; some were settled on the land, some allowed to return home later, and many thousands of the most virile were taken into slavery. Some of these slaves remained in Kabul until the abdication of Amanullah in 1929.

There were a number of outraged squeaks from England; a few despatches appeared in *The Times* to be answered rather surprisingly by a Miss Lillias Hamilton, M.D., Doctor to the Amir's Court, a resourceful woman who had introduced vaccination to the country and founded a hospital at Kabul.* The main point of her letter was that anyone judging what had happened to the Kafirs by English standards of ethics was talking through his hat.

There were many protests from missionaries to whom the Amir replied, blandly: "I did not find any Christians among them."

It was a little difficult for the Government to censure Abdur Rahman. Officially his subsidy had just been increased from 12,000 to 16,000 lakhs of rupees. To the British he had fully justified their selection of him as Amir of Afghanistan and, apart from the few foibles remarked by Lord Curzon, like flaying people alive who displeased him, blowing them from the mouths of cannon, or standing them up to the neck in pools of water on the summits of high mountains and letting them freeze solid, he had done nothing to which exception could be taken. Nothing happened—a curtain descended on Kafiristan. The next time it would rise on Nuristan, The Country of Light.

We passed a steep valley on the right leading to Mir Samir and for a moment we saw the top of it remote-looking and inaccessible far away to the west. Above us an eagle glided along the crests.

* *The Times*, April 4th, 1896.

Here at this small valley junction we came to the first of five suicidal bridges, at each of which the track crossed from one bank to the other. They were all exactly the same, a single juniper trunk more than twenty feet long, split in half and extended over the torrent by cantilevers of wood and stone. Because the trunks rested on their round sides, they wobbled from side to side when trodden on in an alarming manner.

But it was the unfortunate horses who really suffered. They had been really happy in the meadow higher up. Now they had to swim for their lives with their loads half under water, sometimes downstream of a bridge, sometimes far above it, whilst Badar Khan and Abdul Ghiyas shouted encouragement from the bank. But not Shir Muhammad; his little grey mare was the only one the other horses would follow, so that it was she who had to swim while her master sat with his feet tucked up on the saddle. Why his was the most spirited horse no one ever discovered. Not only did he allow it to wander on without giving it any help or encouragement but by sheer neglect it became horribly galled under the saddle. It was only the last bridge made from two parallel tree-trunks with rocks in the space between them (the trunks were crooked) that they were able to cross at all, at the rest they were made to flounder miserably in the river.

At this last bridge we came on an old bearded man sitting under a willow tree with two small boys, who were both wearing waistcoats with orange backs and oatmeal hats several sizes too large for them. With his two grandchildren he had made the journey up from Pushal, the capital, to meet us. This was the *Isteqbal*—the traditional journey of half a stage—that is made by people in the Moslem world to greet a friend who is travelling. The old man was Sultan Muhammad Khan, an ex-captain of the Royal Afghan Bodyguard, who although born a Kafir, had learned this pleasant custom in the years when he was at Court and had come up to escort us to his house, the news of our arrival having been brought to him by the disagreeable man on the horse.

After we had sat with him for some time in the shade of the willow tree, he proposed that we should continue.

"It is only a short walk," he remarked.

Thinking that it might be perhaps a matter of half an hour we set off. The journey took seven hours.

We emerged from the Chamar gorge at a place where it joined another river, the Bugulchi, that rises under the main Hindu Kush range and leads into a part of Badakshan so remote that even the quarter-inch map showed a large unsurveyed blank, and entered the valley of the Ramgul, long and narrow between jagged mountains and thickly wooded with holly oak; crossed the last bridge before the Chamar joined the Ramgul and then, horror, started to climb again up a steep, dusty valley full of bushes on which grew a stalkless fruit, red like a cherry but more bitter, until we came out on a hillside among terraced fields of wheat and barley still young and green, deserted in the midday heat.

Soon even these evidences of human occupation ceased and the track wound interminably along a desolate hillside dotted with the stumps of dead and dying juniper trees, like the remains of a forest destroyed by shell-fire. The heat was appalling. We both had a raging thirst but there was no water, except where five hundred feet below the Ramgul raced down, as green as the fields on either side of it, mocking us. Only the Captain and his two small grandsons seemed impervious to heat and distance, racing ahead and then waiting courteously at the difficult bits to allow Hugh and myself to go first, so that at each steep place, we all stood bowing and smiling politely at one another until I could have screamed.

After four hours of this the track descended steeply to the river and we met the first women we had seen in Nuristan. All were unveiled, but it was difficult to form any opinion about their charms because, as they passed us, staggering under the weight of enormous conical wicker baskets piled eight feet high with firewood, they latched a cloth across their faces. Dressed in dark brown coats with wide sleeves, like the fringed *bezih* worn by the men in the *aylaq*, and with a sort of hood of the same material, they looked like overworked members of some austere religious order.

At a narrow place between the river and the steep side of the mountain, we crossed a stone wall built of round stones the size of cannon balls. Originally it must have been extremely solid, now it was broken down, indistinguishable from the ones that divided the path from the fields on either side.

"Here were the outer forts of Pushal," said the Captain, "but after we were conquered by the Afghans, they were broken and thrown down.

"And there is your camp site," he added.

"And about time, too," said Hugh in English. Like me he was at the end of his tether. Apart from short halts we had been on the move since six. It was now four-thirty and we had not eaten all day.

It was a splendid camp site in a field by the river and was shaded by a vast walnut tree. It was the camp site of our dreams —but Abdul Ghiyas rejected it. Now that the Captain had taken us under his protection and the risk of assassination had receded, he was anxious for the bright lights of the city. We were too tired to argue with him.

The next possible place was in a grove of mulberry trees. It was full of girls and young women. There had been an air of sadness about the others in their drab working clothes: these were far more gay. They wore white and red trousers with red dresses over them. Under their skirts they wore petticoats with contrasting hems which showed. Their hair was covered with a sort of cream-coloured coif and under it they seemed to wear some kind of cotton cap. Their arms were bare and they wore heavy bracelets of brass or gold. On their foreheads they mostly had a fillet of round silver ornaments or cowrie shells. They were barefooted. Even at a distance it was obvious that they were extremely handsome.

Some carried babies on their backs in the sack made by the turned-down hoods they wore. The really small ones were asleep in the conical carrying baskets or in small wooden beds, like the baskets suspended on ropes from the trees. One girl was seated on a swing. As she swung high up under the trees she shrieked and showed her petticoats. It was an innocent happy scene.

"Here," we said instantly.

"No," said Abdul Ghiyas, looking at the Captain out of the corner of his eyes. "It is not suitable." It must have been a hard tussle for him to set a good example to the Infidel at this moment.

"Not suitable," said the Captain. Here he left us and hurried on home.

Eventually Abdul Ghiyas chose an awful place for us. It was in an amphitheatre under some cliffs and had previously been used in the time of the old religion as a place of sacrifice, but there the resemblance to something out of the Golden Bough ended. It was a dusty place covered with excrement and squashed mulberries. There were flies by the million, fierce black ants and, when the sun went down, large blood-thirsty mosquitoes. The raffish youths who watched us as we slowly set up our camp, the dust and the general air of stickiness, made me think of Clapham Common and Bank Holidays.

But, as the news of our arrival spread, the smart young men of the town began to arrive. Half a dozen of the most elegant seated themselves on a large rock and watched us languidly. Like members of the Eton Society, they were dressed rather foppishly—big flat caps, embroidered waistcoats, silver medals and lucky charms. One of them was armed with a double stringed stone-bow. From time to time he discharged a pebble at the lizards that crawled over the face of the cliff.

Before these aloof dandies and an audience of at least fifty lesser men we hobbled backwards and forwards, performing our mundane household chores, like actors in some interminable drama in an experimental theatre, until, unable to stand it any longer, we set off to wash in the river.

"God. You're thin!" Hugh said.

It was the first time we had taken our clothes off for a fortnight. During this time our bodies had become unrecognisable. High altitude, insufficient liquid and the wrong food had wrought an extraordinary change. All the muscles in our arms and legs had melted away to nothing—they were like matchsticks. Our ribs were starting through the flesh. We were as repulsive as the survivors of a journey in open boats.

"If von Dückelmann only began to lose weight when he got

to Nuristan, I can't bear to think what we shall look like in
another ten days."

"If the rest of Nuristan is like the place we're camping in,
we shan't be alive to find out," Hugh said. His teeth were
chattering. So were mine.

We were standing up to our waists in a bay of the river,
the only possible wash place. The water was bloody cold.
The current moved in a circle so that the dirt remained where
it was. We had already lost the soap.

Back at the amphitheatre a game had started—a game of quoits
called *auzil*. Like everything else these people did, it took an
excessive Herculean form and consisted of hurling heavy flat
stones the size of soup plates at a mark the length of a cricket
pitch away. When a particularly good shot resulted loud
cheers rose.

Meanwhile the boys, who infested the place, were amusing
themselves in their own fashion; creeping up behind someone
smaller than themselves and violently hurling him to the ground,
where the victim would lie blubbering for a few moments until
he himself would get up and do the same to someone even more
diminutive.

Whilst Abdul Ghiyas held off the spectators who fought
among themselves for the empty tins, I started to cook. Unable
to stand the thought of Irish stew, and as a revenge on our drivers
for forcing us to camp in this spot, I concocted a loathsome
mixture of soup and pork which I knew would be unacceptable
to them on religious grounds.

The food no sooner started to warm up than a whirlwind
descended on the amphitheatre, which extinguished the stoves
and covered everything in dust. To escape from it I moved
everything to the shelter of some smelly rocks at the foot of the
cliff. In this unbelievably horrid situation I finished cooking
our dinner.

"Apparently this place belongs to a Nuristani General who
lives at Kabul," Hugh said as we digested the ghastly dinner I
had prepared.

"Well, if I were a General I'd get a fatigue party to clean it
up."

When we had finished we gave out chocolate to the watchers, but it was like attempting to feed the five thousand without the aid of a miracle.

It had been among the most awful days I could remember. To escape from the crowds, who showed no signs of dispersing, and from the giant mosquitoes that were sucking my blood, I took my bedding to the top of a high rock.

"If anything falls from the cliff you'll be killed," Hugh shouted up to me.

"Good!"

"Abdul Ghiyas says if you sleep up there you may be murdered."

"It's a risk I'm prepared to take."

He picked up his own bedding and started to move towards the cliff.

"I'm coming up there, too."

"Why don't you find a rock of your own? I need this one myself."

"All right, I will," he said huffily.

Before falling asleep, having long since lost all sense of time, I looked at the calendar in my diary. The date was the twenty-third of July. Only fourteen days had passed since we had set off from Kabul. It seemed like a lifetime.

CHAPTER EIGHTEEN

A Room with a View

BY half-past four the following morning a large audience had already gathered and was waiting with ill-concealed impatience for the curtain to rise.

Soon, bursting with energy, butter-carriers going on leave from the *aylaq* began to trot into the arena. It was difficult at this hour to greet them with much warmth.

Breakfast was an abomination: sugarless tea, chocolate that had melted and set again, and some old mutton *kebab*, a hang-over from *Id-i-Qorban* that Abdul Ghiyas had conserved for such an emergency. There was no bread; Shir Muhammad having eaten the lot in the night.

Whilst we were eating, a tremendous wind began to blow up the valley from the south. Like magic the audience began to disperse uttering cries of warning, while girls, previously invisible, who had been working in the fields, scuttled for home emitting tiny frightened squeaks. It was obvious that some cataclysm was at hand.

Soon we were at the centre of a violent storm. There was a continuous rumbling and forks of lightning tore down on us from the sky. With the background of bulbous rocks, beetling cliffs and twisted junipers it was like a landscape by a Chinese painter of the thirteenth century.

Thunder and lightning were succeeded by torrents of rain. Crouching under one of the rocks we each smoked our last cigarette. My pipe was somewhere on Mir Samir; Hugh had dropped his in the Chamar. At any rate we had no more tobacco.

When the rain stopped a small boy who spoke Persian arrived

with a message from the Captain inviting us to his house.   After
packing everything we set off with him, each of us enveloped in
an aura of steam that proceeded from our wet clothes as they
dried in the hot sun.

He was an odious little boy; the sort whose very appearance
invites ill-treatment.   Unwisely he decided to play a practical
joke.   After leading us through a maze of sodden undergrowth
he eventually returned us to the place where we had started.

All the time, as we floundered after this juvenile delinquent,
Hugh had been getting more and more red in the face and
breathing heavily.

"What is the reason for this?" he said.

The boy laughed and stuck out his tongue.

"You little —— Take that!" said Hugh, "and that! . . .
and that! . . . and that!"

It seemed to make very little impression on him.   His bottom
and ears seemed to be made of cast iron.   All the way up the
steep climb to Pushal he continued to loiter and Hugh continued
to cuff him.   In this way, profoundly depressed, hating Hugh
and the little boy equally, I arrived at Pushal, the capital of the
Ramgul Katirs.

Knowing something of the irregular way of life pursued by
the Kafirs before the conquest, it was easy to see that strategic
considerations alone had governed the choice of the site on which
it stood, a large rock poised above the river.   On the rock, in
indescribable confusion, the houses were piled one atop the other
like stone boxes, many of them two-storied, with large unglazed
windows and some with little galleries, which overhung the
river supported by wooden struts.

There was no main street in Pushal because no two houses
were at the same level.   The way through it was like a gully,
far too steep even for our horses, which had had to cross the
river and ford it again lower down beyond the town.   There
were no shops, no *chaie-khana* but, as in Panjshir, the roofs were
covered with apricots and mulberries.   Among the fruit,
watching us go by, stood wraithlike figures in white so muffled
up that it was impossible to say whether they were men or
women.

The Captain's house was at a place called Asnar, half a mile beyond Pushal, one of several standing among rocks and apricot trees. It was a two-storey building with a slightly pitched roof with boulders on it to stop it blowing away. It was not in fact his house at all but belonged to his son-in-law who came to meet us as we came steaming up followed by the drivers, and escorted us into it.

His name was Abdul Motaleb, which translated means The Slave of the Summoner. Like some of the others here in the capital, he was dressed like a Pathan in white *shalvār* trousers and a turban. He had a soft face, a fine wavy beard and bore no resemblance to any other Nuristani we had so far seen (not that any of them bore much resemblance to one another).

The ground floor of the house was mainly store-rooms. We went up a flight of stone steps on to a platform supported on tree-trunks. Above the door a pair of magnificent ibex horns sprouted from the wall. Like all the other houses I saw in Nuristan it gave me the impression of being still in the course of construction.

The doorway that was partly filled with hurdling was not on the same level with the platform but was a foot or so above it, so that it looked more like a window.

Once over the threshold and inside it was as dark as night. Facing the entrance was the kitchen from which came a dim red glow and a scuttling sound as the owner's wife made herself scarce. We passed through a bare room slightly less dark with a broken-down bed in it, a wooden framework covered with interlaced woven thongs, like an Indian *charpoy*, then through another completely empty, then into a third, with a large, square window and solid wooden shutters that opened inwards. The shutters, like the double doors, were decorated with crude orange stripes. The floor was of mud; the ceiling laths were willow and were supported by solid beams of poplar, the space between the laths being filled with the dead leaves of the holly oaks that grew in thousands on the mountain-sides. On the wall hung a Martini-Henry rifle with the date 1906 on it and a *jezail*, a heavy Afghan musket with a barrel four feet long.

Soon a boy appeared loaded with carpets and quilts, which he spread on the floor. It was the same little boy whom Hugh had kicked so enthusiastically. As he went out he glared.

"My son," said Abdul Motaleb proudly.

Soon the boy was back. This time he carried two wooden bowls of apricots, one of which he put down in front of Hugh.

"Have some of these," said Hugh with his mouth full. "Excellent apricots."

"I think I'd prefer to have some from the other basket. After the way you kicked his bottom they're probably poisoned."

As we sat there, another storm developed and went rumbling away up the valley. This time it continued to rain steadily. Looking out of the window on to a river in spate and mountains shrouded in mist, I experienced a sensation forgotten since childhood; the mixture of cosiness and despair that I used to feel looking out from a seaside hotel on a wet day.

Distinguished visitors began to arrive: the Captain, together with a vigorous-looking old man whose beard was dyed with henna, and another like the man with the skull-cap we had met in the upper valley with the hard face of a professional killer.

The old man was very lively, remembering vividly the happenings of sixty years back.

"I was fifteen years old when the great Amir attacked us. His army was in three columns and we fought with them long and hard, using our bows, spears and swords and what few guns we had." (For 'guns' he used the word 'artillery' and I wondered if they had had some ancient cannon.*) "But it made no difference, in the end we were beaten. I and many others were taken prisoner and brought to Kabul as slaves. There I remained twenty-five years; first, while I was still young, as a page at the court of the Amir; later as a bodyguard until the new Amir, his son, was slain at Qala Gosh." (This was the Amir Habibullah who was murdered while asleep in a tent on a hunting expedition in the valley of the lower Alingar. I wondered if the bodyguard had been on duty at the time.) "When that happened I was allowed to return to the place where I was born."

* According to Robertson, *The Kafirs of the Hindu-Kush*, the Wai, one of the Eastern tribes, owned a cannon.

"What do you remember of the life before you were converted, when you were Kafirs?"

"We used to make wine and hunt bear. There was much killing in those days and I was a great swimmer but I do not remember that time with much pleasure. Now there is no longer any wine made," he said rather wistfully.

The coming of Islam to Kafiristan seemed to have had the same deadly effect as Knox and the Reformation on Scotland.

The talk of killing gave the murderous-looking man an opportunity to butt in. It turned out that he had been twelve years a bodyguard to a former prime minister.

"Have you *ijazat*, permission to be here?"

"What sort of permission?"

"Written permission."

"Yes."

"Here," he said happily, "we shoot people without permission," and went on to tell a gloomy story about an Afghan who had married an American girl and fled with her to Nuristan for sanctuary. It ended badly for both of them. I was not surprised; to me it seemed an unsuitable place to choose for such a purpose.

"If I didn't feel so ill, this man would frighten me," Hugh said.

By a system of barter too tedious to relate, Abdul Ghiyas, who himself looked like death, obtained a chicken and cooked it together with wild onions and apricots, a mixture which in retrospect sounds awful but at the time seemed very good.

Later, to escape the hoi-poloi who had been admitted to rummage in our belongings, we went for a walk in the rain with two young bloods. They were coarse-looking youths and they had not improved their appearance by painting their eyes red and tinting their eyelids with antimony. They said their names were Shyok and Paluk, at least that is what they sounded like, but they also admitted to more conventional Mussulman names.

Shyok and Paluk were tiresomely fit; hurling great stones about; leaping into the branches of mulberry trees and gibbering down at us, and all the time challenging us to feats of strength that were impossible for people in our condition.　By comparison with them we seemed like corpses.

The place seemed deserted.　Warned of our arrival women and girls kept out of sight.　There were no longer the happy groups of girls playing together.　Flitting among the trees were the same ghostly white figures who had looked down on us from the rooftops of Pushal.　They were *madares*, theological students from one of the eastern valleys come to the capital of Ramgul to study at a college run by the *mullahs*.

At this moment one of them came into view, a pouting creature with soft doe eyes, running rather feebly, closely pursued by Akuts, our friend with the cut on the nose, and disappeared from view behind some large walnut trees.

Later the Captain visited us.　He was very smart in a double-breasted gaberdine overcoat and wore a turban wound round a flat-topped *kullah* like a pill-box set with coloured stones. With him was the Company Promoter whom we had last seen in the upper valley.　He wore a dark brown Chitrali cap, a wine-coloured silk shirt, chaplis from Peshawar and carried an American Carbine.

Because we admired this weapon, news of our interest spread quickly.　Men with rifles began to pour into the house: ·303 Lee-Enfields identical with the sort issued to the British Army, with the correct-looking serial numbers but marked V.R. 1912, made at the tribal gun factory at Kohat on the frontier (the bolts were genuine).　There was a Prussian rifle called a Dreyse with the date 1866 on it, one in which a needle pierces a paper cartridge and strikes a detonating composition between it and the bullet. Where the ammunition for such a weapon came from was a mystery, as it was for the long-barrelled Imperial Russian rifle inlaid with brass and a Canadian Ross rifle.　All were in a disgraceful condition, particularly the barrels.

"I didn't think you were allowed to have rifles," said Hugh.

"No," everyone replied happily and ambiguously, "we're not; but in Nuristan there are many robbers."

Apart from the work in the summer pastures and the carrying

down of the butter, the men seemed to have little to do, most of the labour in the fields, except for some ploughing, being done by women.

"In the autumn," they said, "when the crops are lifted and we bring the horses down from the *aylaq* we play *buz-kashi*. We use a dead goat with its head cut off. It is a very strong game when we play it," they said, and all grinned. "And we go hunting; and in the winter we sleep.

"At the *aylaq*," they said, "we make the butter and curds and store it in the rivers until it is needed. When it is needed we bring it down to the valley and it is boiled. Then it is carried away."

For some time we had been mystified by what happened to the dairy produce that seemed to be constantly on the move but never eaten. No one ever offered milk or butter to us, nor could we buy any.

"But what do you do with it?" we asked them.

"We have not enough grain to make bread. We take it over the *Kotal* Arayu and down the Panjshir to Gulbahar and exchange it for grain."

This meant taking it back up the hill again. It seemed crazy to us. I wondered why they didn't boil it up at the *aylaq*.

"Are the men who carry it paid anything?"

"Each man carries four *seer* (about sixty-four pounds) and for each *seer* he receives thirty Afghanis. But that is a short journey; we also go to Kashkar."

At first we thought they said Kashgar.

"But that's in China!" The thought of a man making such a journey loaded with sixty pounds of butter was impossible to contemplate.

"They mean Chitral," the Captain said. "They call Chitral Kashkar. It is a long journey: from Pushal up the Bugulchi, then to the east over the *Kotal* Suan into the country of the Kantiwar people; then by the valley of Kantiwo and into the country of the Presun people; then eastwards to the head of that river and beyond by the *Kotal* Mrami and the *Kotal* Papruk to the Bashgul river; north again to Dewane Baba (Ahmad Diwana) and then to Kashkar."

"How long does it take?"

"Two days to the Kantiwar; two and a half to Papruk; two days to Dewane Baba and two days by the *Kotal* Semeneck to Kashkar."

"What do you exchange your butter for in Kashkar?"

"For caps." Everyone smiled and pointed to his porridge plate.

"But it's fantastic," Hugh said to me. "Nine days to buy caps, eighteen there and back. Why don't they make them here on their looms?" Most of the houses, when the weather was fine, had looms outside them on which the brown material for the men's trousers were made.

"If you were going to buy a bowler, you wouldn't make it yourself. You'd go to Lock. It's just that these people are particular what they wear."

"It is the custom for the hats to come from Kashkar. It has always been so," the Captain said.

"What about your boots (the red *chamus*, which the Ramgulis called ūtzār)?"

"*Before*," someone answered, as if referring to a period of unspeakable iniquity, "they were made by our slaves. Now they are made by the people of Kamdesh on the Bashgul River."

I wanted to find out whether they ever relapsed into the old religion. Instead Hugh asked them a lot of questions about taxes, a subject that seemed to fascinate him. Unlike the Tajiks in Panjshir they paid none on their animals, only on their land. "Two Afghanis for every *jarib** we possess."

And about military service. "Only five in every two hundred are conscripted but many go willingly. We have always been soldiers."

Just before he left the old man, who had been a slave in Kabul, came up to Hugh.

"Tell your companion," he said, "that tomorrow an old man will die. There will be work for his little book and camera."

We slept badly. Our air beds had slow punctures and the floor was hard. Also we discovered that we both had dysentery.

We were woken before it was yet light by Abdul Motaleb and Aruk who wanted to sell us their hats. With clotted tongues

* *Jarib*—a quarter of an acre.

and half-closed eyes we were forced to haggle with them. What they asked in exchange seemed ridiculous. Neither wanted one of the daggers Hugh had brought out from England. They wanted Hugh's telescope. But perhaps in terms of the journey involved to fetch these tubes of cloth, their demand was not altogether unreasonable.

Glad to escape from the house and these interminable negotiations, we set off for the funeral with a party of twenty men, all in their best clothes. They sauntered along, while in the fields the women worked, bent double at their allotted tasks or else staggered past us loaded with four Kabuli *seer* of butter on their way to a boiling-up place.

"A bullock is to be slaughtered," said Abdul Ghiyas. There was quite a feeling of holiday in the air. It was not like a funeral at all.

The path by the river was suicidal. I wore gym shoes, the only things my feet could endure. Walking along in a daze I stepped in a puddle and fell over a precipice, landing miraculously unhurt on a small ledge ten feet below the track, which itself overhung the river by fifty feet. Twenty-four faces, mostly bearded, looked down at me in surprise to find that I was still alive.

As I was being hauled up the cliff a *Mullah* appeared.

"They must not go to the funeral," he said, pointing at us rudely, and went on to say some unpleasant things about Christians in general.

We had no strength to argue with him. We let the others go on without us. Instead we crossed the river by a tamarisk trunk and sat under a walnut tree.

Here we experienced a rare moment of peace. The air was full of butterflies: humming-bird hawk moths; clouded yellows; small blues; painted ladies; Hugh reeled off their names, remembered from his schooldays. Behind us in among the oaks a woodpecker was drilling a hole; flying upstream were a couple of kingfishers.

On the opposite bank was a small village called Lustagam. It was built into the side of a cliff and of the same stone, so the houses looked more like caves.

Hidden from the track by a large rock, we were able to observe the passers-by without ourselves being observed, a rare privilege in Nuristan. They were nearly all women carrying triangular baskets stacked with firewood, so heavy that we could see their fingers trembling with the effort as they walked.

The older women all had their hair parted in the centre but the younger ones wore it in a becoming fringe. In terms of years it was difficult to say when they ceased to be young. Perhaps the worn-looking ones were in their middle twenties.

Pushal, to which we presently returned, was completely deserted, except for a few old women like witches and small children. The doors of the houses were all shut, so we went into a low stone hut which was without a door. It was a public washplace. Inside it a spring gushed into a hollowed-out tree-trunk set in the ground which had circular basins cut in it at intervals. It seemed an unsatisfactory arrangement, the last person at the end of the line getting the dirty water from all the others.

Gradually the men of Pushal drifted back from the funeral. Not one but three bullocks had been slaughtered and shots fired. It had been a great day. Their faces were slightly greasy from the funeral baked meats but they made a brilliant spectacle. They wore striped and checked shirts, mostly red, European waistcoats but with dozens of added pearl buttons, and charms and sacred amulets together with military medals with the lettering erased by years of polishing. Perhaps the medals came from India but their origins had long been forgotten. "My father gave them to me," was what the owners said.

Their Chitral caps were ornamented with top-knots of coloured beads, their red scarves were tied with terrific dash and their puttees were laced with black and purple cords. They all wore faded blue cotton trousers.

Seeing me with a camera they at once began to strike attitudes. They were as vain as peacocks. Great group photographs were taken.

On the way back to the house at Asnar, we met two strange-looking middle-aged beings with blond beards and pale patchy complexions. Like the *madares*, they were dressed in white, but of a different sort. They shook our hands wetly but when

I tried to photograph them, they yelped and went off headlong down the hill screaming at the top of their voices.

"It's we who should be running," Hugh said when the extraordinary creatures were out of sight. "That's about all we've got left to catch."

"What's that?"

"Leprosy. They're lepers."

Everyone in the party, with the exception of Shir Muhammad, was now suffering from dysentery. We all munched sulphaguanadine tablets but even these failed; instead of getting better we began to get worse.

It was only when returning from a particularly trying excursion into the Indian corn that I discovered the reason.

"You know those little huts they build over the streams," I said. There was one outside our house, built over the stream from which the drinking water was fetched. It was a pretty little hut; Hugh had particularly admired it. He called it a gazebo.

"What about them?"

"I've found out what they're for. No wonder we're getting worse."

"I don't believe it."

I told him to go and look for himself. Presently he tottered back into the room with a ghastly smile on his face.

"It's true. But I still can't understand it. *You* only drink sterilised water, yet you've got it as badly as any of us."

"Abdul Ghiyas makes the soup with it."

"But boiling kills germs."

"You'd have to boil that stuff for a long time to kill anything. If the germs are as tough as the children, you'd need sulphuric acid."

"There's only one thing to do," Hugh said. "We must get out of here tomorrow."

How the children ever survived the first five years of their lives in the Ramgul valley was a mystery. There were some of them outside on the platform now. Mostly wizened, undernourished creatures, they tottered precariously about on the edge of it, a fifteen foot drop on to sharp rocks, butting one another in the stomach with their little bullet heads. Assuming that they did this sort of thing every day of their lives, it seemed inevitable that the death rate must be enormous. Yet I never saw a serious disaster.

It seemed impossible too that they could ever grow into the robust giants that their fathers were or the beauties that the women became, at least until they were fifteen or so. As Abdul Ghiyas said, quoting an old proverb in a rare moment of confidence when speaking of them, "The most precious possessions that man can desire are a mare of Qatagan and a young Kafir slave girl."

The children were covered with sores, but then so was everyone else, and as time passed so were we: attacked by an abominable fly, a small yellow-backed variety that drilled holes in us, making a sort of bridgehead for larger filthier flies. This fly had the facility, like a fighter attacking out of the sun, of being able to pick a blind spot and alight on one's nose without being observed. For some reason known only to themselves they were particularly attracted to Hugh's. Soon it was covered with craters that gave him a particularly dissipated appearance of which he was acutely conscious.

On this, our last evening in the village, I spent several hours haggling with the Company Promoter for a complete male costume. At last a bargain was struck. At the same time Hugh concluded a deal with the Captain in which he, Hugh, was to receive two exquisite Gardener tea bowls in exchange for a silk scarf from Meshed and a pack of playing-cards.

All the time the negotiations were going on Aruk and a ruffian wearing a red scarf lay about in a dark corner fondling one another; a manifestation of affection that revolted us all, particularly the Captain.

"If you wish to behave thus, go out!" he shouted in a parade ground voice. They went out. Later the brute with the red scarf returned and fell asleep in a corner. It was a curious capacity the Nuristanis had for being able to fall asleep anywhere without bothering whose house they were in.

At three in the morning we were woken by loud crashing sounds coming from the field below the house, followed by a series of tremendous explosions. We rushed out on the platform. There was pandemonium. Dogs were barking; people were rushing among the trees waving resinous torches, shouting excitedly; while standing on the platform outside his front door Abdul Motaleb was firing shot after shot from his Martini-Henry as fast as he could load it into the field below, from which rose a ferocious threshing noise.

"What is it? What's an itz?" All I could hear was "*Itz itz itz itz.*"

"A bear. There's a bear in the Indian corn."

All at once the noises in the field ceased. There was silence.

"The *itz* is dead," announced Abdul Motaleb.

"Why don't you go and look," Hugh said to him, "if you're so sure."

In the daylight, the Indian corn, which had been twelve feet high, looked as though a hurricane had been through it. There were some impressive footprints but no bear.

There was not much more sleep that night. At four Hugh started blundering about in the dark. I asked him what he was doing.

"Getting ready to leave, of course."

Knowing that it would make not the slightest difference to what time we left, I remained in the comparative comfort of my sleeping-bag for another hour. One of the surprising things about the country was that, while outside in the open Nuristan was a perfect hell of insect life, inside the houses there seemed to be no bugs or vermin.

In spite of my unwillingness to rise, an early start seemed possible. But it was not to be. Abdul Ghiyas went off to wash in the river, where he must have engaged in some kind of ritual for he stayed away two hours. Hugh himself had sent his boots to be repaired the previous day but by eight o'clock they had still not arrived at the house. Driven nearly frantic by these reverses he raged up and down bootless and finally despatched Badar Khan to look for them—he also failed to return.

At last, when everybody was finally gathered together, just as we were leaving, a messenger arrived from the Captain. In his hands he held the Meshed scarf and the pack of cards.

"The Captain's wife refuses to part with her tea bowls," he said. Then he whispered something to Abdul Ghiyas who looked serious.

"*Seb*," said Abdul Ghiyas. "The Captain's wife says that if the bowls leave Asnar, *she will cut off his supplies*."

CHAPTER NINETEEN

Disaster at Lake Mundul

ESCORTED by Abdul Motaleb, a *Mullah* (a surprisingly mild *Mullah* for the Ramgul where the *Mullahs* had shown themselves extremely hostile) and his grandson, a boy of ten, we set off through Lustagam and downhill past a burial ground full of rough stones set on end with something like a wooden cot for a gigantic baby in the middle of it. I wanted Hugh to ask Abdul Motaleb whether this was something left over from the old religion, but he breathed hard through his nostrils and preserved a grim silence. He had had a provoking morning and in my heart I sympathised with him.

The *Mullah* and the boy led the way. The *Mullah* carried a stone bow and from time to time he shot at a lizard to amuse his grandson, making better shooting than the young men of Pushal.

A couple of miles beyond Lustagam a steep valley entered the Ramgul from the east. It led to the Kulam river, a day's journey away, which rises somewhere near the head of the Wanasgul in the country of the Kantiwar Katirs.

"We are not at the moment on good terms with the Kantiwar people," said Abdul Motaleb. "They claim that the grazing at the head of the valley is theirs."

Here he left us.

Here and all the way down the valley the waters of the Ramgul were tapped off into the surrounding fields in ways that made the feats of irrigation accomplished by the Tajiks of the Panjshir seem comparatively insignificant. In the Ramgul when an irrigation ditch came to a place where cultivated land ended and cliffs began, it was carried round the face of the cliff, sometimes as much as thirty feet above the river, in hollowed-out half tree-trunks supported on stone buttresses, like a viaduct for a model train; while at the far side of the obstacle there were complicated junction boxes with two or three wooden conduits branching off from them.

Beyond Pātchāh, a large village of about forty houses built on a sharp ridge of rocks, the inhabitants crowded the rooftops to watch us go by and then trooped down to follow us.

A little beyond the village, rising straight up out of the fields by the river, we came to an enormous rock—*Sang Neveshteh* (in the Katir, *Pshtreal*). On the smooth lower part of it was an indecipherable inscription.

"It reads thus," said the *Mullah*. "In the reign of the great Amir, Abdul Rahman Khan Ghazi, in the year 1313 (in the Christian chronology 1895) the whole of Kafiristan was conquered by him and the inhabitants embraced the true and holy religion of Islam.—Righteousness and virtue have triumphed and untruth has disappeared," he added sententiously.

Near it he said there was another inscription. To Hugh and myself, with the sun beating on it, it might have been anything or nothing.

"What is it written in?" Hugh asked. He had recovered from the bad start.

"It is in the Kufic script. It is the inscription the Emperor Timur made when he turned aside to come here on his way to invade Hind, in the year 800" (A.D. 1398).

Whether Timur Leng, the atrocious Mongol, reached the Ramgul or whether it was one of his generals; whether or not any inscription, other than that of Abdur Rahman, even exists has never, so far as I can discover, been properly verified. Until some qualified person visits the *Sang Neveshteh* even the existence of the second inscription must remain a matter for conjecture. What is certain is that Timur Leng did invade some part of Kafiristan from the west. His method of crossing the mountains was so novel and his observations on the character of the Kafirs so interesting that it seems worth referring to it briefly.

In March 1398, according to his autobiography, *Malfūzāt-i-Timūrī*,* he appointed a viceroy at Samarkand and, having left a garrison to defend it, "I placed my foot in the stirrup at a lucky moment and directed my course towards Hindustan."

With his army he crossed the Oxus at Termez by a bridge of boats and eventually arrived in Andarab, the next valley to Panjshir. There the people were full of complaint, saying "Infidel Kators and the Siyah-Poshes exact tribute and black-mail every year from us and, if we fail in our exact amount, they slay our men and carry our women and children into slavery."

Determined to punish them, Timur left part of his army with his son, Prince Shah Rukh (the same Prince who loved Herat so much and who built the towers I had so miserably failed to photograph), and crossed the Hindu Kush to a place he calls 'Paryan', which has been identified as Parwan (the town at the foot of the Bajgah Pass, near Gulbahar at the south end of the Panjshir where we had begun our journey).† The other wing of his army had already crossed by the Khawak Pass into Panjshir and Timur says he detached a force of ten thousand‡ under Prince Rustam and a General with the delightful name of Burhan Aghlan Jujitar, his chief nobles and sent them eastwards into Kafiristan against the *Siah-Posh* Kafirs in the north.

After ordering most of the nobles and all the soldiers to leave horses, camels and superfluous baggage at Khawak, he began the crossing of the mountains of 'Kator':§ the mountains dividing Panjshir from Kafiristan which we crossed at the Chamar Pass. The conditions were very bad. There was a lot of snow and a hot wind made the going so soft that the army could only move by night when it froze hard. There was no sign of the Kafirs who had all taken refuge in inaccessible caves

* The following pages are lifted almost in their entirety from this chronicle to be found in Elliott and Dowson's *History of India*, Vol. III, London, 1871.

† Colonel Gardner's castello was said to be near Parwan. See Chapter VII, p. 88.

‡ The tens of thousands employed in the actual campaign against the Kafirs are almost certainly an Oriental hyperbole and must be taken with a large pinch of salt.

§ Probably by the Darra Hazara.

on the mountainside, rendering themselves even more invisible by blocking the entrances with snow. Some of the nobles who still had their horses with them, with a stubbornness worthy of a British officer refusing to be parted from his bed roll, were forced to send them back.

From the top of the range there was no way down for the army except by sliding down the slopes of snow and ice on their behinds. Timur himself had a wicker basket prepared with ropes, each 150 yards long, attached to the corners.

"Since I undertook this expedition against the infidels," he wrote, "and had made up my mind to undergo all manner of trouble and fatigue, I took my seat in the basket."

Across the centuries one can detect the unspoken wish that he hadn't come. The basket was let down to the fullest extent of the ropes, then a platform was cut in the snow for the basket and the lowering party to stand on. This was repeated five times until Timur got to the bottom.

The valley they were in was probably the Upper Alishang. Soon they arrived at a Kafir fort. It was, of course, deserted; the Kafirs were all on the heights above. The Mongols attacked the heights but the Kafirs held out for three days until offered the choice of perishing or becoming Muslims and reciting the creed; they chose apostasy. Timur appears to have been delighted. He dressed some of them in robes of honour and dismissed them. Such examples of his clemency are rare.

That night the Kafirs put in a heavy attack on his position and a hundred and fifty of them were taken prisoner—all were put to death instantly: it is scarcely to be wondered at.

The following day Timur's troops attacked from all four sides and destroyed the remnant, men and women, "consigning them", as Timur grimly puts it, "to the house of perdition"; using their skulls to build towers on the mountains. He also had an inscription cut recording "That I had reached this country in the month of Ramazan, May 1398; that if chance should conduct anyone to this spot he might know it."

There was no news of the army to the north commanded by Burhan Aghlan Jujitar. He had done badly in a previous engagement and Timur had no faith in his abilities. Now Timur dreamt that his own sword was bent, and took it to be an omen of defeat.

With one of his more junior commanders, Muhammad Azad, he sent 300 Tajiks and 100 Tartars to the *Siah-Posh* country to find out what had happened. After a dreadful journey Muhammad Azad reached the enemy stronghold, to which Burhan Aghlan Jujitar was supposed to be laying siege, to find that the *Siah-Posh* had deserted it and that there was no sign of any of his own side.

What had happened was as follows: Burhan Aghlan Jujitar had also found the fortress deserted but he had allowed his army to be lured into a defile, where the Kafirs, waiting in ambush, fell on it. He himself had fled and his troops had been defeated, 'drinking the sherbet of martyrdom'. Now it was Muhammad Azad with his four hundred who counter-attacked and defeated the Kafirs, getting back all the armour and booty that had been lost.

Timur says he found an easier way out of Kafiristan. In eighteen days he reached the fort at Khawak. Burhan Aghlan Jujitar languished in disgrace, having failed to defeat the Kafirs with ten thousand, but Mohammed Azad, who had succeeded with his four hundred, was honoured.

That Timur was in Alishang seems absolutely certain. There is a strong tradition in the district that he visited it. As short a time ago as 1837, when the indefatigable Masson visited Najil, he wrote:

'Their malek, Osman, from his long standing and experience, enjoys a reputation out of his retired valley. He boasts of descent not exactly from Alexander the Great, but from Amir Taimur; and when rallied upon the subject and asked how so diminutive a being can lay claim to so proud an origin replies that he has only to put out one of his eyes, and lame one of his legs, and he would become Taimur himself. The tradition goes that Taimur procured a wife in this country.'

As we stood there we were surrounded by the inhabitants of Pātchāh who had followed us down to the rock. Some of the

men wore domed skull-caps. With their stone bows and wild
air it was not difficult to imagine that Timur himself might appear
at any moment.

From now on the country became more lush with many more
trees. There were two kinds of mulberry, the ordinary sort
and one called *shāhtūt*, the king mulberry. On one tree that
had been grafted with the dark ones, both grew together. The
shāhtūt were full of juice and with our troubles forgotten for
the time being we hung in the branches of the tree stripping it
like monkeys, with the *Mullah* higher than anyone. Besides the
mulberries there were plums; small, soft rather tasteless apples;
and a sort of sloe called *yakmah*.

Soon we overtook a man trotting downhill with a big block of
salt on a carrying frame. He took us a quick way by narrow
paths through thickly wooded country where watermills whirred
merrily and wild raspberries and buttercups grew in little meadow
clearings. It was like a summer morning in England, but a
long time ago.

At midday we came to Jena Khel, a place with only a few
scattered houses where there was a circle of stone seats in an
apple orchard, a sort of tribal meeting place.

"We are now in the district of Raro," said the *Mullah*. "This
is the place of the *Alaqadar* of Laghman, the magistrate of this
part of the Eastern Province. He is under the orders of the
Naib ul Hukumah, the Governor, who is a Pathan."

Here, watched by hordes of children, some of them with blue
eyes and striking faces like Slovenes of the Carso near Trieste,
we sat waiting for the horses to come up.

I asked Hugh what we should have for lunch. It was a
familiar joke that never lost its savour.

"I would like cold salmon, cold game pie, two bottles of
Alsatian wine, a long French loaf and some fresh butter."

"We've got cold meat loaf, cold Irish stew, if you can face
it, and one of those dreadful jam puddings—the sort with no
jam in it—and, if you're still hungry, some of these apples
that have gone to sleep." I pointed to the windfalls around us.

We had almost reached the bottom of the last provision box. In one of the compartments there was a sheet of official injunctions intended for the troops. They were printed on leprous yellow paper.

'THIS IS GOOD FOOD,' it said. 'DON'T SPOIL IT,' and across the bottom in very bold type, 'DON'T FEED FLIES.'

"If we'd only dropped some of this pudding on Cassino instead of all those bombs, the Germans would have surrendered," said Hugh with his mouth full of dough.

I was glad to see that his interest in food was growing.

As the afternoon advanced the woods were filled with an autumnal light. There were masses of hollyhocks from which rose the humming of countless bees. There were grapes too, as yet unripe, growing on trellises sheltered by the walls of the few houses. For some reason the appalling yellow fly had suddenly vanished. With the re-introduction of wine-making the place would have been a paradise. For us this short hour was one of the most idyllic of the whole journey.

But it soon came to an end and the track began to wind up the mountainside, higher and higher, and we were once again in the wilderness, struggling across places where the track had been washed away bodily by the storms of the last few days, where what had originally been soft mud had dried out with a jagged rocklike surface. After rounding seventeen bluffs, a journey of perhaps five miles that took several hours, we came to Gadval, the *Mullah's* village. Like all the other villages we had passed, it was dramatically sited on a cliff and, as at Pushal, the necessary houses were situated over the streams that ran down through it.

The *Mullah's* house was directly above the river with a grassy platform in front of it on which we camped.

In the river below a man was fishing, stripped to the waist. He had a weighted net which he cast into the pools, while a boy with a long pole stood by to clear it if it stuck on the rocks.

"I didn't think the Nuristanis ate fish," said Hugh.

"The Kafirs, no; the Nuristanis, yes," said the *Mullah*.

"It's a strange thing," Hugh said. "There are no trout on this side of the Hindu Kush, nowhere south of the main range. Yet all the rivers towards the Oxus have huge trout in them."

For dinner he made a terribly rich soup from half a dozen different Swiss packets, all of which had burst. By now everything we possessed was squashed flat. Unwisely he insisted on administering it to Abdul Ghiyas who, unlike the rest of us, had not benefited by the departure from Pushal. After eating it Abdul Ghiyas complained that his head was going round. So was mine.

Hugh was upset. "I can't find anything wrong with it."

As soon as he had finished his helping, which was very large as no one else wanted any, he tucked into a big bowl of *mast* provided by the *Mullah's* household; I groped for Alka Seltzer (one of the few treats we possessed now that we were out of tobacco).

It was dark now. As I scrabbled amongst my possessions for the Alka Seltzer, watched by an audience of grave, elderly gentlemen, Hugh continued to pester me about food.

"What would you like to eat now."

"Nothing. Go away!"

"All right! I won't ask you again. Personally," he said, "I'm starving."

Much later some hot fish arrived. The name sounded like *mahseer* or it might have been *machhli*, the Indian word for fish, but, as it was decapitated, there was no means of telling what it was. It was delicious but I was not equal to it. I toyed with it in a half-hearted way by torchlight until it grew cold and unappetising.

As we continued downhill the next day the people began to dress differently. They no longer wore the strange uniform of the higher valleys; instead they wore white turbans and thin *shalvār* trousers, and they had a more civilised air.

By contrast the road became more difficult. Frequently it was blocked by huge boulders and there were places where, when the cliff was sheer to the river, instead of climbing over the top it continued round the edge supported precariously on flimsy wooden galleries.

At such places the horses had to cross and re-cross the river, moving from one island of sand or shingle to another or down the opposite bank where dwarf willows grew. With them went Abdul Ghiyas, Badar Khan and the *Mullah* (after we had spent the night in his garden he had insisted on accompanying us still farther). Shir Muhammad took no notice of his horse, he continued to follow us down the right bank and left her to follow the others as best she could.

Five hours downstream we came to the junction of the Linar, the valley that leads to the Arayu Pass, the route by which the butter runners make the journey into Panjshir. Half-way across, waist deep in the strong current, with our feet slithering on the round slippery stones, we were overhauled by an oldish man carrying a wooden cage in which there was a fighting cock partridge. Having crossed over himself and put down the cage, he came back to help us over as if we were elderly ladies. He was on his way to match his bird in a fight and showed us the curved spurs it wore. They were like razors.

We had to wait a long time for the horses. They had been forced to climb over a bluff two thousand feet high. When at last they came slithering across the river we saw that Abdul Ghiyas was covered in dust and dirt. He was past speech.

"His horse fell over a cliff," said Badar Khan, "and he was on it."

Abdul Ghiyas at this moment seemed on the point of death. Forced to walk because of the difficult ground he had become a shambling wreck, roasting in his windproof suit. Shir Muhammad was an extraordinary sight too with his cotton trousers looped up to show his bandy legs and feet encased in unlaced climbing boots several sizes too large for him. (I had bequeathed him mine, having decided to finish the journey in gym shoes.)

We descended a steep combe where the undergrowth was shoulder high and entered a childhood paradise, a dim and mysterious place where the track, which wound along the top of a high wall, was completely roofed in by trees and so overgrown with vegetation that we could only feel it underfoot but not see it. With the sun filtering down and everything green and cool it was like being under water.

Then all of a sudden we came out into the sunlight on to a high hill above a village that nestled between humps of lichen-covered rock. Far below the river, now wide and slow-moving, wound between green fields until it entered a lake hemmed in on three sides by mountains. This was Lake Mundul. With the curious rocks in the foreground, the winding river and the mountains hemming it in, it was like a landscape drawing by Leonardo.

Eager to reach the water's edge we raced down the track towards it.

Once by the river, here a hundred yards wide, we crossed a dyke into a field of short, cropped grass that was full of buttercups. It was like the shores of an estuary where it meets the sea. There was a beach and at the mouth of the river there were sandbanks. Far out in the lake itself where it was shallow two solitary willows grew, and closer in to the shore there were beds of reeds with backwaters winding through them. A cool breeze was blowing down the valley bowing the reeds and ruffling the water.

For the two of us it was a moment of sheer delight that was certain to be ruined as soon as the dozen hangers-on from the village caught up with us. On the far bank Badar Khan and the *Mullah* were moving downstream with the horses, Abdul Ghiyas having been unequal to the crossing, Shir Muhammad disinclined to make it.

"Unless that *Mullah* knows a ford, they'll have to go back," Hugh said. "I don't think there's a way across."

Horror of horrors, before we could stop him and without a word of warning the *Mullah* mounted Shir Muhammad's horse and with Abdul Ghiyas's on a leading rein plunged them both into the river and began to swim them across.

So far, whenever the horses had forded a river, they had always had all four feet on the bottom and elaborate precautions were always taken to ensure that only the lower halves of the loads would get wet.

Now we watched in silent agony as everything we possessed, with the exception of what was loaded on Badar Khan's beast, cameras, films, notebooks, clothing, to say nothing of the flour and the Irish stew sank beneath the water.

At first Hugh was paralysed; then he started bellowing at the *Mullah* to go back, but it was too late, he was already half-way across. Hugh now turned his attention to Badar Khan, but that prudent man had no intention of crossing a river of unknown depth.

When the *Mullah* emerged from the river, proud of what he had done and smiling, I thought Hugh was going to strangle him. "Go away," he croaked in fury. "You're a disgrace. You, a *Mullah*." It seemed dreadful after he had entertained us so hospitably, but it was difficult not to be angry. Only my inadequate command of the language prevented me from joining in. "And you too," he shouted at the twelve villagers, one of whom it turned out was the headman of Mundul, the village we had just come from. "Go away!"

To escape from them in our moment of agony, we hastened through a swamp up to our knees in water and took refuge on a little promontory that stuck out into the lake. Soon we were joined by Abdul Ghiyas and the horses and here we made our camp. Shir Muhammad did not appear. If he had been where he should have been, on the other side of the river with his horse, at least part of the disaster would have been avoided. He lurked somewhere out of sight among the oaks that grew down to the water's edge, waiting for the storm to blow over.

We were not left in peace for long. Soon the headman detached himself from the little group of villagers who surrounded the *Mullah* like rugger players shielding one of the team whilst he changes his trousers, and came splashing through the shallows towards us.

"Go away!"

"We are coming!"

"Go away! What can you do? The *Mullah* has ruined a camera costing twenty thousand Afghanis not to speak of everything else we possess."

"We are countrymen," answered the headman sturdily, "and we shall go where we wish."

"You are not Muhammadans!" This from Abdul Ghiyas who had found the *Mullahs* in the Ramgul excessively devout, even to his taste.

Before his voice finally gave out Hugh resorted to his favourite weapon. "If you don't leave us alone, I shall speak to General Ubaidullah Khan at Kabul and you will be punished."

In spite of this threat they all moved up the hillside and descended on us from the rear, where they squatted down a few yards away and grumbled among themselves—all except the wretched *Mullah*, who was far away at the edge of the dyke, alone in his agony.

This disaster had the curious effect of putting everyone in excellent spirits, so that when Shir Muhammad quietly slipped into the camp as though nothing had happened, he failed to get the rocket he deserved.

Everything was soaked, except one camera, which by extraordinary good fortune had been transferred to Badar Khan's horse at the last moment. It seemed unlikely that any of the film would survive. All the cartons were full of water and we spent a long time emptying them.

"What about Badar Khan," I said, after we had emptied the final carton and hung our bedding up to dry.

"Let him wait a bit, and the *Mullah*. We shall have to make peace with the *Mullah* eventually, but he deserves to suffer."

After forgiving the *Mullah* we undressed and crossed the river on foot. It was up to our necks but the bottom was firm sand and we brought all the gear over in two journeys assisted by two men of the Kulam Katirs, who had come over the mountains by a remote route with a consignment of butter.

All this time Badar Khan sat on the bank, watching our efforts and doing nothing to help. He rode across without even getting his feet wet.

While we were returning to the camp the weather began to change; the wind dropped; black clouds formed over the lake and from high in the mountains came a premonitory rumble. In the woods the pigeons rose in alarm; rooks circled above the trees cawing sadly. Suddenly there were hordes of flies and large fish began to rise in the lake. For the first time since leaving the mountain we erected the tent. The villagers left for home at a steady trot.

After the storm had passed there was furious insect activity. The camp site was like some kind of by-pass; not to be deflected from a pre-determined destination hordes of ants tramped remorselessly over us.

Towards evening the weather cleared and we set off to explore the lake towards the south with the headman, who had returned and with whom we also made our peace—poor fellow he had done nothing wrong.

The part of the lake on which we were camped was about three-quarters of a mile long, then it turned sharply in an S bend and opened out into a stretch of water more than a mile in length and four hundred yards broad. At the far end towards the south there were more mountains at right angles to the valley.

"Last year because the King (Zaher Shah) wished to come here for fishing and hunting he sent his *Mīr-i-Shīkari*, his head game-keeper, to see if it were possible for a party of people to get here. The *Mīr-i-Shīkari* came with horses by the Kotal Arayu out of Parian but he found the way too difficult for a King."

"That's the way we're going out, over the Arayu," Hugh said. "But why doesn't he come from the south?"

"Because it is very difficult with horses. From here to the Lower Alingar at Nangarāj is three days through the country of the Pashaie people.

"Is it possible to do it in winter?"

The headman slipped his shirt off his shoulders to show a scar a foot long which extended from shoulder to elbow.

"This happened last year in deep winter when there was much snow. It was a black bear that did it; as big as a Nuristani cow. I went down by the Alingar. I was many days on the road to the hospital at Kabul."

Just before it grew dark two cormorants came flying up the

lake and landed on one of the sandbanks. To us it seemed a remarkable place to find them.

"I think I shall write a piece for the *Royal Central Asian Journal* about Lake Mundul and seeing cormorants," Hugh said when we were wedged uncomfortably in our tent. "Very few Europeans have ever been here."

"If you do that somebody is bound to write a chilly letter saying that it's a very well-known lake and that it isn't at all remarkable to find cormorants on it."*

In the night as a result of the storm, the river rose three feet. After an unsuccessful attempt to catch fish with an ugly artificial French fish, which I eventually lost, I spent the rest of the morning on one of the sandbanks. It was the sort of place you see from a train or from a ship and can never visit. In the afternoon I visited a valley that led to the west, a deep gorge between high cliffs, full of boulders. Half a mile up there was a bridge over a torrent leading to some small fields at the foot of one of the cliffs. Hidden away behind the Indian corn there was a tiny hovel, with the exception of the *aylaq* in the high valley, the loneliest house I had seen.

The place seemed deserted. Apart from the humming of insects, there was absolute silence. Inside the house there was no one but the tools belonging to the occupants were leaning against the cliff, a wooden hand plough, a long-handled spade and several hoes. Whoever they were had been threshing; there was chaff everywhere and there were flails lying about, long poles with flexible whips on them. All the time I had the uncanny feeling of being watched.

The next day, the twenty-ninth of July and the twentieth of our journey, we left for the Arayu.

* Hugh did write his piece and by an uncanny coincidence this is exactly what did happen.

CHAPTER TWENTY

Beyond the Arayu

BEFORE leaving Lake Mundul an argument developed over the route, Hugh maintaining that we should go by the valley as far as Mundul village, Abdul Ghiyas favouring the mountainside.

Eventually the mountain was decided on and we found ourselves stuck high above the valley unable to go backwards or forwards. In this way the journey to Mundul village took three hours instead of thirty minutes. The horses had to be unloaded three times and Shir Muhammad's kicked me in the stomach. Before this happened I had never realised that horses kick sideways. Temporarily I began to wonder why I had become an explorer.

Once again, with pain and difficulty, we crossed the Linar, the river where we had met the man with the bird cage, and turned westward up the gorge for the Arayu and home. We soon found out that the gorge was impassable.

"You know what this means," Hugh said. "Over the top!"

We climbed two thousand feet straight up the mountain until the river looked like a narrow ribbon below; through a dry uncultivated wilderness, where the only trees were the holly oaks and the earth was nothing but pulverised rock.

All day the track switchbacked up and down; at one moment a hundred feet above the river, the next a thousand, so that our progress resembled a temperature chart in a funny drawing.

In the middle of the day, when the sun was intolerable, we reached an oasis, a place called Warna, where there were two or three houses and, best of all, a waterfall and a patch of grass. In Warna no one bothered to collect the mulberries when they fell and the air was heady with the smell of them as they lay fermenting under the trees in drifts six inches deep.

Here Abdul Ghiyas bought a chicken from a smelly old man and salted it for dinner. We shared two apple puddings between us. Although a very long way from home an end-of-term air pervaded the party.

The old man decided to accompany us up the valley, thereby adding materially to our discomfort. Never in my short acquaintance with Asia had I encountered anyone or anything, dead or alive, who smelled like this old man. Although I couldn't say why, he reminded me of the Crimean War.

"He is a Tajik," Abdul Ghiyas explained, as if it was an extenuation. "Twenty years ago he came over the Pass with some merchants and got left behind. He has been here ever since."

"If he smelled like he does now twenty years ago," Hugh grumbled, "I can't say I blame them."

We were climbing high along the side of the gorge now. Its far bank was in shadow and there were the scours of waterfalls and patches of old snow. Abdul Ghiyas was very ill. We noticed that whenever there was an opportunity, which was frequently, he drank the water from the stream. We told him that if he continued to do so he would die.

I dreamt of all the cool drinks I had ever had in my life. The ginger beer I had drunk as a child; foaming lager; draught Worthington; Muscadet kept in a stream until I was ready for it; pints of Pimms; buckets of ice. . . .

There were clouds now, hemming in the sun but not obscuring it, concentrating it on our heads like a burning glass. All the time, to windward, was the awful old man whose clothes were like cerements.

"I wish to God he'd go away," I said at last.

Hugh's reaction to this was even more violent.

"If there weren't any witnesses, do you know what I'd do? I'd push him over the edge."

At last the sun began to sink and, as it grew cooler, we came to Linar. On the outskirts of the village grew a magnificent mulberry tree, *shāhtūt*, loaded with fruit.

As the only really fit man left among us and as a punishment for his behaviour at the lake, Shir Muhammad was ordered to remain behind to collect a basketful. The last we saw of him was swinging aloft in the branches like a great overgrown schoolboy.

In the village Abdul Ghiyas halted. "I have an aunt in Linar," he said. "Here we should stop the night."

At this moment angry cries rose on the air from the direction of the *shāhtūt* tree. It was obvious that Shir Muhammad had been caught by the owner.

"Perhaps after all," Abdul Ghiyas went on, "it is better to continue."

As we passed through the inhabitants of Linar turned out in force. They were a wild-looking independent lot. For some reason they took exception to Abdul Ghiyas in his windproof suit. They left the rest of us alone, but, as Abdul Ghiyas lumbered up the road, they treated him to a sort of slow hand-clap.

The air began to grow cold. A few miles farther on the track descended sharply and at the junction with another valley, the Makhin Kadao down which an icy wind was howling, Abdul Ghiyas halted.

"It is time to camp."

It was a crazy, windy place to choose for a camp. Without saying anything Hugh hurled his ice-axe to the ground and set off alone up the Makhin Kadao. There he sat down at the foot of a cliff with his back to us. I must say that at this moment he had my sympathy.

Whilst we were standing in the middle of the gorge in some indecision, Shir Muhammad came stumbling down the hill towards us. His nose was bleeding and he had a beautiful black eye. He had apparently been caught up the tree by the owner, an old woman, who had summoned her son and two hefty daughters. They had given him a fearful beating. He had also lost the basket, but he still had his shirt full of *shāhtūt*, although they were a bit squashed.

Mustering this sad, mutinous little force, I drove them before me up the Linar gorge, cursing the lot of them. It was not difficult for me to work up a rage at this moment. All of a sudden I felt that revulsion against an alien way of life that anyone who travels in remote places experiences from time to time. I longed for clean clothes; the company of people who meant what they said, and did it. I longed for a hot bath and a drink.

The track immediately climbed a thousand feet out of the bottom of the gorge. Whenever we came to a small table of level ground that might accommodate two men without horses, Abdul Ghiyas suggested that we should stop. He was very sick but we had to go on until we found a suitable place.

"*Seb*. Here!"

"No! GET ON!"

After a long hour we came to a fine place; close to the river and with fresh water from a spring.

"Abdul Ghiyas!"

"*Seb?*"

"What about this? Good place."

"The old man says there is a better farther on."

The old man, now that he was cooling off in the streaming Asian wind, was less objectionable.

When it was dark, after being twelve hours on the march we came to the place recommended by the old man. He was right; it had been worth the extra effort. Almost immediately Hugh arrived. He seemed in excellent spirits. The men ate their delicious chicken; we ate horrid tinned bacon-and-egg mixture and delicious apple pudding and some of the *shāhtūt* that had survived the battle at Linar. As a result of enjoying this modest feast Hugh was very ill.

Without their pipe, which had broken down, and having still a little tobacco, Badar Khan and Shir Muhammad constructed a pipe from mother earth, boring a hole in the ground for the bowl and connecting it by an underground passage with another smaller one that served as the mouthpiece. They applied their lips to the ground, sucking horribly. It was a disagreeable spectacle.

On August the first, early in the morning, we reached Achagaur, the last village in Nuristan.

The men of Achagaur all wore heavy sleeveless knitted pull-overs with a sophisticated pattern of black and white dicing on them. They gave us melted butter and bread. We gave them Irish stew. Here they still spoke the Katir.

"We are Koreish Katirs," they said, "from Arabia, as are the Linar people of the same tribe as the Prophet."

"When did you come here?"

"We cannot tell. We do not know."*

We asked them how they traded with the Panjshir people.

"We meet them beyond the Arayu—in a lonely place. They bring us salt and we exchange butter for it."

Up beyond the last houses the valley of the Linar was nothing like the Chamar Valley. Because the bottom of the valley was blocked with stones, there was hardly any grass and therefore there were few cattle and sheep. The last dwelling of all high up in the valley was the herdsman's hut and from it a family sprawled out who themselves looked like animals.

To the left, in the direction of the Panjshir, the valley swung round and became a vast cul-de-sac of peaks. Straight ahead, far up the valley and high above us, was the Arayu Pass, like a funnel with a track winding interminably up through it. To think that this was one of the principal butter routes out of Nuristan into Panjshir was a sobering thought.

All of us, proprietors and drivers, even Shir Muḥammad, were now ill. For this reason our caravan presented a curiously scattered appearance, as it wound its way up the dreadful slope, exposed to wind and sun and the whistles of the marmots who were out in force among the rocks. As one or the other of us succumbed, a ruthless atmosphere prevailed; no one waited for anyone else and those who had fallen out had to catch up as best they could when they finally emerged, green-faced, from behind the inadequate boulders that covered the lower slopes.

The climb began in earnest at a quarter to ten and took three hours. The last few hundred feet were moraine and the way through it was marked by cairns, two stones on top of one another. But it was worth all the suffering. Once again, as

* This was nonsense. They all looked like Rajputs, and are—descendants of the Keruch Rajputs of the Indus Valley.

on the Chamar, we stood on the great dividing ridge of the whole massif. To the left the ridge plunged down in snow-covered slopes straight into a glacial lake; to the right of the col the mountains were smoother, more rounded. Ahead was Mir Samir.

Here on the Arayu, one of the lonely places of the earth with all the winds of Asia droning over it, where the mountains seemed like the bones of the world breaking through, I had the sensation of emerging from a country that would continue to exist more or less unchanged whatever disasters overtook the rest of mankind.

We went down towards the north, following the cairns and later the stream from the top of the watershed, with the cold yellow mountains all about us standing alone, like sentinels.

It was mid afternoon before we stopped. In spite of everything, I was mad with hunger. Hugh, having a queasy feeling, was more finicky.

"It's your turn to cook," he said. "I want green tea and two boiled eggs."

"Well, I want a damn great meal."

There was a screaming wind. Boiling water at 15,000 feet or thereabouts is a protracted operation using nothing but solid fuel. Whilst I was waiting for the egg water to boil, I fried two eggs in thirty seconds and ate an entire apple pudding, cold.

Hugh looked like death but he was in a fury. At first I thought he would have some kind of seizure.

"Look at you. Hogging it. You only think of yourself. When are you going to cook something decent for *me*?"

"You asked for boiled eggs. I can't think of anything more difficult at this height. You can cook them yourself and anything else you want in the future."

I set off over the green grass down the valley alone.

In spite of this ridiculous tiff, rarely in my life had I felt such an ecstatic feeling of happiness as I did coming down from the Arayu. The present was bliss beyond belief; the future looked golden. I thought of my wife and children; I thought of the book that I had already written; I even thought about the Everest Foundation and the grant that up here seemed certain to materialise (it didn't—one can hardly blame them).

I went down past high, cold cliffs already in shadow where the first tented nomads were, down and down for two hours.

Eventually I came out in a great green meadow with a river running through it like a curled spring. The sun was just setting, the grass that had been a vivid green had already lost its colour, the sky was the colour of pearls.

Under the wall of the mountain on the left there were four rocks, each forty feet high and fifty long; built out from under them were the stone houses and pens of the summer *aylaq*. Women and children dressed in white were standing on the roofs watching the herds come slowly down from the fringes of the mountain. Standing in the river two bullocks were fighting.

Before going to the *aylaq* I waited for Hugh to appear.

"You know I've had the most extraordinary feeling coming down," were his first words when he appeared. "As if there was never going to be anything to worry about again."

"I expect it's the altitude."

The night was a bitter one. The wind howled over the screes but we dined on rice pudding (the rice was provided by the headman, our own provisions were exhausted) and, although we were blinded by the smoke of the *artemnesia* root, we were content to be where we were.

All through the next day we still had the same feeling of extreme happiness. Until late in the afternoon we went down; always with the great bone-coloured mountains on either side and valleys choked with the debris of glaciers, leading to regions of snow and ice and to rocks too sheer for snow to cling to them.

We came to cornfields and a village called Arayu, full of savage dogs and surly-looking Tajiks and mud houses like those of Egyptian *fellahin*.

This patch of cultivation was succeeded by a mighty red-cliffed gorge where there were caves in which we sheltered from the midday sun. But not for long. The path to Parian and Shāhnaiz led up out of it high over the mountain. At the watershed we turned still more to the north going downhill again now and into a final narrow valley where the wind threw the spray from a river in our faces. It was spray from the Parian, the Upper Panjshir. We had made it.

We crossed the river by a bridge, went up through the village of Shāhnaiz and downhill towards the Lower Panjshir.

"Look," said Hugh, "it must be Thesiger."

Coming towards us out of the great gorge where the river thundered was a small caravan like our own. He named an English explorer, a remarkable throwback to the Victorian era, a fluent speaker of Arabic, a very brave man, who has twice crossed the Empty Quarter and, apart from a few weeks every year, has passed his entire life among primitive peoples.

We had been on the march for a month. We were all rather jaded; the horses were galled because the drivers were careless of them, and their ribs stood out because they had been in places only fit for mules and forded innumerable torrents filled with slippery rocks as big as footballs; the drivers had run out of tobacco and were pining for their wives; there was no more sugar to put in the tea, no more jam, no more cigarettes and I was reading *The Hound of the Baskervilles* for the third time; all of us suffered from a persistent dysentery. The ecstatic sensations we had experienced at a higher altitude were beginning to wear off. It was not a particularly gay party.

Thesiger's caravan was abreast of us now, his horses lurching to a standstill on the execrable track. They were deep-loaded with great wooden presses, marked 'British Museum', and black tin trunks (like the ones my solicitors have, marked 'Not Russel-Jones' or 'All Bishop of Chichester').

The party consisted of two villainous-looking tribesmen dressed like royal mourners in long overcoats reaching to the ankles; a shivering Tajik cook, to whom some strange mutation had given bright red hair, unsuitably dressed for Central Asia in crippling pointed brown shoes and natty socks supported by suspenders, but no trousers; the interpreter, a gloomy-looking middle-class Afghan in a coma of fatigue, wearing dark glasses, a double-breasted lounge suit and an American hat with stitching all over it; and Thesiger himself, a great, long-striding crag of a man, with an outcrop for a nose and bushy eyebrows, forty-five years old and as hard as nails, in an old tweed jacket of the sort worn by Eton boys, a pair of thin grey cotton trousers, rope-soled Persian slippers and a woollen cap comforter.

"Turn round," he said, "you'll stay the night with us. We're going to kill some chickens."

We tried to explain that we had to get to Kabul, that we wanted our mail, but our men, who professed to understand no English but were reluctant to pass through the gorges at night, had already turned the horses and were making for the collection of miserable hovels that was the nearest village.

Soon we were sitting on a carpet under some mulberry trees, surrounded by the entire population, with all Thesiger's belongings piled up behind us.

"Can't speak a word of the language," he said cheerfully. "Know a lot of the Koran by heart but not a word of Persian. Still, it's not really necessary. Here, you," he shouted at the cook, who had only entered his service the day before and had never seen another Englishman. "Make some green tea and a lot of chicken and rice—three chickens."

"No good bothering the interpreter," he went on, "the poor fellow's got a sty, that's why we only did seventeen miles today. It's no good doing too much at first, especially as he's not feeling well."

The chickens were produced. They were very old; in the half-light they looked like pterodactyls.

"Are they expensive?"

"The Power of Britain never grows less," said the headman, lying superbly.

"That means they are very expensive," said the interpreter, rousing himself.

Soon the cook was back, semaphoring desperately.

"Speak up, can't understand a thing. You want sugar? Why don't you say so?" He produced a large bunch of keys, like a housekeeper in some stately home. All that evening he was opening and shutting boxes so that I had tantalising glimpses of the contents of an explorer's luggage—a telescope, a string vest, the *Charterhouse of Parma*, *Du Côté de Chez Swann*, some fish-hooks and the 1/1000000 map of Afghanistan—not like mine, a sodden pulp, but neatly dissected, mounted between marbled boards.

"That cook's going to die," said Thesiger; "hasn't got a coat and look at his feet. We're nine thousand feet if we're an inch here. How high's the Chamar Pass?" We told him 16,000 feet. "Get yourself a coat and boots, do you hear?" he shouted in the direction of the camp fire.

After two hours the chicken arrived; they were like elastic, only the rice and gravy were delicious. Famished, we wrestled with the bones in the darkness.

"England's going to pot," said Thesiger, as Hugh and I lay smoking the interpreter's King Size cigarettes, the first for a fortnight. "Look at this shirt, I've only had it three years, now it's splitting. Same with tailors; Gull and Croke made me a pair of whipcord trousers to go to the Atlas Mountains. Sixteen guineas—wore a hole in them in a fortnight. Bought half a dozen shotguns to give to my headmen, well-known make, twenty guineas apiece, absolute rubbish.

He began to tell me about his Arabs.

"I give them powders for worms and that sort of thing." I asked him about surgery. "I take off fingers and there's a lot of surgery to be done; they're frightened of their own doctors because they're not clean."

"Do you do it? Cutting off fingers?"

"Hundreds of them," he said dreamily, for it was very late. "Lord, yes. Why, the other day I took out an eye. I enjoyed that.

"Let's turn in," he said.

The ground was like iron with sharp rocks sticking up out of it. We started to blow up our air-beds. "God, you must be a couple of pansies," said Thesiger.